The Political Economy of Food and Nutrition Policies

The Political Economy of Food and Nutrition Policies

EDITED BY PER PINSTRUP-ANDERSEN

Published for the International Food Policy Research Institute

The Johns Hopkins University Press
Baltimore and London

The Johns Hopkins University Press, 2715 North Charles Street,
Baltimore, Maryland 21218-4319
The Johns Hopkins Press Ltd., London

Library of Congress Cataloging-in-Publication Data
The political economy of food and nutrition policies / edited by Per
  Pinstrup-Andersen.
     p.   cm.
  Published for the International Food Policy Research Institute.
  Includes bibliographical references and index.
  ISBN 0-8018-4480-0
    1. Food supply—Government policy. 2. Nutrition policy. 3. Agriculture and
state. I. Pinstrup-Andersen, Per. II. International Food Policy Research Institute.
HD9000.6.P643   1993
363.8'8—dc20   92-25287

A catalog record of this book is available from the British Library.

Contents

PART III   Improving Labor Productivity through Nutritional Improvements: An Expedient Political Justification?

PART IV   Implications for the Design of Programs, Policies, and Research Needs

PART V   Conclusions and Policy Implications

Tables and Figures

Preface

Results of economic analysis of existing and alternative policy options are an important input into policy decision-making. However, policy makers must take into account economic as well as political and institutional considerations in policy design and implementation. The interaction between the two sets of considerations, the political economy issues, is of particular importance for sound and sustainable policies. Explicit consideration of such interactions is also important to interpret the results of economic analyses and their likely effect within a given political environment. Thus, while information from economic analysis may be necessary for rational decision-making, it is often not sufficient to guide decision-making toward feasible and sustainable policies.

Policy advisors and policy makers frequently ignore results from policy-related economic analyses because the analyses fail to take into account the political and institutional environment within which decisions are made. Thus, while positive economic analysis of policy-related issues plays and will continue to play an extremely critical role in providing knowledge needed to ensure sound development strategies and policies, normative policy analysis is likely to be more useful and relevant to action if based on a political economy framework.

During the last ten to fifteen years, a vast literature has developed on political economy issues and relationships. However, the utilization of the related research methodology in the area of food and nutrition policies has been relatively limited. Similarly, although anecdotes are plentiful, structured documentation of political economy aspects of food and nutrition policies is very limited. This book attempts to provide the latter. No attempt is made to develop a new theory. The aim is the more modest one of providing empirical evidence of important political economy issues in food and nutrition policy and how these may be considered in future policy analysis. While this book complements past food policy research undertaken by IFPRI and others, I hope it will contribute to making future policy analysis more relevant for those who must make policy decisions and for those who must bear the consequences of such decisions.

The contributions made by the chapter authors and a large number of reviewers, both inside and outside IFPRI, as well as financial support by the United Nations University (UNU) and the United Nations Development Programme (UNDP) are gratefully acknowledged. The initial phases of the project leading to this book were undertaken in collaboration with the International Union of Nutritional Sciences (IUNS).

Introduction

The failure of developing countries to alleviate food insecurity and malnutrition among their poor is frequently explained as resulting from lack of political will. A government's inability to design and implement cost-effective policies and programs to deal with the nutrition problem is often attributed to "politics," which many see as irrational and unpredictable. Therefore, the design and implementation of programs and policies to improve food security and nutrition are often based not on an understanding or prediction of public sector agencies' behavior but on the convenient assumption that the public sector is a monolithic agent that will adopt and implement nutrition-related policies either because they are cost-effective or out of a genuine concern for human welfare that overrides other policy goals.

Political trade-offs, conflicting goals among public sector agencies, rent-seeking by public and private sector agents, opportunities for coalition building, and related political economy issues are ignored along with a vast literature on neoclassical political economy. Some advocates of improved nutrition feel so strongly about the overriding importance of alleviating malnutrition that their approach is non-negotiable: trade-offs between cost-effectiveness and political factors are unethical, they feel, and should not be pursued.

Past efforts to design, institutionalize, and implement multisectoral nutrition planning seem to have suffered from some of the above perceptions. Although considerable work has been done to make these interventions cost-effective, virtually no research has been conducted to understand the goals and behavior of the various agents and institutions within and outside government, which in the final analysis would determine whether the planning efforts would succeed. Instead, it was generally recommended that nutrition planning be institutionalized so as to have the power to dictate or prescribe action to sectorial ministries and other agencies. Such an approach would presumably override all other goals, if needed, to meet nutrition objectives. Thus, knowledge of the various agencies' goals and behavior was not essential.

Multisectoral nutrition planning has failed as a planning and implementation tool for a number of reasons (Field 1987; Berg 1987b; Levinson, forthcoming), one of the biggest being the failure to explicitly consider political economy issues. Though the importance of such consideration is now well known from experience with many nutrition-related programs and policies, very little research has been done to increase the understanding of how efforts to improve the nutrition status may be compatible with other goals and interests in the public and private sectors.[1]

The purpose of this volume is to unravel the mysteries surrounding public sector agencies' behavior with regard to food and nutrition. Attempts are made to peek inside the black box of the political economy of food and nutrition. Following the neoclassical political economy tradition, the book generally conforms to the assumption that decision-makers and those who may influence them are rational and pursue various goals—reflecting their self-interests—within existing constraints. Therefore, it should be possible to develop a quantifiable theory of the public sector's food- and nutrition-related behavior with predictive capability similar to existing theories of consumer and producer behavior.

This book aims to provide qualitative evidence and analysis of past behavior, a necessary step toward a more formal theory. By adding to existing knowledge of the various public sector agencies' reasons for their actions and possible reactions to outside influences, the content of this book should be useful to professionals involved in the design, implementation, and analysis of policies and programs with implications for food security and nutrition. Explicit consideration of economic as well as political trade-offs is likely to result in more realistic advice to governments, identification of opportunities for coalition building, more effective government action, and reduced food insecurity and malnutrition.

The book is divided into five parts. Part one (chapters 1 through 6) provides evidence of national political economy issues related to food and nutrition. Chapters 1 and 2 provide conceptual underpinnings for a theory of the political economy of food and nutrition policies. In chapter 1, de Janvry and Subramanian analyze the origin and economic and political rationale for various types of food price policies and nutrition-related transfer schemes. They conclude that policies to keep food prices low pass through a program cycle. The cycle evolves partly as a result of interactions among various agents who attempt to influence and, in turn, are influenced by the program or policy, and partly as an outcome of external factors. De Janvry and Subramanian identify and discuss three basic forces that determine how the state designs and implements policies and programs: system imperatives, that is, political and econom-

1. A few researchers, e.g., Uphoff (1981) and Field (1977, 1983a, 1983b, 1985), have studied various aspects of the political economy of nutrition. Political economy studies of food and agriculture, e.g., Anderson and Hayami (1986), Bates (1981), de Janvry and Subbarao (1984), Hopkins (1986, 1988), and Nelson (1989), are also highly relevant to the content of this book.

ic constraints; electoral politics, bureaucratic behavior, and rent-seeking; and lobbies and pressure group politics. They conclude that cheap-food policies are seldom cost-effective in alleviating malnutrition. Rent-seeking behavior tends to redistribute benefits away from the malnourished and causes such policies to overexpand, thereby making them unsustainable in the long run and vulnerable to severe cuts or termination during periods of macroeconomic crisis.

In chapter 2, Petit develops a conceptual framework for political economy analysis of food and agricultural policies and tests its applicability on a case study of the United States Dairy Production Stabilization Act of 1983. He develops and substantiates two hypotheses. First, in the short run, policies are outcomes of conflicts among economic interests regulated through the political process, and, second, macroeconomic variables play a critical role in the long-term evolution of policies. However, the influence of macroeconomic variables is mediated by the political process. Thus, the authors of chapters 1 and 2 agree that food and agricultural policies are strongly influenced by attempts of various public- and private-sector interest groups to capture benefits in the short run, while political and macroeconomic constraints or imperatives are important determinants of the evolution of policies.

Case studies in Sri Lanka, Colombia, the United States, and Nicaragua are presented in chapters 3 through 6. These case studies focus on selected time periods during which changes of particular interest to the topic of this book took place. First, Sahn and Edirisinghe examine the political economy of the transition from a welfare-oriented state employing a basic-needs approach to a more market-oriented or liberalized economy during the late 1970s and the first half of the 1980s, with emphasis on the implications for food and nutrition. A number of important political economy issues emerge from the analysis. First, sharp reductions in transfer programs including food subsidies were successfully initiated in the late 1970s without social or political unrest. This is in contrast to similar attempts undertaken earlier in Sri Lanka and elsewhere, which caused severe unrest. Second, the liberalization of the economy in the 1970s triggered expanded inflows of capital from outside the country, which, together with the investments in human capital during the previous periods of welfare or basic-needs orientation, contributed to rapid economic growth. This illustrates the importance of the historical context and the danger of simplistic comparisons between a welfare and a free market approach. The importance of international political economy issues is demonstrated by the large inflows of foreign capital in response to domestic policy changes. By distancing themselves from a welfare orientation with heavy government intervention and by adopting a free market system more acceptable to the international community, these countries gained access to more foreign resources.

In chapter 4, Uribe Mosquera analyzes the political economy factors behind the creation, implementation, and termination of the Colombian Food and Nutrition Program (PAN). The key question Uribe Mosquera asks is why an apparently well-designed, successful, cost-effective, and well-targeted program was dismantled after only a few years of existence. He identifies five principal reasons. First, in a democratic system with a one-time, four-year presidential term, development priorities and strong political commitments to specific policies are difficult to maintain over time. Second, PAN was institutionalized in a way that infringed upon the autonomy of well-established sectoral agencies. Third, the action orientation of PAN was in conflict with the planning approach and philosophy of the host institution, the National Planning Department. Fourth, PAN was weakened by successive divestments; as some of the functions of PAN were removed, the program became more vulnerable to criticism and further cuts. Fifth, the program lost most of its constituency after the government under which it was designed finished its term. PAN was effectively targeted to the poorest households at highest risk of malnutrition, but PAN's beneficiaries had little political voice, and no serious efforts were made to develop coalitions with more powerful groups (although producers of the processed foods used in the program provided some support).

Andrews and Clancy (chapter 5) examine the history of food stamps in the United States in a political economy framework. Approaching the theme from a broad historical perspective that recognizes significant structural changes in political, social, and economic institutions, they conclude that food stamps are fully institutionalized in the United States economy. Although the influence of various support groups, such as farmers and food advocates, changed over time, the authors conclude that the changing of political values toward reduced government intervention is unlikely to result in the dismantling of income-maintenance programs without reversing the broader patterns of structural change.

Utting (chapter 6) analyzes the political economy aspect of food policy changes in Nicaragua between the revolution and the mid-1980s. Although the political will to bring about improved food security for the poor existed in postrevolutionary Nicaragua, a series of economic and political constraints limited the government's options. The postrevolutionary government introduced a series of structural changes in the economy, including agrarian reform, credit and input subsidies for agriculture, the strengthening of the food distribution system, large subsidies of goods and services including food, broadly based health and education programs, and large increases in the money supply to finance increasing government expenditures. Explicit food subsidies were used to maintain reasonable producer prices and to improve poor consumers' access to basic food staples. After a few years, however, it became clear that the subsidies were unsustainable, and the government increased consumer prices drastically.

In spite of some expropriation and central planning, the postrevolutionary government maintained a mixed economy with considerable policy-making participation by various groups. Food policies were particularly influenced by trade unions and producers' and consumers' associations. The analysis presents an interesting picture of how these groups influenced food policy, how their influence changed over time, and how attempts to ignore basic macroeconomic constraints will make policies unsustainable.

In chapter 7, based on a study of the local power structure in an Egyptian village, Adams concludes that a small group of rich peasants providing poorer households with a stream of patronage services is able to dominate local affairs, including the food and nutrition programs and policies and the associated benefit distribution. According to Adams, government officials, particularly agricultural extension workers in the countryside, were unable to significantly influence the existing power structure because they lacked the means and the skills to provide sufficient patronage either to the poor (to alleviate the need for existing exploitative links with the rich farmers) or to the rich (to warrant a coalition).

As illustrated by the example of Nicaragua (Utting), consumer groups may play an important role in shaping food and nutrition policy. However, as Pinstrup-Andersen discusses in chapter 8, it is more common to consider households as passive recipients. Yet, if programs and policies are designed and implemented with insufficient regard for the preferences of the intended recipients and for the economic, social, and cultural constraints under which they make decisions, the results are likely to be disappointing. Program participation and cost-effectiveness will be low, the impact on nutrition will be small, and public resources will be wasted. This is because the *household* and not the *program implementor* decides whether and to what extent to take advantage of existing programs.

The household response and the opportunity for enhancing program and policy effects through a fuller understanding of the preferences, goals, and socioeconomic constraints of the intended target groups are often ignored. Real participation by the target group in program design and implementation is critical yet rare. As a result, many programs and policies are based on incorrect perceptions of households' goals, preferences, and constraints or, worse, on what they ought to be rather than what they are.

Of course, improved information and promotion may change preferences and behavior. However, in the absence of such change, attempts to impose society's goals and preferences where they conflict with those of the household are likely to fail.

Of particular importance in this regard is the society's role in protecting powerless or less powerful household members, such as preschool children, from discriminatory household practices. Attempts to circumvent the head of the household, to reach individual household members through programs such as food supplements for preschool children and direct feeding programs are widespread. Households try to counter such efforts, and leakages of program benefits are high. A much better understanding of these and related political economy factors operating within the household would help make government intervention more effective.

Two of the critical political economy questions related to nutrition are whether improved nutrition results in enhanced economic growth and, if so, whether public investment in improved nutrition will yield a return equal to or higher than investment in other economic growth-enhancing changes. If the answer to both questions is yes, investment in nutrition is clearly justified at the macroeconomic level. Furthermore, conflicts among interest groups are then easier to deal with because, at least in theory, no group needs to lose. Potential losers can be fully compensated with a net economic surplus, presumably but not necessarily to be captured by the poor.

Latham (chapter 9) and Strauss (chapter 10) examine these issues in part three of this book. Flawed analytical methodologies make it difficult or impossible to interpret the results of many of the studies of the productivity effects of improved nutrition. However, several studies that do not suffer from serious methodological problems provide strong evidence of a significant increase in labor productivity as a result of improved nutrition of adults. The evidence is particularly strong when severe iron or energy deficiencies are alleviated. Adult stunting that resulted from malnutrition during early childhood also appears to have a negative effect on productivity.

Thus, although the authors conclude that the return on investment in improved nutrition is positive, very little is known about the magnitude of the return. Is it higher or lower than that obtainable from investment in education, bridges, and roads? The question is difficult to answer because of complementarities among investments in nutrition, education, and physical infrastructure. Strong evidence exists, for example, that malnourished children do not do well in school. However, the task of separating the effects of poor nutrition from the effects of poor educational facilities, poor infrastructure, and the complex factors associated with poverty and malnutrition is difficult, to say the least.

Having examined the role of political economy issues at the national, local, and household levels and the extent to which improved nutrition can be justified by its impact on economic growth, the book continues with part four, where the implications for future action and research needs are assessed. In chapter 11, Field addresses one of the most critical questions this book raises: how to incorporate political sensitivity into program design and, in so doing, how to integrate political calculations with the economics of choice. No one is against good nutrition, and nobody favors malnutrition. However, as Field points out, nutrition is a weak political issue for four principal reasons. First, it lacks salience. In any government, a nutrition concern is difficult to activate or sustain. Second, nutrition suffers from poor advocacy. Third, it lacks policy definition and guidance, and efforts to improve nutrition suffer from a lack of a natural institutional home. Finally, nutrition is very susceptible to rhetoric and tokenism, and it is difficult to determine the extent of real political commitment.

Field identifies various relevant government groups and assesses their power over and interest in nutrition-related action. He asserts that the priority given to nutrition by a government is determined principally by the posture of its political leadership and, to a lesser extent, the initiative of senior officials in agriculture and health. He argues that more emphasis must be placed on implementation, and he concludes that the promise of successful programs lies in good strategy management that is relevant to existing conditions.

The importance of integrating political and economic factors is not limited to action programs. As Jonsson and Hopkins discuss in chapters 12 and 13, this integration is of equal importance in research needed to support action.

Jonsson argues that policy research must be based on a detailed understanding of the causes and nature of malnutrition, and on a sound conceptual framework. Policy research based on simplistic or incorrect perceptions about the problem is widespread and results in mistaken guidance for action. The author proposes a conceptual framework and identifies and discusses the key relationships and the most urgent research needs. He points out that most research on food and nutrition policy in Africa is undertaken by non-African institutions, and their research methods frequently ignore the specific political context of the study country. It is important that future methods and priorities reflect the characteristics of the study population and its environment.

Among the research priorities the author identifies are: the impact of present and alternative policies and programs for women, including the gender division of labor and ways to enhance women's control of household resources; the effects of structural adjustment on nutrition and the social conditions of women and children; the effects of universal primary education on nutrition; and the enhancement of communities' ability to solve their own nutrition problems. Participation by the poor and malnourished in the design and implementation of policy research is important to assure relevance.

Hopkins identifies four political economy questions to be included in nutrition-related policy research. First, what political and economic factors induce a state to make direct nutrition interventions? Second, what goals shape government nutrition-related policy? Third, what effects do political and economic factors have at different stages in the policy process? And fourth, what are the economic and political determinants of nutritional status?

Hopkins points out that nutrition traditionally has been a personal or family rather than a state responsibility. He identifies three conditions under which nutrition is likely to become important to the state: acute food shortages, new information about the relationship between food, health, and productivity, and the increasing power of undernourished groups.

The author distinguishes three major stages in the policy process and illustrates how competing economic and political factors shape the outcomes: the formation of interests, in which the priority given to nutrition in public policy is settled; interest incorporation, in which effective goals of particular policies are formulated; and policy implementation, during which distortions in priority and intent take place. Hopkins then identifies a number of research priorities related to the entire process. He argues that such research is needed to recognize interests that are served in existing situations and to identify prospects for changing interests through research. Where political support for the most cost-effective strategy is absent and those without adequate nutrition lack political power, the political economy approach to research can at least suggest how political support can be obtained through leakage of program benefits to nontarget groups and how to do so in the most cost-effective manner.

In the concluding chapter, Pinstrup-Andersen attempts to draw general lessons from the previous chapters and other relevant literature. He concludes that in order to understand the complex process leading to specific nutrition-related action and to predict how this process will respond to alternative stimuli, it is essential to identify not only the key actors but also their goals and rationales, to assess their relative power within the process, and to attempt to model their behavior. It is also essential to better understand these actors' interactions, their dependencies and competitive relationships, their vested interests, and opportunities they may have to coalesce into mutually beneficial groups to the exclusion of others.

Policy analysis based on a solid understanding of the political economy issues is likely to result in information that is more relevant to the policy decisions at hand, more realistic within the existing power structure, and therefore more useful for the decision maker.

PART I

Political Economy Issues at the National Level

1 The Politics and Economics of Food and Nutrition Policies and Programs: An Interpretation

ALAIN DE JANVRY AND SHANKAR SUBRAMANIAN

Government interventions in the pricing of food and in the determination of entitlements to food are so pervasive that it is impossible to analyze the nutritional status of a population without an understanding of the politics of food policies and their economic consequences. If one were to argue that the fundamental determinant of political mobilization is the expected economic payoffs for different social groups resulting from alternative policies, the main contribution of economic analysis to a political economy of food and nutrition policies and programs would be to identify these payoffs. This is a daunting task, because these policies and programs have complex dynamic repercussions at all levels of the economic system, from household welfare to macroeconomic aggregates.

Expected economic payoffs, however, are only the basis on which to endogenize government behavior. The state is activated by complex and contradictory forces, especially the management of economic and ideological system imperatives in either crisis or planning modes, the requirements of electoral politics and bureaucratic behavior, and the demands of lobbies and pressure group politics, much of which originates in the expected growth and welfare payoffs of alternative policies and programs. We attempt to show how these different forces result in specific food policy interventions. Of particular interest are the factors that explain the origin of programs, their subsequent expansion or contraction, and the changing biases in the allocation of their benefits. We develop a program-cycle approach to explain what appear to be frequently repeated sequences in the history of food and nutritional interventions, starting with a broad review of various types of policies and programs that have been used by the state to alter food prices and redefine food entitlements. Our focus is on food-price and subsidy policies to the near exclusion of purely nutritional interventions, such as supplementary feeding programs and nutrition education.

Types of Food and Nutrition Policies

Food and nutrition policies may be classified according to the level of governmental cost involved and by their distributional consequences. The typology suggested is as follows:

1. *Cheap-food policy at no direct cost to government.* Food prices may be suppressed, either across the board or selectively, by imports at an overvalued exchange rate or through concessional aid, state monopoly procurement and sale, or export taxes and levies.
2. *Untargeted food-subsidy schemes.* Food prices are lowered by the introduction of a consumer subsidy. Producer prices may be at the same level or above consumer prices. Part of the demand may be fulfilled by imports subsidized by the state. Little or no restriction is placed on access to subsidized food, and coverage of the population is often fairly uniform.
3. *Targeted interventions.* Access to subsidized food or to nutritional supplements is restricted geographically, by means tests, or to segments of the population that are considered to be at high risk of malnourishment, such as school children, pregnant mothers, and babies. The benefits of cheap food to the poor can also be restricted by subsidizing only those foods that, while nutritionally sound, are considered inferior by the rich.

An analysis of the origins, impact, and outcome of food and nutrition policy in several countries shows that these three types of state intervention have very different macroeconomic, distributional, and nutritional outcomes. Consequently, this classification is useful in elucidating both the rationale for and the limits to intervention by the state in the area of food and nutrition.

Cheap-Food Policy at No Direct Cost to Government

Cheap-food polices may originate as a side effect of a strategy of import-substitution industrialization and its attendant overvaluation of the domestic currency, as was the case in much of Latin America in the 1950s and 1960s, and in parts of Africa until the introduction of recent macroeconomic reforms. Cheap-food policies have been often reinforced by access to imports of concessional food aid. Since food prices are a major determinant of the real wages of urban workers, a cheap-food policy is favored to keep wages in industry low. While agricultural production tends to be hampered by low producer prices, access to institutional rents created by the state allows selected commercial farmers to produce profitably, often for the export market.[1] Lacking access to cheap credit, subsidized irrigation, seeds, and other inputs—the sources of

---

1. By institutional rents we mean surplus appropriation by social classes through their control of or access to public services and resources.

institutional rents—peasant producers are at a disadvantage. Peasant incomes and the production of peasant foods (often wage foods) tend to stagnate or decline (de Janvry 1981).

In the short run, income is transferred from producers of food and exporters to the urban classes who have access to cheap food. The shares of urban workers and industrial capitalists in the amount transferred depends on the extent to which real wages are allowed to rise. In Latin America and Africa, several factors have combined to make a cheap-food policy based on an overvalued exchange rate unsustainable in the long term. On the external front, the exhaustion of import-substitution industrialization and the debt crisis have produced a shortage of foreign exchange, making it difficult to import foodstuffs. In Latin America, the economic crises have led, in the last instance, to the imposition of austerity programs involving, among other things, cuts in real wages and food consumption for urban workers. Domestic production of wage foods has also stagnated because of the disincentives posed by cheap-food prices and exclusion from institutional rents, and because of the bias toward producing commercial crops for export to help alleviate crises in the balance of payments.

Governments have also attempted to procure foodstuffs at below-market prices to provide cheap food to certain groups. In order to control the disposition of domestic production, restrictions may be placed on the movement of food between and within regions, as has been the case with maize in Kenya and cereals in India. Levies may be instituted upon millers and processors, and the state may attempt to monopolize all purchases of food grains. As Bates (1981) notes, such measures applied in many African states through parastatal agencies may not have succeeded in intercepting more than 20 to 30 percent of marketed output. At the same time, state-sponsored agricultural development projects provide institutional rents to large farmers in the form of subsidized irrigation, fertilizers, credit, and other inputs. Bates (1981) finds that "the poorer, small-scale, village-level farmers do not secure farm inputs that have been publicly provisioned and publicly subsidized. . . . The evidence suggests that the benefits of these programs have been consumed chiefly by the larger farmers." The net effect is uneven development in the countryside; peasant production stagnates, while cheap-food production is sustained through highly subsidized commercial farming.

A third mechanism for depressing domestic food prices is the use of export taxes and levies, such as those used to lower meat prices in Kenya and Sudan (Bates 1981) and rice prices in Thailand (Trairatvorakul 1984). As Trairatvorakul's study shows, a reduction of the export tax on rice and a corresponding increase in domestic price would have a decidedly inequitable outcome: most of the gains would accrue to the better-off part of the population, while urban consumers and many rural poor would lose. In spite of the export taxes, rice production in Thailand has not stagnated and has shown an increasing trend ever since the 1950s, which would suggest that the producer price has remained above the cost of production.

In sum, with the rather striking exception of Thailand, the extractivist approach to cheap food seldom benefits the rural poor. In the long term, the peasant sector is forced into decline by the combination of low prices for commodities they produce and exclusion from the compensatory institutional rents provided to the politically powerful commercial farmers.

Untargeted Food Subsidy Schemes

Pinstrup-Andersen (1988a) provides a review of consumer food subsidies in a number of countries. A few are discussed below from the political economic point of view.

The Egyptian food-subsidy scheme after 1973 and the Sri Lankan food-subsidy scheme prior to 1979 are prime examples of largely untargeted interventions providing explicitly subsidized food virtually to the entire population. Both schemes had rather modest beginnings in the rationing programs started during the Second World War. The expansion in the scope and extent of the subsidies initially came about as a result of the socialist orientation of the Sri Lankan and Egyptian regimes and their concern with equity and income redistribution.

Until about 1973, the Egyptian scheme involved only a small governmental outlay, based as it was on procurement of crops at below-domestic-market prices, on imports at an overvalued exchange rate, and on access to foreign food aid. Several factors conspired to force a rapid expansion in the food subsidy outlay after 1973, and government expenditure on food subsidies rose from 4 million Egyptian pounds (£E) in 1970 to 605 million £E in 1980, both at 1975 prices (Scobie 1983).

Chief among these factors were (1) the inability of the government to pass on to consumers the substantial increase in world food prices that took place after 1973; (2) the increase in import prices that resulted from the devaluation of the Egyptian pound in 1980; (3) the rapid increase of imports of cereals and other foodstuffs that resulted from low prices; (4) the high income elasticity of demand for these commodities in a rapidly growing economy; and (5) the slow growth in domestic food production, which barely kept pace with population growth.

Recent attempts to increase the price of subsidized foodstuffs have proved infructuous—in both 1977 and 1984, outbreaks of rioting forced the government to rescind announced price increases. The failure of the government's attempts to modify the subsidy system and the strength of popular opposition to these attempts may be attributed to the regime's lack of legitimacy at a time when rapid economic growth stimulated by the open-door policy *(infitah)* has gone hand in hand with increasing income inequality and extensive poverty. However, Egypt has been able to sustain an expensive and untargeted food-subsidy scheme because of increased revenues from the booming oil sector and the Suez Canal, large remittances from Egyptians working abroad, and its geopolitical position in the Middle East, which gives it access to substantial amounts of United States and Arab aid and credit.

Egyptian food policy has had a variety of effects on income distribution and nutrition. In the period before 1973, the provision of cheap food was based on domestic procurement and imports at an overvalued exchange rate, resulting in an income transfer from exporters and producers to consumers. After 1973, the state shouldered much of the burden, and input subsidies to producers increased at much the same rate as food subsidies. An important change has been the protection of the meat, livestock, and feed sector after the mid-seventies, which resulted in large transfers to this sector, amounting—in 1980—to some 73 percent of the total transfer from agriculture (Braun and de Haen 1983). Alderman and Braun (1984) show that the average transfer to rural households is larger than that to urban households, leading to an improvement in income distribution, since average incomes are lower in rural areas.

Within the rural population, there is a net transfer away from large farmers and toward all other groups, as large farmers produce a larger proportion of field crops that bear a high implicit tax rate and a smaller proportion of meat and livestock products that benefit from protection. While the net transfer due to producer and consumer subsidies has a rural bias, there is an urban bias in transfers arising from the purchase of subsidized foods from governmental outlets. Moreover, richer urban households buying larger amounts of subsidized commodities have a disproportionately larger share of this type of transfer. On the other hand, richer households buy more meat, resulting in larger transfers to the livestock sector, which is dominated by small farmers and landless workers. In addition, the income transfer due to the subsidy system accounts for increases in daily per capita calorie intake of 100 to 200 calories for the poorest urban and rural quartiles of the population.

The long-term outcome of Egyptian food policy is unclear. Recent studies have focused on the macroeconomic implications of the subsidy, which in recent years reached a level of 10 to 15 percent of total government expenditure. The rapid increase in outlay on subsidies in the 1970s coincided with a fall in public investment in agriculture, which since then has somewhat recovered. Using a programming model, Braun and de Haen find that a removal of price distortions would cause production of some crops to increase and that of others to fall; however, the increase in aggregate output would be limited because of constraints on resources, water, input management, and extension services. They conclude (Braun and de Haen 1983, 16) that "subsidies do not automatically support or impair economic growth. That depends on the accompanying government policies." Scobie (1983) finds that an increase in expenditure on subsidies causes an increase in the rate of inflation and a fall in the market value of the Egyptian pound. Import demand for food is inelastic because of the import subsidies. As a result, a rise in world food prices or a fall in foreign exchange availability has the effect of curtailing imports of intermediates or capital goods and is felt mostly by industry. For example, a 10 percent rise in the cost of food imports would produce a drop of 1 to 2 percent in industrial output.

The Sri Lankan food-subsidy scheme was an important part of the state's social welfare programs (this section is based largely on Taylor, Horton, and Ruff 1983). The net effect of its progressive social policies was to raise life expectancy and adult literacy, and to lower fertility and infant mortality to levels that correspond to countries that have far higher levels of per capita GNP. The food subsidy scheme began during the Second World War and provided a subsidized rice ration to almost the entire population. At the same time, producer price supports were established, the area under irrigation was increased, and subsidized inputs were provided. Under the impetus of these measures, rice production almost tripled in thirty years. The price and quantity of the rice ration were adjusted periodically as new governments were voted in and in response to large increases in world food prices. In 1953, an attempt to cut food subsidies and raise the cost of public services was abandoned when food riots erupted. Until about 1972, the expenditure on subsidies was partly offset by profits from the sale of imported sugar and wheat. With the increase in world food prices after 1973, this source of revenue was exhausted and the outlay tripled between 1970 and 1975, reaching a level of 18 percent of total government expenditures. Between 1973 and 1978, the price of the ration was increased and the quantity was curtailed in an attempt to hold down costs. The new government that came to power in 1977 was determined to liberalize the economy. At first, it raised the quantity of the ration and then, in 1978, introduced a means test limiting eligibility to the lower half of the population. In mid-1979, food stamps were issued to those who were eligible for rations. At the same time, the ration system was dismantled and food prices were allowed to rise to world-market levels. The initial value of the food stamps was such that most recipients could get more food than they had been able to obtain under the ration system. By 1982, however, inflation had so reduced the value of the stamps that government expenditure on them had declined to 5 percent of the budget.

Sri Lanka's food-price policy entailed subsidies to both consumers and producers—if domestic prices are compared with world market prices using the official exchange rate. If a less favorable exchange rate—one applicable to certain nonessential imports and most exports—is used, transfers to producers would have been negative for many years. These figures do not include transfers on account of input subsidies and do not give any indication of whether rural households, when considered as both producers and consumers, gained or lost. Other studies show that the subsidy redistributed income to the poor and improved income distribution. Gavan and Chandrasekera (1979) suggest, however, that the ration scheme was inefficient because it did not substantially increase calorie intake by the poor and because many of the recipients of the ration already had adequate diets.

The Sri Lankan subsidy scheme became difficult to sustain after some thirty years of operation due primarily to increasing costs and requirements of foreign exchange arising from the increase in world food prices. Herring (1985) points out that the Sri Lankan economy underwent little structural change and remained dependent on a few plantation commodities for its exports. The crisis of the mid-1970s was the result of a "drastic and long-standing deterioration in the terms of trade," which fell more than threefold between 1960 and 1975 (Herring 1985). While the volume of exports remained fairly constant over this period, the volume of imports declined by almost one half. As Herring emphasizes, Sri Lanka's annual average growth rate between 1960 and 1977 compares quite favorably with those of other countries in the region. Taylor, Horton, and Ruff (1983) conclude that the subsidy's role in crowding out domestic investment may have been overstated. The state's overriding concern with rice led to the neglect of other food crops, whose output did not increase to the same degree.

It is worth emphasizing that the untargeted food subsidies in both Sri Lanka and Egypt provided substantial increases in real incomes and food intake to both the rural and the urban poor, which is seldom the case with the extractivist policies discussed earlier. Both schemes were successful in this respect for two reasons: (1) access to subsidized food was well-nigh universal; and (2) agricultural production was stimulated not merely by raising producer prices but by various developmentalist measures, including the extension of cultivation and irrigation and the provision of cheap fertilizer.

Targeted Interventions

FOOD SUBSIDY SCHEMES. The food rationing schemes in India, Pakistan, and Bangladesh were all instituted during the Second World War with a view to securing and meeting urban food requirements in a war economy. All are targeted to some degree, either by the provision of a cheap, nutritionally adequate inferior foodstuff whose income elasticity of demand is negative, or by specific geographical coverage.

Until it was terminated in 1988, the Pakistani ration system provided wheat flour perceived by consumers to be of low quality because of its high extraction rate. There was no means test, but the perceived low quality of the flour made the system self-targeting to some degree. Furthermore, ration shops were found primarily in urban areas.

The Bangladesh ration scheme is also urban-oriented. The proportion of food distributed by the government outside major urban areas and to groups other than government employees, the armed forces, and the police has decreased considerably and is now under 20 percent. The net effect is to worsen income distribution, since urban incomes are higher, on the average, than rural incomes. About a quarter of the food distributed is procured domestically, the rest is accounted for by foreign aid and imports. The amount of subsidy as a proportion of government expenditure has been quite large, ranging from 8 percent to 13 percent over the period 1972–73 to 1975–76, which included a famine year.

The ration system in most of India, excluding the food-deficit state of Kerala, is likewise urban-oriented and does not use a means test to determine eligibility. The provision of coarse food grains, a possible self-targeting commodity, is insignificant, and the ration system concentrates on the provision of subsidized wheat, rice, and sugar. The explicit food subsidy to consumers is small in comparison to other subsidies, averaging not more than 4 percent of the subsidies for irrigation, fertilizers, and rural development between 1974 and 1982 (de Janvry and Subbarao 1984).

Until 1977, procurement was based on compulsory levies on millers and the restriction of trade between deficit and surplus areas. Procurement prices were often below wholesale prices and, it has been argued, often below the cost of production in some areas, especially for rice (less so for wheat). Restrictions on private movement of grains have been abolished, and procurement prices now play the role of harvest time support prices. The discriminatory pricing of rice and wheat before 1977 has led Mitra to argue that it represented an attempt to transfer income from rice producers, mostly in the south and the east, to wheat producers in the north of India. The evidence for the period after 1977 suggests that the net effect of the food subsidy and price supports has been in income transfer to large farmers, urban workers, and capitalists (de Janvry and Subbarao 1984). The only available microlevel studies on the food subsidy are for the state of Kerala; they show that ration coverage is high, that income distribution is improved by the ration scheme, and that there are substantial improvements in various nutritional indicators (cf. George 1979).

While the ostensible purpose of targeted food subsidies is to provide cheap food and real income transfers to the poor while excluding the rich (or those not nutritionally at risk), the rural poor are often excluded from these benefits, which accrue largely to city dwellers and large farmers.

FOOD SUPPLEMENTATION PROGRAMS. Direct food supplementation programs seek to identify target households or individuals who are particularly vulnerable to the effects of malnutrition and to restrict the provision of food supplements to them in order to reduce leakage to others who have adequate diets. These programs often involve the provision of specially formulated foods or milk to children at school or to infants and pregnant or lactating women at health centers. While leakage to households that are not targeted may be small, there is usually a substantial reallocation of intrahousehold consumption, leading, in effect, to a transfer of real income to the household of the targeted individuals, and to only a small net increase in the nutritional intake of the targeted individuals (Pinstrup-Andersen 1985). A review of over two hundred reports of food distribution programs for children by Beaton and Ghassemi

(1982) (quoted in Pinstrup-Andersen 1985) found leakages of the order of 30 to 55 percent. Moreover, direct feeding programs tend to have high administrative and infrastructural costs compared to food-subsidy or food-stamp programs.

The Chilean food-supplementation program uses the school system and the network of national health clinics to provide food supplements to school-children and pregnant women. One component of the program, the milk distribution scheme, was started in 1924, when Chile's first social security measures were passed. The program provided milk to working mothers who had children under the age of two. The school feeding program began in 1928. As Hakim and Solimano (1978) point out, the impetus for the milk distribution program came from groups of physicians who, concerned over the high rate of infant mortality and the incidence of malnutrition and ill-health, agitated for reform and the expansion of health care. The coverage of both programs was limited by the extent of the health care and school systems. As late as 1951, the milk distribution program covered only some 10 percent of those eligible. After the election of a populist regime in 1952 and the consolidation of all government health agencies into the National Health Service, the milk program expanded rapidly and coverage was extended to all children under the age of six, requiring large milk imports, which were opposed by domestic milk producers. After the Frei administration came to power in 1964, the milk program expanded substantially, reaching nearly half the eligible population. Some 20 percent of the milk distributed during the Frei years was donated by the United States. After 1968, milk imports were restricted because of foreign-exchange shortages. Salvador Allende became president in 1970, and one of his popular campaign promises was a half liter of milk a day for children under the age of 15 and for pregnant or nursing women. Milk distribution increased almost three-fold over the 1970 level, and the milk program achieved a coverage of 90 percent among school children and about 50 percent for other target groups. The milk program was continued after the overthrow of the Allende government. In explaining the continuing popularity of the milk program, Hakim and Solimano (1978, 59) assert that "unlike such issues as agrarian reform, expropriation of industry, or wage policies, the milk program was not the object of national political conflict or controversy." Before the Allende years, the milk program was financed largely by social security funds, and the expenditures were uncontroversial. The only opposition came from domestic producers, and the expansion of the program was limited only by the availability of scarce foreign exchange for milk imports.

The effectiveness of the Chilean nutritional supplementation programs has been studied by Harbert and Scandizzo (1982). They used data from a 1974 nutritional survey on the intrahousehold distribution of consumption and incidence of malnutrition. Over and above the effect produced by the equivalent income transfer, they found a statistically significant increase in protein intake among young children below the age of two. This increase was two to six times that, due to the increase in real household income. The school lunch and complementary feeding programs provided 33 percent and 50 percent of daily calorie requirements and cost U.S. $60 and U.S. $38, respectively, per beneficiary. For countries with per-capita incomes below that of Chile, expenditures of this order would represent a sizeable fraction of GNP and government expenditure, as was pointed out by Hakim and Solimano for the pre-1973 nutritional supplementation programs.

This survey of policies and programs designed to reduce the cost of food illustrates a number of common features.

1. Most policies and programs did not originate in an evolutionary fashion, but in response to marked economic crises or ideological discontinuities, such as severe food shortages, shifts in growth strategies at the macroeconomic level, and shifts in ideology in conjunction with transitions to socialist or populist regimes.
2. Many cheap-food programs have improved the nutritional status of the population they have reached, while failing to implement other redistributive measures, such as asset transfers or wage policies. This indicates that food and nutritional policy, however effective it may or may not be in a cost-benefit sense, is politically a more legitimate instrument of income transfer than these other measures.
3. Cheap-food policies and programs have often benefited groups not at nutritional risk, while bypassing or injuring the neediest. This suggests that these policies and programs create institutional rents that are appropriated through the logic of the political economy, that is, in terms of electoral politics, bureaucratic behavior, and lobbies and pressure-group politics.
4. The continuation of cheap-food policies and the magnitude of nutritional programs are generally severely constrained by macroeconomic circumstances and the fiscal capacity of the state. As these programs expand in response to demands for institutional rents, the constraints create increasingly explicit trade-offs between short-run gains and long-term growth, pointing the way to future crises and an eventual scale-down.

Elements of a Political Economy of Food and Nutrition Policies

There exists a "program cycle" in the way most public interventions to cheapen food, either through cheap-food policies or through untargeted and targeted food subsidies, have originated, expanded, contracted, and eventually ended. This cycle finds its logic due, in part, to the interactions of varying actors as the program creates new political forces and runs into economic constraints but also as a result of the broader historical evolution of economic and ideological conditions, starting with extensive state interventions after the Second World War and ending with enforced neoliberalism in the context of the debt crises and stabilization policies of the 1980s. The cycle is consequently not one that evolves solely as a result of its own internal dynamic but is a result of both an internal dynamic and a particular set of unique circumstances. Three basic forces determine how the state—both the various branches of government and the civil and military bureaucracy—defines and implements policies and programs: system imperatives; electoral politics, bureaucratic behavior and rent-seeking; and lobbies and pressure group politics.

System Imperatives

Whatever the prevailing economic system, the state is entrusted with ensuring that a set of key macroeconomic and macropolitical variables remains within a commonly accepted range. In other words, whatever the form of the state, there are some common functions that it must fulfill within the limits imposed on it by its legitimacy (or lack thereof) and its administrative and financial capacities. In terms of economic performance, this range is bounded by such variables as the perceived minimum acceptable rate of growth, a maximum rate of inflation, and a maximum rate of unemployment. It is also expected to remove a number of transaction costs that would exist if market forces were left alone, especially the provision of public goods and the internalization of externalities. These government interventions create net social gains, thus increasing the size of the economy.

On the political side, limits are set by civil insecurity and by the delegitimatization of the social relations that have brought the state to power. Actually reaching these limits triggers a crisis response. This can occur when disruptions created by a war economy or by large-scale droughts devastate food supplies, resulting in extensive scarcities and runaway inflation, or when stabilization policies are introduced to handle a sudden crisis in the balance of payments. Anticipation of reaching these limits induces the state to implement reforms in a planning mode. Examples are the introduction of import-substitution industrialization policies, as a result of reduced opportunities for international trade, or the shift to neoliberal policies brought about by the subsequent exhaustion of the import-substitution model. Alternatively, political limits can be changed by major ideological swings, as when a new government assumes power on the basis of a populist or socialist program with either extensive electoral commitments to welfare programs or sufficient autonomy to carry these out on its own initiative.

In all cases, the state's capacity for autonomous action is bounded by economic and political limits, which, in turn, create imperatives for the state to act in a crisis or a planning mode whenever they are, or are in danger of, being transgressed. Attempts at implementing policies and programs in response to these imperatives are constrained by the limited legitimacy and managerial and fiscal capacities of the state, which influence the potential success of state initiative.

In examining the origins of cheap-food policies and food-subsidy programs, we see that most were started in response to economic and political system imperatives acting upon the state: (1) food-price controls to stem inflationary pressures associated with war scarcities and droughts were introduced in India, Pakistan, and Bangladesh; (2) cheap-food policies were instituted as part of the import-substitution industrialization strategy in most Latin American countries in the 1940s and in the African countries in the 1960s to subsidize industry by lowering the nominal wage bill in the industrial and public sectors, and to increase the size of the domestic market for nonagricultural goods; and (3) food-subsidy programs aiming to benefit the entire population were instituted during transitions to socialist or populist ideologies when the state, its autonomy enhanced by the transition, entered into a progressive alliance with subordinate classes and was able to engage in redistributive measures, as was the case in Egypt and Sri Lanka.

The extent to which policies to cheapen food are implemented, in both magnitude and duration, depends on the restrictiveness of a certain number of constraints. The limits to imposing price controls are dependent on the prevention of black-market operations and smuggling; reproducing the food-supply flow in spite of low prices; and legitimizing income transfers from producers to consumers. The limits of cheapening food via overvalued exchange rates as part of import-substitution policies are determined by several factors:

1. The more inelastic the aggregate supply in agriculture, the fewer real effects low prices will have and the closer they will be to the structuralist goal of a pure income transfer away from producers. As the development strategies advocated by the Economic Commission for Latin America made clear, import-substitution industrialization policies in Latin America were grounded in the belief that prices had essentially no impact on the level of agricultural output.

2. The capacity of the state to compensate the losers, in this case farm producers, through access to institutional rents arising from subsidized credit and inputs, and public spending on research and infrastructure, is critical. While it is the market mechanism (low product prices) that serves to levy a tax, the compensation of institutional rents are determined by the forces of the political economy: productive and social sectors favored by the state are selected to receive compensation. If sufficient, a competitive rate of profit can be maintained in certain sectors of agriculture, as, for example, in Brazil, where large farms producing export crops were booming under import-substitution industrialization in spite of overvalued exchange rates. By taxation through market distortions and compensation through the political economy, the state is thus eventually able to neutralize the political effects of its economic program.

3. Negative political effects on agriculture are also warded off by weak farm

lobbies and limited electoral politics, an achievement of bureaucratic-authoritarian regimes that has typically been associated with the later phases of import-substitution industrialization models, when social contradictions lead to the destabilization of democratic forms of government.

4. Sustaining cheap food over time through an overvalued exchange rate is conditional upon the ability to maintain equilibrium in the balance of payments, which is aided by the presence of a booming export sector (oil), the buildup of debt, access to foreign aid, effective foreign-exchange controls, and rationing.

When policies of cheap food and food subsidies are introduced as part of a broad ideological shift implemented by government, two main factors limit their magnitude and duration. First, a contradiction exists between the ideological goals of the state and its imperative of sustaining accumulation. Since the state cannot neglect the latter, principally because it depends on surplus generation in civil society to generate its own budget, redistributive programs that hamper growth can operate only within narrow limits. This is particularly true if the financing of food subsidies competes with public or private investment. In this case, the very beneficiaries of redistributive programs may be better off in the long run if the surplus that is redistributed and consumed were to be invested.

A second contradiction exists between the progressive alliance—the state and subordinate classes—and the dominant classes. If the latter is fundamentally motivated by capital accumulation, while the former is motivated by social welfare, the same contradiction between growth and distribution resurfaces in the form of class conflicts.

We thus derive a number of testable propositions from these observations. If these policies and programs increase in scope and magnitude with the goals they are supposed to fulfill, they will be reinforced by the strength and sudden onset of inflationary pressures, the degree of commitment to an import substitution industrialization strategy, and the strength of endorsement of a socialist or populist ideology. These policies and programs will also expand in scope with a relaxation of the limits that bind them: the inelasticity of aggregate supply in agriculture, the economic capacity of the state to distribute compensatory institutional rents, the ability to tax agriculture, the ability to sustain over time an overvalued exchange rate, and reduced conflicts both between ideological goals and accumulation functions of the state, and between the goals of the state-centered progressive alliance and the dominant classes.

Electoral Politics, Bureaucratic Behavior, and Rent-Seeking

Once cheap-food policies and food subsidies have been introduced in response to economic and ideological system imperatives, their expansion or contraction and the distribution of the welfare gains they create fall in the realm of two very different sets of social forces. On the one hand, the state is activated from within in response to electoral politics, bureaucratic behavior, and rent-seeking by its agents. On the other hand, the state is activated from below in response to lobbies and pressure groups that seek to appropriate the benefits of low-priced food. In starting as system imperatives and subsequently trans-formed into elements of political calculations and struggles, the policies and programs of low-priced food eventually become increasingly contradictory regarding their original economic and ideological purposes. This has two im-plications. First, the social distribution of program benefits becomes increas-ingly determined by relative social positions in the political economy, which means, in particular, that they may well be appropriated by those who do not need them the most, while the needy may either be marginalized or, worse, adversely affected by backlash effects of the programs on free-market prices. Second, the cost of the program eventually becomes disproportionately large in relation to the capacity of the state to fulfill its system imperatives, resulting in the need to relax the imposed policies or scale down the programs being implemented.

To understand how the state is activated from within, we observe that the government and bureaucracy are highly divided institutions and that the partic-ular motivations of state agents deeply affect the determination of public policy and the distribution of institutional rents. There are two basic behavioral pat-terns at work here: one is the search for political and bureaucratic clienteles to maximize the probability of remaining in office, the other is rent-seeking by politicians and bureaucrats trying to appropriate institutional rents on their own behalf.

The particular policy instruments through which the state provides for cheap food result in very different configurations of gains and losses across social groups and over time. The distribution of economic payoffs does not, however, tell us how cheap food is used for the sake of political patronage and clientele-seeking. As is the case with all institutional rents, the key question is how to target the benefits so that they reach the relevant clientele, and, thus, elicit political support. The lower the degree of political legitimacy of the state with politically essential groups, the more necessary it is to channel attractive institutional rents toward them. Failure to ascertain what the relevant rents are and how they will be received can result in costly political mistakes (Hopkins 1984a). Since democratic institutions serve as a test of government perfor-mance, mistakes made in the handling of institutional rents can result in serious food riots and delegitimization of the state.

Clientele-seeking through cheap-food programs results in a major con-tradiction. The most malnourished people are rarely the relevant clientele for political support, so programs that would effectively reach the poor generally lack political support, while the benefits from projects with strong political support tend to be diverted toward the less needy. The most visible symptom of this clientelistic distortion is the urban bias that food-subsidy programs have in India, Pakistan, and Bangladesh. Not only do they benefit the politically relevant urban population while bypassing the rural poor, but they benefit many urban groups that are not at nutritional risk, the bureaucrats in particular, while having a backlash on the rural poor who pay food prices on the residual free market that are both higher and more unstable than they would be without government procurement and food subsidies (Hayami, Subbarao, and Otsuka 1982).

The handling of cheap-food policies via overvalued exchange rates can also be motivated by clientele-seeking. Lattimore and Schuh (1976) have examined the hypothesis that Brazilian government intervention in the pricing of beef has the objective of holding down prices for this commodity, which is consumed by middle- and upper-income consumers and hence is politically important. The instrument used to achieve this goal is the overvaluation of the exchange rate for beef. The level of intervention is measured by the difference between the world price, expressed in national currency evaluated at the free market exchange rate, and the domestic price, which thus incorporates the effect of overvaluation. Regression coefficients significantly different from zero are found in the relation between this level of intervention and both the free-market import price and the rate of increase in the general consumer price level. This empirically observed behavior is interpreted as supporting the hypothesis that a cheap-beef policy originates in the political motivation of seeking clienteles among the middle- and upper-income classes.

The extent of appropriation of institutional rents by politicians and bureaucrats, including the military, depends upon the degree of accountability of the state, the class origin of the state bureaucracy, and the composition of the coalition formula in power. As is typical of postcolonial and bureaucratic-authoritarian regimes, the state enjoys a considerable degree of relative autonomy that eventually allows agents of the state to capture abundant institutional rents. Particularly in relatively stagnant economies, where control of the state means control of the rules of zero-sum games, access to power in the political and bureaucratic hierarchies may be the surest road to wealth. The class origins of state agents also influence the form under which rents are appropriated. In Latin America, the urban bureaucratic class is a direct beneficiary of cheap-food policies while the politically relevant social sectors in agriculture are compensated for low prices by institutional rents. In India, by contrast, the rural origin of an increasing majority of representatives in the Lok Sabha and control by the agrarian lobbies of the Agricultural Prices Commission lead to a coalition formula at the state level where the urban-based bureaucrats derive benefits from food subsidies, while the farmers gain from product price supports, expansion of effective demand through urban food subsidies, and input subsidies. The difference between producer and subsidized consumer prices as well as the input subsidies are paid by the state, at the cost of lower public investment.

Because of the state's monopoly in the production of many key intermediate goods and services and the observed complementarity between private and public investment, insufficient public investment seriously limits economic growth (Bardhan 1984b). A coalition that feeds on rents, and particularly on food subsidies, while effective in ensuring the status quo in the situation of a zero-sum game, eventually negates the capacity of the economy to reproduce the very source of rent on which the coalition is grounded.

Analysis of the state activated from within, by either clientele-seeking or rent seeking, thus provides us with a number of testable hypotheses regarding the magnitude of cheap-food interventions and the distribution of welfare gains. Clientele-seeking tells us that cheap-food interventions will be more actively promoted if they generate political support and if politicians and bureaucrats have a better knowledge of the relation between subsidies and induced political support. The targeting of benefits toward the clientele most relevant for political support often does not include those most at nutritional risk. Rent-seeking tells us that politicians and bureaucrats will promote cheap food to their benefit if public accountability is low and if the political coalition in power is more inclined to a short-run sharing of the spoils from public revenues than to promoting accumulation or defending its legitimacy.

Lobbies and Pressure-Group Politics

In addition to electoral politics and bureaucratic behavior, lobbies and pressure groups form an important mechanism through which food subsidy programs expand or contract and through which the distribution of their welfare gains becomes transformed. The less autonomy the state has, the more these demands determine the making and implementation of policy. At the limit, lobbies and pressure groups are able to make public policy if they are able to appropriate particular institutions of the state, thus effectively balkanizing the state apparatus, as is common in less developed countries, or, if the dominant class acquires monopoly power over the state, reducing it to the orthodox Marxist vision of the instrumental state. Short of these local- or global-monopoly theories, there are basically two ways of looking at how pressure groups affect cheap-food policies and programs. One is through rent-seeking, the other in terms of demands for compensation when some of the net social gains from development programs have to be transferred to the absolute or the relative losers.

Rent-seeking can be conceptualized as a situation in which there exist both political and economic markets. In economic markets, the equilibria between demand and supply are derived from consumers maximizing utility and producers maximizing profit. In political markets, equilibria are reached when neither supporters or opponents of a program nor politicians are willing to alter the form of intensity of government intervention. A change in government intervention away from this equilibrium would lead losers to offer to pay up to a certain amount to prevent the change, while gainers would be willing to offer up to a certain amount to secure it. Obviously, if all markets and information were perfect and organization costless, the amount offered by losers to oppose the change would always exceed the amounts offered by the gainers. The key asymmetry is in the political economy: according to relative social positions, the income changes determined by political interventions vary greatly. As a result, redistributive government interventions can occur in favor of the groups that are politically more effective at managing this transformation (Brock and Magee 1978; Rausser, Lichtenberg, and Lattimore 1983).

For programs of food subsidies this means once again that the demands of the most malnourished will rarely have the same political clout as the demands of the better organized—hence the urban bias in most food-subsidy programs. If, in addition, farm lobbies are powerfully organized, this will mean either favorable farm-price support levels with a price wedge financed by the state, as in India, or generous institutional rents as in Brazil and Colombia. Another useful interpretation of pressure-group politics in regard to food subsidies is to look at them as demands for compensation for either absolute or relative losses incurred by the poor. Short-run compensation may thus be sought for the negative real-income effects of inflation, devaluation (Jamaica), or of an increase in the price of food to stimulate supply response in agriculture (China). Long-run compensation may be demanded in the context of successful but inequalizing growth. This has been the case of the Latin American growth paths under late import-substitution industrialization as well as neoliberalism, and of Egypt, Tunisia, and Morocco in their transitions to open-economy models. The food riots that followed attempts to reduce the compensatory subsidies to the poor in the latter three countries were explicit protests against the social implications of open economy models.[2] In these cases, food subsidies can reach enormous magnitudes over time because they are used as substitutes for the structural reforms that alone would make growth compatible with equity. In Egypt, where foreign-exchange constraints have not been limiting, these compensatory subsidies could be maintained without much difficulty. In Sri Lanka, an increasingly limiting foreign-exchange constraint due to sharply falling international terms of trade legitimized the attempt to resolve the trade-off between food subsidies and long-term growth and employment creation in favor of the latter. Though the poor were given transfers in the form of food stamps, the falling real value of these stamps led to a rapid increase in malnutrition and morbidity (Herring 1985). In this case, democratic mobilization behind the issue of long-term growth and employment permitted the legitimiza-

2. For a similar interpretation of the Egyptian food riots, see section 3.4, "The Moral Economy of Food Prices" in Dethier (1985). As Dethier points out, quoting Soshan (1980), many historians "reject the simplistic correlation between social disturbances and high food prices. In their view grain riots . . . not only express discontent with actual deprivation, but are a reaction to structural changes in the political economy [of the country]."

tion of liberalization policies that exposed the poor to higher food prices and the uncertainties of an open economy.[3]

The state activated from below by lobbies and pressure-group politics gives us a set of hypotheses about the direction and magnitude of cheap-food policies and programs. Food subsidies will tend to increase with greater political organization and representation of consumer interests, greater inequality in the ability of different groups to transform political contributions into subsidies, greater use of the state as an instrument for compensatory redistribution than for equity-promoting structural reforms, and rapidly inequalizing growth. The magnitude of food subsidies will tend to increase with the relaxation of constraints on the availability of foreign exchange, public revenues, and food surpluses.

The Program Cycle and the Politics of Scaling Down

We have argued that, in general, policies and programs to cheapen food at the consumer level have been initially introduced as part of broad economic and ideological system imperatives. Like all institutional rents, these subsidies subsequently create their own political clienteles in response to electoral politics and bureaucratic behavior, lobbies and pressure-group politics, and the dynamic interactions between them. This political momentum tends to amplify the scope of the subsidies and redefine their clientele away from the groups most nutritionally at risk. The contradictions that cheap-food policies (through overvalued exchange rates or forced deliveries at low prices) create on the supply side tend to displace the crisis at the state level by forcing introduction of either a price wedge between farm and consumer levels, or compensatory institutional rents for selected farmers, financed, in both cases, out of public revenues. Unless the state has abundant foreign-exchange reserves (generally from oil, debt, or aid), this displacement creates a fiscal or legitimacy crisis for the state.

The politics of scaling down subsidies to meet the limits of the state have been successfully managed in Sri Lanka (between 1977 and 1979) but have more often led to food riots, such as those in Egypt, Morocco, Tunisia, and earlier in Sri Lanka (1953). Elements of a successful scaling down of food subsidies include: (1) gradually reducing the subsidies and targeting the remaining subsidies toward the politically most demanding sectors; (2) legitimizing the cuts by blaming them on uncontrollable external events, such as IMF-imposed austerity policies, falling international terms of trade, or shrinking foreign-exchange transfers; (3) making explicit the long-term contradictions between subsidies and growth under a democratic form of government (in this case, the program cycle starts and ends with the constraints of system im-

---

3. Comparing the Sri Lankan and Egyptian experiences, Hopkins (1984a) has argued that differences in the degree of legitimacy of the state were a major explanatory factor.

peratives); and (4) substituting structural reforms such as land reform and employment-creation programs.

Conclusion

Using a combination of historical analysis and political economy, we have seen that cheap-food policies seldom translate into effective nutrition policies. Most importantly, extractivist cheap-food policies should be restricted, because they have ultimately contractionary effects on economic growth, while policies that seek lower food prices through technological change and irrigation in agriculture are expansionary. Food subsidies that reduce investment in equitable forms of growth, such as developing irrigation on small farms for the production of staple foods, should also be resisted, because they reduce the welfare of the rural poor and the rate of economic growth. Only when food subsidies are fully financed by foreign aid, as in the case of Egypt, does this trade-off disappear.

When food subsidies have a positive impact on nutrition, a large part of the benefits are often appropriated by social groups that have political power but are not at nutritional risk. The political dynamics of rent-seeking tends not only to redistribute benefits away from the poor and ill-fed but to make these programs overexpanded, creating increasing macroeconomic trade-offs between short-run welfare gains and reduced growth in the long term. Nutritional programs thus tend to progress through cycles that make them particularly vulnerable to scaling down and eventual dismantling at times of macroeconomic crisis.

Promotion of equitable growth thus requires a combination of targeted subsidies to protect the poor until the income effects of increased investment materialize and the diversion of all other subsidies to investment in activities such as agriculture, which has high potential for productivity improvement, dispersed asset ownership, labor-intensive technology, and the provision of staple goods for the domestic market with flexible prices.

2 Determinants of Food Policies: An Attempt to Understand Government Behavior

MICHEL PETIT

To better understand why governments do what they do and to assist in predicting how policies might change in the future, this chapter addresses the question, What are the determinants of food policies?

There has been growing awareness of the importance of this central question in recent years, particularly among economists concerned that politicians ignore their policy advice. It has been increasingly recognized that the blame should not be placed on supposedly incompetent politicians but on too narrow economic analyses. Both Hagedorn (1983) and Rausser (1982) have expressed this view. Hagedorn writes:

> The adjustment of present policy research to the requirements of effective political counseling in democratic societies must be based on the following . . . two inter-related domains: the market and the political coordination of agriculture and agricultural policy. . . . Agricultural economists usually restrict their research to the analysis of the market coordination mechanism. . . . Their domain should be adjusted . . . to cover the political coordination mechanisms, i.e., the various institutions regulating the politician's decisions and the policy process.

At the same time, and somewhat independently, a new political economy has emerged. Referring to the "public choice" literature, Muller (1979) writes:

> Public choice can be defined as the economic study of nonmarket decision-making, or simply the application of economics to political science. The subject matter of public choice is the same as that of political science: the theory of the state, voting rules, voter behavior, party politics, the bureaucracy, and so on. The methodology of public choice is that of economics, however.

Today, the body of literature that can be placed in the "new political economy" category includes such works as those by Olson (1965) on collective action; Downs (1967) on the theory of democracy; Tullock (1965) on bureaucracies; Krueger (1974) and many others on rent-seeking; Stigler (1970) and his followers, and Peltzman (1976) on regulation. Two sets of preoccupations have converged on the study of how policies are determined, which must be clearly distinguished. One begins with a dissatisfaction with the insufficiencies of available economic tools to handle important practical problems, whereas the other aims at extending the application of existing tools and at forging new ones or new links among new ones.

The starting point of this chapter is the need to better understand why agricultural policies are what they are. In this context, the choice to conduct the analysis in terms of political economy stems from the conviction that policies are not designed to reach some economic optimum, be it the most efficient allocation of resources in the long run or the fastest rate of capital accumulation. Rather, following the classical economists, distribution is viewed as essential. Policies are then interpreted as resulting from the struggle among competing interests trying to influence government behavior. Note that this implies a "classical" rather than a "new" definition of political economy (Petit 1985b).

Emphasis will be placed on the positive and predictive rather than on the normative or prescriptive. This should not be construed as implying that it is useless to prescribe policy changes. Rather, it reflects the conviction that in order to prescribe, it is first necessary to describe and interpret the forces at play in the phenomena one wishes to influence. The assessment of the consequences of various policy alternatives will only be touched on here tangentially. Such questions are important, but they are only related to our central question inasmuch as the behavior of the actors involved in the policy process is influenced by their expectation about the likely or possible consequences of the policy alternatives being considered. Expected, rather than actual, consequences are what matters in determining policies.

This chapter is organized in two main parts: (1) the development of a tentative conceptual framework and (2) its application to a case study—the U.S. Dairy Production Stabilization Act of 1983. This partial illustration of the conceptual framework will provide us with clues as to how it can be generalized and applied, particularly to the analysis of food and nutrition policy issues in developing countries.

Toward a Conceptual Framework

It is important to recognize the simple fact that the policy-making process occurs through time. Two dynamic features appear immediately: the process is sequential, and uncertainty plays an important role. These features are discussed first, as they must be taken into account in any conceptual framework designed to analyze the determinants of policies. Two broad hypotheses are then presented as the foundation of the conceptual framework. Finally, the consequences of these hypotheses for interpreting the policy debate and the timeliness of issues are discussed.

Dynamic Features of the Policy Process

The policy process is sequential because it occurs through time. Events, that is, policy decisions and positions taken by the various actors involved, are ordered according to a chronology. Each actor is conscious of that chronology; his behavior is influenced by past events. Furthermore, he knows that what happens today will affect his position tomorrow. Thus, expectations about the future influence his behavior. In most instances this means that the time horizon of each actor extends beyond the date current issues under discussion will be decided. Actors pay attention to the stakes involved in current issues as well as to their future position in the policy process.

Uncertainty results from the mere fact that the consequences of any policy decision occur only after the decision has been made. When an issue is being debated, these consequences are necessarily uncertain, since nobody knows exactly what the future will hold. This influences the behavior of all actors, who display the various attitudes that are familiar to the students of behavior under uncertainty (gambling, hedging, wait and see, seeking more information, etc.).

In such a context, static models are useful, but they suffer from serious limitations because they tend to neglect these dynamic features of the policy process. This is true of the models of individual behavior, although there is no a priori reason to reject the hypothesis that individual actors pursue rational strategies. Their actions are consistent with their objectives, given their perceptions of them and of the constraints that limit what they can do. If one recognizes that these perceptions change through time and that the objectives are closely related to the constraints, it is not too difficult to conceive dynamic models of individual behavior of the actors in the policy process. But interpreting the interactions among policy actors is more difficult. Simple paradigms, such as the Coase's theorem of the Prisoner's Dilemma[1] or the concept of political markets (Rausser 1982), however useful, remain far short of capturing the essential dynamics of the process. What is needed is a broad historical perspective, à la Schumpeter.

Two General Hypotheses

Because we are unable to propose here a broad historical perspective of the type alluded to above, the purpose of this section is more modest. We formulate two general hypotheses that are useful for interpreting actual cases of policy process but which need to be more specific before we can claim to present a theory of the determinants of food and agricultural policies.

1. In the short run, policies can be viewed as the outcomes of conflicts of economic interests regulated through the political process. These out-

---

1. For a discussion of these concepts and of their relevance for explaining the famous "tragedy of the commons," see Lipton (1985).

comes are always subject to revision, and policies evolve from one such revision to another. The importance of each revision and the time span between two successive revisions vary tremendously, and do not seem to obey a simple, general rule.

2. In the long run, economic variables play a critical role in the evolution of policies, but this influence is always exerted through the mediation of the political process and, as a result, it does not follow a purely economic rationality.

Discussion

Direct observation discloses that special-interest groups always attempt to influence public officials. This is obvious in democratic societies; it is also true in other societies, even where political power is more concentrated. There is an abundant literature on how special-interest groups influence public policies. The most interesting treatment is by Olson (1965), who has shown that any group is faced with the problem of eliminating free riders—those who benefit from the collective action even though they do not pay for it—or at least minimizing their numbers.

In most developing countries, economic interest groups are not very well organized, nor is their role very visible. This does not mean that governments are not subjected to the pressures of special interests. On the contrary, it is often useful to raise the question of whose interests are actually taken most into account by government policies. What role do unorganized masses play? Are urban workers and consumers more likely to be heard than the dispersed rural dwellers? Can the latter be totally ignored? At what cost? For how long? These broad questions suggest that conflicts of interest play as important a role in the policy process of developing countries as they do in developed countries. More research is needed before hypotheses can be proposed to render account of these conflicts.

When interest groups can be clearly identified, many other questions remain open. It is true that, in spite of well-known analytical difficulties, cohesive and organized groups may often be viewed, for the sake of analysis, as individual actors following a rational strategy—that is, their behavior is consistent with their objectives and their objectives reflect their situation. But there is no such a thing as a perfectly homogeneous group. Members' interests are diverse. Some are identical or sufficiently similar that a collective effort to enhance them makes sense; other interests differ, and some even conflict. Group managers know this very well; they must find ways to mobilize members around joint objectives and pacify those who are hurt through compromises.

Groups are constantly under stress—some die, some split, new ones emerge, new alliances are formed, new conflicts arise. It is this dynamic process that must be interpreted and for which relevant and powerful hypotheses are missing.

Whatever these limitations of our knowledge are, it is clear that individuals having similar interests often attempt to act collectively in order to enhance these interests. In order to be influential, they must be organized. This need results from the fact that interest groups interact with another category of actors in the policy process—government agencies. Public authorities never constitute a monolithic group. There are many different agencies, each with their own bureaucracies. In addition, each one has a separate function, and hence a specific set of priorities and a specific constituency. For instance, in many countries the ministry of agriculture is viewed as, and often actually is, the ministry of the farmers. Recognizing that government agencies do not constitute a monolithic state apparatus does not rule out the possibility of coordination among them. Ideology, in particular, seems to play an important role in this respect. Yet it is useful to view government agencies as distinct policy actors.

The policy process results from the interactions among all these actors, in which conflicts of interest, particularly conflicts of economic interest, play a critical role. Eventually, a policy decision has to be made by a public authority and, until revised, that decision is publicly enforced.[2] In that sense, policies are viewed as resulting from conflicts of interest regulated through the political process.

Changes in conflicts of economic interest lead to changes in organizations and in their relative influence, that is, to political changes that may be more or less important. These in turn lead to changes in policies, which then influence the distribution of economic interests. This recursive model of interaction between the economic and the political is probably oversimplified, but it does suggest a dynamic process that is self-sustained.

In the long run, economic forces play a critical role in determining the evolution of policies. By economic forces we mean long-term trends resulting from the behavior of a small number of individual actors—be they large firms or government agencies. For instance, the long-term rise in the price of labor relative to other prices in many developed countries cannot be attributed to the role of any single actor. It is true that government policies may have favored this evolution, but they did not cause it. Such a change in relative prices had a tremendous impact on the evolution of agriculture and, as a result, on agricultural policies. Similarly, variations in the balance between supply and demand on agricultural markets, the level of agricultural prices, or the public-budget cost of farm programs, have historically played an important role in the evolution of market-intervention policies in Europe and the United States (Petit 1985a).

The articulation between these long-run determinants of agricultural pol-

2. Of course, there are instances where enforcement is not effective. But the very fact of discussing agricultural and food policies implies that many such policies matter, and hence they are somehow enforced.

icies and the policy process in the short run must be spelled out. Long-term economic forces influence the relative position of the various actors in the policy process and thus their conflicts of interest. Hence, one can understand that in the long run, economic forces play a critical role, but that this influence is not exerted according to a purely economic rationality.

Consequences: The Role of the Policy Debate and Timeliness of Issues

In order to influence public officials, organizations express their views, privately and publicly, and provide information to support them or to counter those of their adversaries. In other words, they participate in the policy debate. Clearly, this debate is an important part of the policy process. In open democratic societies the debate is more public and, therefore, more visible to outside observers than in societies where political power is concentrated in the hands of a dictator, a small group, or even a single political party. But even in extreme cases, there is no doubt that a policy debate takes place, even if most of it occurs behind closed doors. Its existence is important for the study of policy determinants, inasmuch as it provides information about an important aspect of the process. One should, however, keep in mind that such information is always partial.

The debate usually revolves around a limited number of issues, and the nature of these key issues changes through time. Participants and close observers are very conscious of the timeliness of issues. But how can this timeliness be interpreted? Why is one issue timely today but not yesterday or tomorrow? This again illustrates the dynamic nature of the policy process. In the social bargaining that takes place during the policy debate, each party attempts to obtain as good a result for itself as possible. The starting point of the debate is existing current policies. Various groups exert pressures to revise them in contradictory directions. If nothing has changed since the last revision, there is no reason to believe that the policy will be revised. Thus it is a change in the distribution of economic interests or in the distribution of power among government agencies that can lead to a revision, and the debate revolves around such potential revisions. They define whether or not an issue is timely or not.

To understand the strategies of the various parties involved and their interactions, the analogy of the theater, rather than that of a formalized game, may be useful. Each actor has his part to play, usually with some initiative to write his own lines. Some actors have a lead role, others are more secondary. What goes on in center stage is important, but important events also occur backstage. The analogy can be extended to the role of the chorus in ancient Greek drama, which is composed of observers commenting and often lamenting but having no influence on the outcome. Many academic economists, this author included, belong to the chorus.

The Making of the U.S. 1983 Dairy Production Stabilization Act

In November 1983, President Reagan enacted the Dairy Stabilization Act, which introduced important changes in United States dairy policies. It included a diversion plan whereby farmers who agreed to reduce their dairy production would receive a significant payment (U.S. $10/cwt.)[3] This policy decision was the outcome of a very controversial debate, which received much press coverage in the United States. It mobilized the energies of many groups and provides us with a case study to illustrate the relevance and limitations of our conceptual framework.[4] We will present the chronology of events leading to the act, discuss the strategies of the various actors involved, and review the issues underlying the debate. As such, this case study will focus on the determinants of policies in the short run. It is only incidentally that we will reflect on the influence of long-term economic forces.

The Events

The growing surplus of dairy products and the associated budget costs of government intervention[5] led Congress in 1982 to introduce two $.50/cwt. assessments on dairy farmers. This measure did not satisfy any of the actors involved and precipitated the events that led to the 1983 act. Everyone agreed that the growth in production and in treasury costs had to be checked, but solutions to the problem differed. Dairy farmers viewed the assessment as a tax that reduced their receipts but had no positive effect on demand. The administration did not think such a measure would be sufficient to check the growth in production; but it doggedly implemented the assessments as a way to put pressure on Congress to change dairy policy. Legislators sensitive to dairy policy were under great pressure to act, but they knew they had no chance to pass any dairy legislation in Congress unless it was supported by all segments of the dairy industry—and the industry was divided. A large majority of the National Milk Producers Federation, the apex dairy organization, favored a diversion plan, but a minority from the southeastern states and from southern California wanted a straightforward reduction in the level of price supports. Since they were located in deficit areas where very little milk is affected by government intervention, they felt that they would be affected less than producers in surplus areas by a reduction in the intervention price.

Under the initiative and in the presence of a few legislators, a compromise was laboriously worked out between these two groups. The secretary of agri-

---

3. Prices are usually expressed in U.S. dollars per hundredweight (1 cwt. = 100 pounds) of milk.

4. Space allows only a brief presentation here. For more details, see Petit (1985a).

5. For the purpose of this illustration, it is sufficient to mention the main feature of dairy policy prior to the 1983 act: the government purchase of specific products, such as butter, milk powder, and some cheese, in order to support prices.

culture participated in these discussions. Thus the so-called compromise bill was elaborated in the spring of 1983. It included the creation of a diversion program for a 15-month period, an immediate reduction in the price-support level, and authorization for the secretary to further reduce the price support if projected government purchases remained high. Finally, the two $.50/cwt. assessments were eliminated, but a $.50/cwt. assessment was to be collected from farmers who did not reduce their production. A compromise was possible because each group realized that without one there would be no new legislation, which could rapidly become a very dangerous situation.

An alliance was made with tobacco program supporters, tying dairy and tobacco policy revisions together in the same bill, a purely procedural linkage that turned out to be critical in the final outcome. But a major problem arose when the administration insisted that acceptance of the compromise include a provision to freeze target prices for other agricultural commodities. Dairy leaders refused to cooperate, as they did not want to be pitted against other agricultural interests. The stalemate was only broken when the secretary gave up the linkage with the target price-freeze after it had become clear that Congress would not even discuss it. The secretary stated that he would then be neutral on the dairy issue. The Senate voted in favor of the compromise bill, with the decisive battle to be fought in the House. Both sides were fully organized. Dairy organizations, now completely united, launched a very sophisticated lobbying campaign. A coalition was formed on the other side, including dairy processors, consumer groups, and farm organizations who felt their interests were threatened by the proposed bill. The coalition was supported by the administration, including the secretary of agriculture. Finally, the House adopted the compromise bill by a large margin.

Attention shifted to the president. Would he sign or veto the bill passed by Congress? In spite of the administration's serious reservations, he signed it, presumably for political considerations—several Republican senators facing difficult reelection campaigns stated the need for a dairy or tobacco bill. At a time when Republican control of the Senate was threatened, the new political stakes were very high indeed.

Strategies of the Various Actors

As already indicated, dairy interests played a critical role in the policy process. First they were divided and legislation could not move; then they reached a compromise and their pressure provided momentum to the policy process. Accepting a compromise does not mean that an organization changes its long-term objectives. Rather, it should be interpreted as acceptance of the best among a poor choice of feasible alternatives. Since time is required to assess what is feasible at any given point, the process is slow.

The fact that dairy interests are represented by dairy cooperatives, or federations of cooperatives, is probably important in the definition of their strategies. They are undoubtedly concerned about the economic interests of their members, but they also worry about the development of the organization itself. Thus, the opposition of southern cooperatives to a diversion plan may have in part been motivated by the desire to protect their supply of raw material in order to avoid operating at a low level of capacity utilization.

It is striking that once a compromise was reached, all organizations worked hard to support it—forcefully opposing those they defended earlier. All the tricks of the lobbying trade were effectively used.

Other agricultural interests entered the policy debate to oppose the dairy compromise. This unusual situation reflects the conviction of some, such as the meat producers, that they would be hurt. But more important, it reflects an ideological opposition to government interference with market forces and handouts to sectoral interests. The involvement of the pork and broiler producer organizations in the policy debate occurred during the summer of 1983. They resorted to the usual lobbying activities and were active in organizing the coalition against the compromise bill.

A small number of legislators played a key role. They were elected from states or districts where dairy production is important and needed to show that they had been instrumental in bringing about new dairy legislation. Some took great political risks in initiating a compromise that they then had to sell to their constituents, arguing that the choice was between a bad compromise or no new legislation, which meant continuation of the hated assessments. The extent of their legislative victory in the face of a formidable opposition may appear surprising. Why, after all, did so many urban congressmen support a program that most economists viewed as a rip-off by the powerful dairy lobby at the expense of the public interest—an opinion widely reported and supported by the press? Much has been made, in this respect, of the financial contributions by dairy organizations to the electoral campaigns of many legislators. But the amounts involved are such a small percentage of the total cost of a campaign that such an argument cannot explain the result. Actually, many legislators had probably made deals with colleagues, supporting the dairy legislation in exchange for their colleagues' support of legislation that mattered more to them; they could accept these deals because the compromise bill seemed to lead to a faster reduction in dairy surpluses and lower budget costs over one or two years than a straightforward reduction in the price-support level would have.

The main actor in the administration was the secretary of agriculture. His behavior in the dairy-policy debate, shifting from participation in the elaboration of the compromise in April, to neutrality in the summer, and finally to opposition in the fall, can only be understood if one remembers that dairy policy was only one element of his overall plan of action. He needed to maintain the farmers' political support for the administration while implementing the president's general policy orientations. This meant reducing government intervention, relying as much as possible on market mechanisms, and decreasing budget costs.

In this respect, developments in FY 1983 were very embarrassing, since the cost of commodity programs, including the famous PIK (payment in kind) program, had reached an unprecedented level. Forcefully implementing the two $.50/cwt. assessments was an effective way to call the farmers' attention to the surplus problem. Participating in the compromise in April can be interpreted as an exploration of feasible options. Insisting on the linkage with a target price-freeze may have helped establish that the administration badly wanted the freeze and that only Congress should be blamed for the continued high budget cost of agricultural programs.

Finally, the secretary is reported to have recommended to the president that he sign the bill. He may have felt that he had made his point and that if the bill failed to check production, his view would be vindicated, while if it worked, he would be under less political pressure to do something about dairy policy.

The Issues and the Policy Debate

Much of the debate revolved around whether or not there should be a diversion plan. By 1983, growth in production and associated government purchases of surplus dairy products had been such that a social or political limit had been reached. Everyone agreed that something was necessary to check that growth. There was even a consensus on the need to reduce the price-support level in nominal terms. Clearly, this had not existed a few years earlier.

Regional conflicts of interest emerged in the debate. The real stakes behind these conflicts were not clear, however; even today it is not evident whether the main issue was the differential impact of policies on dairy farmers' incomes in various regions, or their impact on regional milk supply and, as a result, on the utilization capacity of the various processing facilities. But what is clear is that the regional issue took a specific form in 1983. Even if it remains an issue in future years, the terms of the regional debate will no doubt be different.

It is interesting to note that dairy farmers' incomes and the level of prices paid by consumers did not figure prominently in the debate. The former was indeed implicit in the position of the dairy lobby, and concern for the latter explains why consumer groups joined the coalition against the compromise bill.[6] But, clearly, other, more immediate considerations regarding the level of government stocks and the projected budget costs over one or two years seem to have weighed much more heavily in legislators' decisions to vote for or against the bill.

---

6. The fact that consumer groups did not win in this debate does not mean that they are powerless in the United States. The existence of a very large food-stamp program and of stricter regulations concerning the quality and the labeling of products testifies to the contrary. But, as with other groups, their power is limited. They could not impose their views on a reduction of the milk-price support this time. Generally, their influence on strictly agricultural policies has never been very large, but they have formed successful alliances with farm groups on several occasions in the past.

Finally, it appears that short-term considerations played a very important role in the politicians' decision. This is often very frustrating for economists, who realize that the policy decision will not solve the long-term issue. Recent development in United States dairy production, after the 1983 act was implemented, largely vindicates the economists' point of view—but in a positive rather than a normative perspective. This feature of the decision-making process also explains why in the long run, economic forces may be determinant. If a problem is not solved because the policy decision process is very myopic, the problem is sure to arise again and to affect the policy debate in the future. Thus the fact that the dairy diversion plan was not effective in bringing about a balance between long-term supply and demand called for and led to new measures.

Conclusion

This case study has illustrated that policies are the outcomes of conflicts of interest regulated through the political process. In the short run, the particular outcome depends very much upon the interests at stake, the ways in which they are organized, and their ability to influence officials. The latter depends, of course, on the institutions shaping the political process. In the long run, long-term economic forces play a critical role, even if this case study does not illustrate it directly. These forces shape the evolution of economic interests and variables that government agencies are sensitive to. Thus they largely determine which issues are critical at any point in time.

To what extent can these general hypotheses and this broad conceptual framework be applied to other agricultural and food policies? In other democratic and developed countries, using such an approach to study the determinants of agricultural policies seems possible and useful, as illustrated, for instance, by research currently being conducted on the determinants of agricultural policies in the European Economic Community (Petit et al. 1987). The only major difficulty is access to information, which is often viewed as confidential by the actors involved.

What about food policies in developing countries? Access to information may also be a problem there. But the major difficulty may be the identification of the interests at stake and of the organizations that represent them, or pretend to do so. In many instances, the conflicts are at least as sharp as in developed countries, but their expression by pressure groups is probably less clean-cut. The political process, being less open, is probably more confused and consequently more difficult to interpret. Research along the lines suggested in this chapter would have to be attempted before a definite conclusion could be reached in this respect.

In many cases, the mass of the population is poorly organized and, as a result, not well represented politically. Yet food or nutrition policies are widespread. This paradox is particularly acute in the case of famines. The victims of famines are usually found among the weakest segments of the population; but the degree of pressure exerted on public authorities in such crises can be staggering. The solution to this contradiction may be found in the fear that those who are not hungry have of those who are. The former are afraid of riots and threats to their property and personal security. Hence, public authorities are under very strong pressure to do something. This explains why authorities are often tempted to hush up and minimize the problem in the instance of a food crisis, thereby making the solution of the problem more difficult. One can understand that even if morally wrong, such behavior is fully rational. The difficulties faced by national authorities are often compounded by the con-tradictions of external pressures.

On the one hand, international public opinion is very critical of national authorities, whom they view as very ineffective because they did not prevent the famine. This blame weakens the legitimacy of the government within its terri-tory. On the other hand, international agencies, such as the International Mone-tary Fund or the World Bank, often exert pressure on national authorities to reduce food subsidies, and it is well known that such curtailments have often led to food riots. Thus the political economy of famines illustrates the complex set of interrelationships among various policy actors in developing countries. Even if specific interest groups cannot always be identified, the analysis of conflicts of interest and their regulation through the political process seems to constitute a promising approach to understanding how food nutrition policies change.

Whatever the merits of this hypothesis for the analysis of food policy-making in developing countries, it is important to remember that the conceptual framework presented here falls far short of constituting a theory of the policy-making process. In particular, even if the individual strategies of the various actors can be interpreted, a systematic body of hypotheses remains to be elabo-rated. In addition, and perhaps more importantly, very limited knowledge is available regarding the interactions through time of the various actors. If the concept of a political market where political agents offer policies in response to a demand by economic agents does not appear very illuminating, one must recognize that few alternative hypotheses have been suggested. In such a state of knowledge, careful case studies are called for, from which it will hopefully be possible to infer general hypotheses in the future. In the meantime, the conceptual framework presented in this chapter provides us with an interesting and useful interpretation of why agricultural polices are what they are in specif-ic cases.

3 The Politics of Food Policy in Sri Lanka: From Basic Human Needs to an Increased Market Orientation

DAVID E. SAHN AND NEVILLE EDIRISINGHE

Introduction

Economists have long debated what strategy will best promote the primary goals of development: economic growth and equitable distribution of income. The fact that a cornerstone of this debate has been the assertion of the incongruity of these objectives has often served to polarize both economists and policy makers into those concerned primarily with growth and those concerned with equity (Kuznets 1972; Adelman, Adelman, and Taft 1973). This dilemma has been further fueled by confusion over how to realize either aspiration.

During the past few decades, the profession witnessed an evolution of ideas on how the objectives of growth and equity are best achieved. One school of thought reflected in the policies of many countries, is that government should intervene strongly and pervasively in the economy. The state is considered to be best equipped to optimally allocate scarce resources for the good of all while fostering the necessary social and institutional changes required to bring about self-sustaining economic growth. Such an approach often leads to a set of policies that include a high level of protection for domestic manufacturing, a plethora of state-owned enterprises, price controls on most, if not all, major commodities, and high levels of government recurrent expenditures devoted largely to maintaining political power, be it through expanding the influence of the military or by subsidizing food to gain favor with the populace. The emerging consensus is that many of the state-run economies have been racked by inefficiency, corruption, and distorted allocation of productive resources. This has retarded the transformation of society as originally envisaged.

Disappointment with the effects of major intervention by the government in the economies of developing countries has given rise to other ideas on how best to foster prosperity and equity. Liberalizing the economy through the reduction of state controls and ownership has assumed a new position of prominence. The tenets of such an outward-looking strategy have been embraced by many countries (Krueger 1980). Ideas currently in use include opening up international trade by removing state protection of industries and promoting exports, decontrolling prices and reducing subsidies, promoting fiscal restraint, eliminating state-owned industries and enterprises, removing cumbersome banking controls, and promoting rational capital markets to encourage savings and more propitious investments.

The extent to which government policies reflect this changing wisdom varies widely among countries. Sri Lanka is one nation that has unquestionably been strongly affected. A reorientation is manifested in the major macroeconomic changes that began in 1977, when a new political party assumed power. Although the new government moved toward a more market-oriented economy, it remained a major actor in the economy as manifested in the growing level of government borrowing and investment from 1977 onward. Thus, while we will show that policy changes in Sri Lanka do not strictly conform to the tenets of a structural adjustment toward a completely liberalized economy, the reordering of priorities away from welfarism and toward economic growth is perhaps nowhere more evident than in the arena of food policies. Similarly, the results of these macropolicy shifts are of greatest concern, as manifested in the food intake and nutritional status of the population. Therefore, this chapter examines the transition of development philosophy in Sri Lanka, focusing on the implications of food-subsidy policy changes for the poor. In particular, we concentrate on the shift from a basic human-needs approach, characterized by extensive government intervention in the economy and large food subsidies, to a more market-oriented approach whereby economic growth itself is expected to provide benefits to all members of society through the market mechanism.

In examining this transition, a political economy perspective is employed. The focus is on the social processes and institutional mechanisms that bring about change. Understanding the nature of these changes in a context broader than mere descriptions of the policy reforms can provide is vital, given that economic liberalization is politically difficult; inevitably, major macropolicy reforms will have immediate losers as well as gainers. In the case of Sri Lanka, it is suggested that the poor—those who had benefited most from heavy government intervention, especially in the food sector—may be the short-term losers. The questions remain whether the poor stand to gain enough over time to compensate for any short-term dislocation and how and with what efficacy has the political process responded to mitigate any potential deleterious short-term effects of macroeconomic changes on the standard of living, especially of the poor.

The Origin of Social Welfare and Food Policies in Sri Lanka, 1948–1977

The recent political economic history of Sri Lanka began with independence in 1948, after nearly 450 years of foreign rule. It was, however, during the last 150 years of colonial rule under the British that the major structural transformation of the social system and economy occurred. This change, in the words of dependency theorists, represented a distortion of the ecological, social, and economic structure of the island. It fully entrenched the export-oriented plantation economy. The three tree crops—tea, rubber, and coconut—accounted for more than 90 percent of the total export earnings at the time of independence (Herring 1981). Therefore, the country was overtly subject to the vagaries of international prices for three primary products. This fact was to remain a permanent fixture of the Sri Lankan economy, as manifested by the fact that in 1984 these tree crops still accounted for 57 percent of the country's exports (Central Bank of Ceylon 1984). Concurrently, the competition for natural resources and capital between the modern capitalist sector and the traditional low-productivity peasant sector was a classic example of a dualistic economy.

Of equal importance was the legacy of democracy that the British left behind. By the time of independence, Sri Lanka had experienced many years of universal suffrage. A commitment to parliamentary democracy became a cornerstone of the political context in ensuing years.

In addition to colonial rule, the events of the Second World War were important in terms of influencing development, food policy, and food subsidies, whose evolution is the focus of the remainder of this chapter. Specifically, food-related transfer payments were a direct legacy of the war. They originated in 1942, when rice rationing commenced in deficit areas because of interruptions in normal import channels due to the global conflict (Edirisinghe and Poleman 1976). Soon rationing of food, which was to protect consumers from soaring prices, spread throughout the island nation. In the decades that followed, the food subsidy grew steadily and remained at high levels until the economic changes that occurred in the late 1970s.

In assessing the growth of the subsidy scheme between 1942 and 1977, a few domestic and international events serve to illustrate the interplay between politics and economics, which led to the formulation of a food policy in Sri Lanka. The maintenance of the welfare program during the period 1948–52 was assisted to a large extent by the boom in the economy induced by the Korean War. Exports fetched high prices and the balance of payments was favorable. This trend reversed in 1952 and resulted in the contraction of trade, worsening of the balance of payments, and depreciation of the rupee. By mid-1952, the import price of rice had increased sharply. The government realized that the budget deficit, partially attributable to food-subsidy expenditures, was becoming a serious burden. At this time, the size of the basic rice ration, which was kept constant at three pounds per person per week since 1948, was reduced by one-half pound per household, but there were no changes in prices.

The most sweeping changes in the subsidy program occurred in 1953. The government's overadherence to an International Monetary Fund (IMF) proposal to phase out the subsidy scheme resulted in a price increase of nearly 300 percent on rice rations. At the same time, postal, telegraph, railway, and electricity rates were also subjected to substantial price hikes. These measures, particularly the ration-price change, became the target of the *Hartal*—a massive protest launched mainly in urban areas. The immediate outcomes were civil disruptions, a few deaths, damage to state property, and increase in the ration entitlement at reduced prices, and the resignation of the prime minister. These events marked the beginning of the "rice issue," which was to loom large in almost every major political campaign in future years.

The elections of 1956, in which the ruling center-right United National Party (UNP) was defeated by a powerful coalition of Marxist and non-Marxist central-left parties led by the Sri Lanka Freedom Party (SLFP), reaffirmed a role for a consumer-oriented food policy. Emphasis was placed on "planned" economic development, socialization and Ceylonization of productive resources, and state patronage to directly assist the poor and the middle class. Relief to the poor was provided through reduction of rice and sugar prices, increases in health and unemployment benefits, village expansion, and colonization schemes. These welfare-oriented policies were reaffirmed by the electorate in 1960. The state grew more powerful, more egalitarian; distributional policies were adopted and welfarism continued to grow.

In the 1965 general elections, food was not a major issue. Rather, the focus was on more ideological concerns, such as the role of the state and freedom of the press. Government did change hands; a coalition led by the United National Party (UNP) ruled from 1965 to 1970. Shortly after this change, however, the focus on food subsidies resumed. Rice prices had soared by 1966 due to a shortfall in world rice output against a backdrop of increasing world demand. These exogenous events once again contributed significantly to balance-of-payment difficulties. An element of economic reality was the IMF conditionality that expenditures on social services be restricted. In December 1966, domestic policy responded to the changing international climate: the basic ration was cut by one half and issued free of charge. This was a strategic compromise between economic reality and political feasibility, the latter of which was necessitated due to the public's long-standing expectation that rationed rice would be available at subsidized prices. The result of the reduction in the ration was a substantial decline in imports. Per capita imports of rice, which averaged 46 kilograms between 1960 and 1966, declined to 29 kilograms between 1967 and 1971. Subsidy changes were accompanied by a massive campaign to intensify domestic rice production.

The changes in 1966 are significant in several respects. First, somewhat drastic subsidy reductions were not followed by food riots. These cuts were preceded by a declaration of an emergency in order to reduce the potential for adverse reaction among the population. In addition to this precautionary action, the decision to provide the remaining ration free of charge may have dampened initial protests over the subsidy cut. At least in the short run, the free issue of rice was able to partly offset the real-income losses due to the cut in the subsidy.

Second, the rice-intensification program that accompanied the subsidy cuts brought to light the crucial role that technological change can play in expanding agricultural production. New varieties of rice accounted for 43 percent of rice production in 1966. By 1970, this proportion had increased to 70 percent. Between 1960 and 1970, paddy production increased by 70 percent. The key to this success, as manifested in the high rate of farmer response to new high-yielding varieties, was undoubtedly facilitated by the relatively high rates of literacy brought about by social welfare programs.

The rice ration was once again a dominant factor in the election of 1970. Restoration of the rice subsidy was a major promise of the center-left coalition, and this coalition registered a landslide victory. One of the first actions of the new government was to restore the size of the weekly rice ration to four pounds. Before long, the global world food shortage was beginning to affect the cost of imports. As a result, by the end of 1973 the basic ration was reduced by 50 percent despite the strongly espoused commitment to social justice and economic equality. At the same time, the guaranteed price to the farmer was increased by 40 percent. A long-term solution to the vagaries of international markets was sought through intensified efforts to increase domestic food production.

While the above discussion focuses on the role of the political process in the growth and maintenance of food subsidies for the past 30 years of Sri Lanka's history, it must be seen in the larger context of a commitment to welfarism. This was displayed in the widespread health and education coverage on the island. In comparison with other countries, the share of GDP allocated to health and educational services was not exceptionally high. However, the government orientation placed emphasis on widespread coverage of these programs. This is largely reflected in the share of health and educational financing assumed by the government, which was markedly higher in Sri Lanka than in other nations (Richards and Gooneratne 1980).

The performance of Sri Lanka in pursuing policies to meet basic human needs has received pervasive attention from academicians and policy makers alike. Suggestions that Sri Lanka has distinguished itself by the "general political commitment to the poor majority" (Gwatkin 1979a) or that it has achieved "remarkable social progress for a country with a very modest economic base and relatively low per capita income" (Gavan and Chandrasekera 1979) are indicative of the types of praise given during the 1970s. Much of this was a result of the high literacy rate, low infant mortality, and long life expectancy that singled out Sri Lanka from all other nations of comparable per-capita income (Morris 1979). In turn, it has been strongly argued that such accomplishments were largely attributable to the welfare policy in general and the food subsidy policy in particular (Isenman 1980).

Despite the global recognition of Sri Lanka's accomplishments in the area of social welfare, some have expressed doubts about the success that Sri Lanka achieved. In this regard, the sentiments that "Sri Lanka has not been the model example of the application of a basic needs strategy" (Richards and Gooneratne 1980) must be considered.

Specifically, it has been suggested that social welfare policies were implemented coincidentally with policies that impeded economic performance in general and growth in exports in particular (de Melo 1981). In addition, Bhalla (1986) asserts that it was the initial level of literacy and low mortality rates at independence, rather than the social welfare expenditures between 1960 and 1977, that brought about exceptional levels of basic-needs accomplishments. This contention has been disputed by Sen (1986), who argues that the social expenditure of the government did indeed contribute to the long life expectancy and high level of literacy in Sri Lanka. He also points out that while eliminating all expenditures on health, education, and welfare would have doubled the annual rate of GDP growth, such a scenario is unrealistic and the actual rate of 2.4 percent between 1970 and 1977 was better than that of many of Sri Lanka's South Asian neighbors (Sen 1980).

It may also be posited that there is a relationship between expenditures on nutrition, health, education, and growth. The reduction in fertility rates, for example, was partially attributable to high literacy rates coupled with low infant mortality and increased receptivity to family planning. The food ration also provided a sort of insurance against disability in old age. This concept of the subsidy as a form of insurance may have also reduced the risk-averse behavior of farmers, as well as disaccumulation in years of poor harvest or during the lean season (Richards and Gooneratne 1980). This, in turn, may have increased farmers' receptivity to adoption of new technologies (Sen 1980).

It is beyond the scope of this chapter to resolve the opposing viewpoints concerning the actual performance of the Sri Lankan economy prior to 1977 and the efficacy of social welfare expenditures. In addition, the question remains as to whether and to what extent the redistributive policies of the government could have been implemented without the market distortions that were extant. It is clear that tea taxes paid for much of the food imports used in the quantity rationing scheme (Thorbecke and Svejnar 1987). Could this revenue have been raised through other means? And could a variety of other policies, such as reducing government involvement in corporations and removal of many trade barriers, have been adopted concurrently with high levels of social expenditures?

Despite the difficulty in presenting a counterfactual argument as to what would have transpired in the economy without the food subsidy and other pillars of the welfare policy, it is clear that both exogenous events, such as the oil shock, world food crises, and low tea prices, and domestic policy choices in terms of reducing the efficiency of markets contributed to a slow rate of growth during the early 1970s. The taxation of the plantation sector, which provided the needed capital to finance Sri Lanka's welfare programs, further squeezed this sector and provided disincentives to greater investment. Other actions, such as the process of moving toward nationalization of the plantations, land reforms, and expropriation of private businesses, may have also contributed to the stagnation of private investment. Nevertheless, the improvement in the terms of trade from the trough in 1975 witnessed a commensurate increase in economic activity in 1976 and 1977 prior to the election. This trend, however, was not sufficient to dissuade Sri Lankans from voicing their disaffection with the state of economic and political affairs.

In 1977, the voters peacefully brought about a change in government. The leftist coalition built around the SLFP was succeeded by the UNP. The mandate for change was overwhelming. However, some compelling questions arise: What are the characteristics and circumstances that resulted in such a smooth transfer of governmental power in 1977? How did the new government succeed in taking such politically precarious moves as drastically reducing food subsidies, decontrolling prices, and devaluating the currency?

The most important characteristics of the transition from a welfare oriented to liberalized economy were the broad consensus among the people that the performance of the previous government had been unsatisfactory in spite of the commitments to welfare and the democratic heritage that allowed the people to vote for change. The inability of the economy to provide sufficient employment opportunities was a key factor. Mismanagement of the growing number of government-owned institutions and discouragement of private-sector initiatives contributed to unsatisfactory levels of productive employment. Controls on trade, shortages of consumer goods, long lines to purchase essential goods, and the existence of black markets all contributed to a general discontent among the electorate (Moore 1985). The disincentive effects were nowhere harder felt than among the large capitalist class, whose economic activity was curtailed in an era of nationalization, currency restrictions, and state-controlled industries. Thus, the leftist coalition, dominated by the SLFP until it was dismantled in 1975, confronted a series of internal and external political and economic events that resulted in a growing dissatisfaction.

The economic picture, coupled with the fact that the left-of-center coalition was both divided and in disarray, resulted in a political crisis that the UNP capitalized upon by providing a platform where abundance of consumer goods, employment opportunities, and elimination of corruption were promised.

The Postliberalization Period

Following the national elections of July 1977, the UNP acted promptly in bringing about macroeconomic changes designed to fuel economic growth. Such efforts revolved around institutional changes and reforms of policies designed to liberalize trade, provide incentives for productive investment, and increase domestic savings. Associated with these reforms were many "lead projects," entailing heavy capital expenditures that were expected to provide the infrastructure for development.

There are numerous features of the government's actions, some initiated immediately and others phased in over longer periods of time. For example, the government undertook promotion of institutional change through a variety of initiatives, including the formation of several new government agencies to guide and encourage both domestic and foreign private investment (U.S. Agency for International Development 1982). In addition, major policy changes were undertaken. These included (Nelson 1985):

1. Immediate unification of the exchange rate at a level that represented a sharp depreciation of the currency; the currency was also allowed to float.
2. Elimination or reduction of price controls on all but a few select commodities, for example, rice, flour, bread, sugar, coconut oil, kerosene, and bus and rail tickets, that were then decontrolled in phases over the next couple of years.
3. Change in the structure of tariffs to allow for some protection of domestic industries that heretofore were protected by a combination of an overvalued exchange rate, quotas, and exchange controls.
4. Phased adjustments in interest rates in 1977 and again in 1980 to more closely reflect the real prices of capital and thereby encourage savings; and the establishment of a National Development Bank in 1979 to improve the flow of credit.
5. Movement toward elimination of public-sector import monopolies except for certain commodities, such as rice.
6. Reductions in corporate tax rates and tax incentives such as special depreciation provisions.
7. Establishment of free-trade zones to encourage foreign industrial investments.[1]
8. Targeting of the food-ration system to only the lower half of the income distribution beginning in January 1978, followed by the introduction of food and kerosene stamp programs tied to a fixed nominal value beginning in September 1979.

In the transition from one political era to the other, a coherent package of policy reforms and a well-developed strategy to turn around economic stagnation was thus presented and operationalized by the UNP.

---

1. It is also noteworthy that despite these major policy and institutional changes, the number and role of public-sector corporations were not reduced significantly. Rather, emphasis has been on improving the efficiency of these corporations while encouraging new productive investments in the private, instead of public, sector.

It is noteworthy that the reduction in the food-subsidy scheme did not bring about the vociferous opposition that occurred during previous attempts to reduce the program. The question is why. The first, and most prominent, reason is that the government did not advertise its intention to remove the most politically sensitive element of the welfare state—the food subsidies. In fact, the new government actually increased subsidies by decreasing the subsidized price of the rice ration after a few weeks in office (Nelson 1985). Thereafter, the process of strategically phasing down food-related income transfers began. Thus, although there was an overwhelming call for new leadership in Sri Lanka, the removal of the food subsidy was not on the platform of the UNP. Only well after the elections, when the country was already responding to the changing economic environment, did the food subsidy in the form of the quantity rationing scheme meet its demise, although this was brought about gradually to mitigate any adverse political consequences.

To amplify, it was not until January 1978 that the government implemented new regulations to disqualify the upper half of the income distribution from receiving subsidized food; the quantity rationing scheme was restricted to the lower half of the population after a means test. This change was preceded by a vast publicity campaign to show that such changes were required to generate more employment. A second phase, one and a half years later, involved the change from ration shops to food stamps. Under similar eligibility criteria, households could receive food stamps whose value was set in nominal terms, which at the time of the transition exceeded the value of the subsidy from the old quantity rationing scheme. By not indexing the value of the stamps to the cost of living or the price of rice, it assured that fiscal costs of the program would be contained. In addition, the inflationary environment gradually diminished the real value of the transfer to the consumers without the need for any government proclamations or further policy adjustments.

The second reason for the new government's successful reduction in the food subsidy bill is that there was little or no concern over the possibility that the sentiments of the urban population would be aroused by Marxist-oriented political parties. The left-wing political parties had been completely rejected at the 1977 general elections. Their power in the trade unions was eroding due to the strength of the newly organized progovernment trade unions. The first truly concerted effort to protest against the rising cost of living by the leftist-oriented trade unions in 1981 was firmly handled by the government. For the first time in trade union history, over 40,000 protesters lost their jobs.

Third, on the electoral front, people were given the opportunity to express their confidence or nonconfidence through a presidential election in 1982 and a referendum in 1983. These were different from the usual format of the parliamentary general elections that have witnessed regular changes in government. For many, voting at the general elections was a show of confidence or nonconfidence in past experiences of localized patron-client relationships. In the presidential elections, it was a choice of a leader for the whole nation. National issues and the personal popularity of the incumbent president were perhaps more important elements in the presidential elections. Although the rising cost of living and the impact of subsidy cuts were the major issues focused upon by the opposition, at the presidential election there was a comfortable victory for the ruling party. This particularly reflected the view of many voters that early positive effects of economic reforms outweighed the more recent negative effects of the elimination of the food ration and other welfare losses.

The real substitution of the general elections was the referendum held in 1983 to prolong the life of the existing parliament for another six years. In this instance, the referendum did not even involve voting for a candidate but instead was a vote of yes or no to continuation of the existing parliament. The referendum gave rise to a debate on many economic and noneconomic issues, but it apparently lacked the form and spirit found in earlier general elections (Silva 1984). The people had already voted for the leader of the ruling party a year before. There was little or no surprise when the referendum supported continuation of the legislature under the president's control.

In sum, the newly elected government reacted quickly to its overwhelming mandate and took strong measures to reverse the slow growth of the economy in the 1970–1977 period. In this case, free elections brought about political change that enabled economic liberalization and decontrols to gain a strong foothold in Sri Lanka.

The Effects of Liberalization

The success of the economic liberalization scheme can be measured by many indicators. The most visible statistic has been the impressive rate of growth in GDP during the late 1970s. The real growth of 8.2 percent in 1978 and 6.3 percent in 1979 leveled off to around 5 percent between 1982 and 1983.[2] The growth in agricultural GDP grew at a rate of 4.3 percent compared with 1.85 percent from the 1970–1977 period. Similarly, unemployment dropped from 14.8 percent in 1978–79 to 11.7 percent in 1981–82, only three years after the change in government (Central Bank of Ceylon 1984). The unemployment rate recorded for 1970 was around 15 percent and rose to 24 percent during the world food crises of 1973 (Sahn 1986).

In terms of the effects on social programs, food-related income transfers, and investments in human capital, the data indicate the dismantling of the welfare state, especially in the food sector. There was a dramatic decline in the percentage of the GDP and recurrent expenditures devoted to food subsidies as well as in the real value of the subsidies to the consumer. Expenditures on

2. These rates of growth may be overstated because of technical problems with the accuracy of the deflators used in their calculation by the Central Bank (see Bhalla 1985).

education and health care have also declined as a share of total expenditures, although considerably less than the food-related income transfers.

The question remains as to what extent the increase in the growth rate over the late 1970s reflects the fact that liberalization was accompanied by a precipitous increase in the flow of resources from international institutions to Sri Lanka. The comparatively low level of investment in the preliberalization period was partially attributable to acutely low levels of foreign aid (Sen 1980); just the opposite was the case after 1977. In fact, the net foreign financing of the cash deficit increased in real terms from 582 million rupees in 1977 to 1,992 million rupees in 1981. In dollar terms, total aid commitments rose from $250 million in 1977 to over $600 million in 1980.

Around one third of the assistance was outright grants, while the remainder was low-interest long-term loans.

This voluminous increase was not indicative of what was transpiring in neighboring Asian nations. The lesson here is that adopting a policy set that was compatible with the basic principles of international lending institutions reaped major benefits in terms of availability of capital. This led to increased economic activity, amply manifested in rapid growth of the GDP directly after liberalization. As argued by Herring (1981):

> International factors in the new strategy, thus, become critical; international support in material terms has arguably been a necessary condition for the liberalization initiatives. The international development community has provided resources to tide the regime over the potentially rocky re-adjustment period.

Concurrent with the increase in foreign investment and grants, the period from 1977 to 1979 was characterized by a recovery of international tea prices, a major source of foreign exchange in Sri Lanka. The overall improvement in the terms of trade was dramatic. Furthermore, the Keynesian effects of removing controls stimulated demand, which was previously constrained by import restrictions. This, too, contributed to an increase in the growth of GDP. So while there is little question that the origins of the improved economic performance were in the reforms adopted by the UNP, international lending facilities and a favorable international climate in the immediate postadjustment period facilitated economic growth.

The postliberalization regime was not without serious problems, however. These became apparent at the end of 1980. Most obvious was a worsening balance of trade, large trade deficits, a growing budget deficit, and an annual inflation that reached around 40 percent in 1981.

One may attribute the worsening macroeconomic environment of the early 1980s to a number of factors. They partially emanate from the need of the UNP government to employ deficit financing to support a series of public-sector investments initiated concurrently with liberalization. The largest was the capital-intensive Mahaweli River Development Program, with the free-trade zone, major housing and urban development projects, and water projects also demanding heavy public-sector investments. The result was that capital expenditures as a percent of total public expenditures increased rapidly from 24 percent in 1977 to 46 percent in 1982.

External events also significantly contributed to the difficulties encountered with the liberalization program in the early 1980s. Most important were the rise in oil prices and the dramatic deterioration in the terms of trade between 1980 and 1983 to levels that prevailed in 1975. These events adversely affected both foreign-exchange earnings and the budget deficit through the fall in export revenues and revenue from export duties.

As a result of growing deficits and inflation, austerity efforts continued after the election in 1983, both in terms of budget cuts and devaluation. Furthermore, a quick examination of the foreign financial assistance contributing to the net cash deficit makes it clear that continued support of international institutions was a critical prerequisite to Sri Lanka's ambitious investment program.

These questions of macroperformance are dealt with extensively in other reports (Central Bank of Ceylon, various years). Similarly, the microimplications of the policy reforms are addressed in greater detail elsewhere (Sahn 1986). However, there is evidence that the government expected that a combination of reduced subsidies, rapid food-price inflation, and decontrol of prices would be accompanied by a deterioration in the equitability of income distribution in Sri Lanka. This is supported by the Central Bank of Ceylon (1981):

> Income inequality tends to widen in the initial stage of economic growth as richer groups increase their incomes at a faster rate than the lower income groups. Given the economic reforms of 1977 and the massive increase in the investment after that date, it is likely that the trend in the distribution of income will be initially adverse; the economic benefits of major economic reforms do not percolate down to the lower income groups in such a short period.

This, coupled with indications that major price increases of staple food commodities, especially rice, would result in a net loss of income for small farmers, landless laborers, and urban poor, supported the view that despite an improved macroeconomic climate, there might indeed be short-term losers from policy reforms initiated in the late 1970s (Sahn 1987). In reality, the real expenditures of the poorest quartile of the expenditure distribution did decline (Edirisinghe 1985; Sahn 1987). The consumption consequences reflected these changes— the calorie consumption of those in the lowest expenditure deciles dropped between 1978–79 and 1981–82, while intake increased for those in the upper expenditure groups (see figure 3.1).

Recognition of the problems accompanying liberalization revitalized the debate on equity versus growth in Sri Lanka. The long-standing commitment of the political process to provide for the poor resulted in a reexamination of how

FIGURE 3.1 Percentage change in daily calories consumed per adult equivalent, by income decile: Sri Lanka, 1978–1979 to 1981–1982

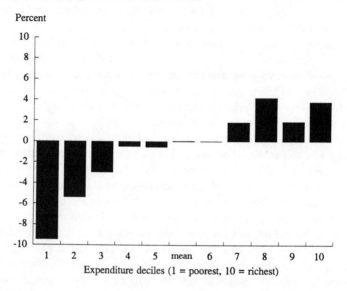

SOURCE: Sahn 1987.

to achieve social goals without jeopardizing investment in physical capital. The government recognized research results that indicate that the real value of the income transfer in the form of food stamps declined and that there was considerable leakage of the food-stamp scheme to upper income groups (Edirisinghe 1985). In 1985, policy reforms were initiated to better target the program.

The revised scheme was to be administered by the Social Services Department instead of the Food Commissioners Department (Sri Lanka Department of Government Printing 1985). The change in the character of the program and the implementing agency was to ensure government determination to achieve efficient targeting of the income transfers. Basically, the new program aimed at redistributing the current outlay of the government transfer to those in the bottom quartile of income distribution. This was warranted because, as of 1982, this quartile received less than 40 percent of the total outlay.

Initial attempts to implement the new program were met with strong protests from both the current beneficiaries and their representatives in the legislature, resulting in a postponement of the implementation.

The goal of improving the efficiency and equitable nature of transfers, even if they were smaller in overall magnitude, is an illustration of Sri Lanka's ongoing concern with the indigent. The roots of these concerns are difficult to delineate. They partially emanate from the political power of the poor, as exerted through long-standing democratic traditions. In addition, the strong intellectual and academic tradition of social welfarism that exists in universities and other institutions in Sri Lanka undoubtedly influences government officials and policy makers, encouraging a concern for and awareness of the needs of the poor. This, coupled with the pride that accompanies the international acclaim received for basic human needs accomplishments, also perpetuated a sensitivity to the needy. This not only portends good things for the poor but for the nation as a whole. The political process reflects the needs of not only the well-to-do but those less prosperous as well.

Conclusions and Lessons

In analyzing the transition in Sri Lanka from what was primarily a welfare-oriented state to a liberalized economy where more emphasis is placed on the free market, a number of consistent themes emerge. Similarly, many issues remain unresolved and lend themselves to further research and analysis.

First, the controversy continues concerning the accomplishments of and returns to social expenditures during the 1960–1977 period. There is little doubt that more efficient operation of social welfare programs would have been feasible. However, one has to view with caution any assertion that diversion of welfare expenditures to investment would have been effective at generating significantly greater growth, especially considering the crucial role of exogenous events and international influence on the Sri Lankan economy. Similarly, the contribution of social welfare programs to economic growth and performance through human capital formation should not be overlooked. Nevertheless, the poor economic performance from 1970 to 1977 was primarily responsible for the election of a new government in 1977, giving it a mandate for the dramatic policy changes that were to occur.

Second, the success of the post-1977 economic reforms hinged fairly heavily on the moral and economic support of the free-enterprise-oriented donor community. In other words, the commitment to promotion of economic efficiency through the market system, rather than government intervention, brought about unprecedented external support. This aid was for investments that actually increased the role of government as an actor in the economy, at least in the short run. In this regard, a number of interesting lessons can be learned. It appears that the government's move toward liberalization by reducing consumer subsidies, decontrolling prices, and devaluing the currency was sufficient to garner support of donors and avoid the monetarist prescriptions that are traditionally associated with the IMF–World Bank structural adjustment programs. Simply, Sri Lanka succeeded in circumventing certain key components of structural adjustment and stabilization, as witnessed by the growth in borrowing and deficit financing that occurred in the postliberalization period. This raises the question as to whether the reduction or elimination of social welfare expenditure was a sine qua non for the external support, despite the government's adoption of an expansionary fiscal policy in the wake of the shift toward a freer market.

Nevertheless, even in the face of pressures from international lending institutions to adhere to certain policies, the most important element that has steered the process of development in Sri Lanka has been the strength of the participatory democracy.

A third consideration is the extent to which the postliberalization economic surge was partially made possible by the extensive investments in human capital that preceded the shift in government priorities. One could hypothesize that in the absence of a relatively educated and healthy population, the effects of the liberalization experience would have been less favorable. On the other hand, one can query why the extensive subsidies and expenditures on human capital development did not fuel rapid economic growth before the policy changes in the late 1970s. Government intervention, mainly in the arena of basic human needs, may be an appropriate prelude to a more laissez-faire approach designed to allow the free market to allocate resources most efficiently.

Fourth, the rather successful and peaceful transition from basic-human-needs-oriented development policies to a free-market economy in Sri Lanka represents a lesson for other nations. There were many periods in Sri Lanka's history in which removal of food subsidies was greeted by anger and violence. This was not the case in 1978. In determining why, a number of propositions arise. One important fact is the phased process in which food subsidies were reduced. Of equal prominence is that the transition took place concurrently with a surge of economic growth and optimism. Just as it has long been argued that social programs are more politically palatable in an expanding economy than in a contracting one, it may well hold that reducing subsidies is more acceptable when the economy is growing and all feel that they will benefit in the not-too-distant future from its continued vitality. This is juxtaposed with reducing food subsidies as part of overall austerity measures in periods of economic retrenchment.

Fifth, such economic policies as devaluation of the currency to promote exports and encourage free trade come into conflict with the large fiscal and foreign-exchange costs of food-subsidy programs. Of course, there are arguments that subsidies moderate wage demands and, thus, export goods may prove more competitive. In theory, lower wages due to subsidies may also promote increased demand for labor. There is, however, no empirical evidence that this theory was realized in the import-substitution economic environment of pre-1978 Sri Lanka, where rigid wage laws also existed.

Similarly, it is noteworthy that the magnitude of recurrent expenditures on food subsidies and other social investments found in Sri Lanka during the 1970s is often the subject of criticism by economists because of the potential link of such spending with budget deficits and, consequently, inflation. However, there is an irony in that the reduction of these expenditures was followed by a period of increased budget deficits, contributing to high levels of inflation. These problems can be attributed to a combination of the government's undertaking other types of investments, especially in the area of infrastructural development, and international shocks to the economy. Undoubtedly, the deficits and inflation would have been exacerbated if recurrent expenditures on transfers would have remained at the historical high levels of the mid-1970s. Nonetheless, it is apparent that even when such expenditures are greatly reduced, if fiscal restraint is not followed in other budget items, the precise macroeconomic problems to which social expenditures may contribute can arise in spite of their reduction. In such a circumstance, those most in need are hurt doubly by the reduction in the income transfers and the ensuing inflation due to international events and government policy in other sectors.

Finally, there are indications of the need for a country such as Sri Lanka to judiciously combine policies such as the promotion of food self-reliance with a liberalized trade regime. While the former is geared to reducing dependency on international markets, the latter tends to increase reliance on other nations. Successful management of such a delicate balance is required so that a disproportionate burden of adjustment does not fall on the indigent.

4 The Political Economy of Colombia's PAN

TOMÁS URIBE MOSQUERA

Introduction

Colombia's National Food and Nutrition Plan (PAN) during the 1975–82 period was a uniquely comprehensive plan, though it was complex and hard to understand. It was not administered by an implementing agency, but, rather, it was a jointly programmed and implemented group of mutually supportive programs by various government and nongovernment entities. At the community level, these programs included health care, water supply, health and nutrition education, supplementary feeding, and agricultural extension. Higher-level support was provided by the health and agricultural sectors, technological research centers, private food suppliers, and the central government itself. The related Integrated Rural Development Program (DRI) was originally conceived as a component part of PAN's food system, together with modern agriculture, food agroindustry, and consumption-oriented interventions.

On a policy level, PAN was mainly concerned with credit and technology for the modern sector of the Colombian food system but also included human-resource policy in education and health. As providers of community services, PAN's implementing agencies concentrated on the urban and rural dwellers of Colombia's "poverty map."

The target population was the food consumers and producers, especially in the poorer households. A further nutrition-based selection in favor of mother-child groups applied in the case of subsidized feeding, both direct (through the Colombian Institute for Family Welfare, ICBF) and through coupons. In order to reach the poorest, systematic use was made of the National Health System, whose primary-level expansion PAN actively supported. DRI's target benefi-

The author's sincerest thanks go to Per Pinstrup-Andersen, Robert Schwartz, and C. Peter Timmer for their comments and feedback on this chapter. He is particularly indebted to Neville Edirisinghe for his very helpful critique of the original version and subsequent revisions of the analysis.

ciaries, by contrast, were the more viable *minifundista* farmers, that is, the better-off fringe of the rural poor.

PAN avoided most of the pitfalls found in other integrated nutrition projects:

1. It was never very expensive. Its share of budget resources peaked at slightly over 1 percent of the central investment budget in 1980–81. The total cost of funding PAN was only $25 million, even though 3 million poverty-map dwellers had access to primary health care and other services.

2. Distortions in resource allocation were minimal. Coupon food prices were left uncontrolled. The scale of *pancoger* (small plot/kitchen plot) agriculture was too small for its interest subsidy on credit (70 percent) to cause any significant distortion. This also applied to the subsidy on agricultural inputs. No subsidy applied to modern-sector distributors or producers.

3. No external dependency was involved. PAN was not dependent on food aid, and external credit financed a significant but hardly impressive 15 percent of PAN's cost (versus 25 percent of DRI's). Finally, neither PAN nor DRI owed their existence to external pressures of any kind.

4. No internal dependency, arbitrariness, or paternalism existed. A 40 to 50 percent cash payment was required of coupon beneficiaries, and foods purchased with coupons differed little from those consumed by poorer communities in most of Colombia, thus maintaining existing food habits.[1] Community-cost participation was also set at a high level by the other community-level interventions. Living on the poverty map and belonging to an eligible beneficiary group insured rights to the respective PAN services.

5. Even when coverage remained small, as was the case with food coupons, administrative efficiency was demonstrably high, with administrative costs shrinking in percentage of the coupon subsidy. The weighted average cost of all PAN interventions in 1980–81 was $8 annually per poverty-map dweller.

6. "Integrated" or "multisectoral" programming did not mean pell-mell juxtaposition of various interventions but local convergence of mutually supportive actions. A local community was not regarded as "covered" until no fewer than three such actions simultaneously converged on the same group.

7. Finally, there was an early and systematic fit of PAN within Colombia's overall national development strategy.

1. Coupon foods included such popular items as grain (rice/wheat/maize) flour and mixes, pastas, biscuits, brown-sugar *panela*, and dried peas. Total administrative costs went down from 41.7 percent of coupon subsidy in 1976 to 1.8 percent in 1981, even as other indicators pointed to a commensurate rise in the proportion of actual coupon utilization.

Yet, PAN was short-lived. Its policy dimension was taken away after 1978, following a change in government, though it had proved successful in the food agroindustry arena and elsewhere.[2] National mass-media education ended in 1980 and between 1980 and 1982, so did most other aggregate PAN interventions, even as PAN and DRI were made to undertake a hasty and ill-planned territorial expansion at the community level. *Pancoger* agriculture was terminated in mid-1982. When the administration changed anew in late 1982, PAN's demise was ordered. It came swiftly, though the plan's name was kept as an appendage to that of DRI, which survived.

The Political and Policy Environment of PAN

Some observers have alleged that PAN and DRI evolved as a result of external pressures, domestic crises, or both. The cessation of food aid and the world-development community's emphasis on "basic-needs" and a multisectoral approach to the solution of rural poverty in the seventies are most often quoted as examples of the former. Social unrest, guerrilla threats, and the government's failure to implement land reform are usually thought to account for the latter. Neither statement is true, and it is unnecessary to go beyond Colombia's institutional history of the last two decades and beyond the policy environment of the mid-seventies in order to understand the gestation and birth of PAN and DRI. The present analysis does not dwell on why they came to be; rather, it concentrates on their subsequent development until PAN's eventual demise—a process all at once subtler, more complex, and harder to explain.

Multisectoral programs at least formally similar to PAN and DRI—with community-level sanitation and health care, subsidized food production and consumption, and informal education or technical training—were started in Colombia in early 1960s, long before the multisectoral and basic-needs approaches became world fads. The interagency Applied Nutrition Integrated Program (PINA), which the Colombian Institute for Family Welfare (ICBF) actively coordinated during most of that decade, and the small-scale integrated rural development projects that the Colombian Land Reform Institute (IN-CORA) began developing at about the same time, are examples. Even as they waned, both precedents were still close enough to people's minds throughout the earlier half of the 1970s to keep alive the policy options of integrated rural development and nutrition programs.

---

2. For example, the production capacity of five priority PAN foods (precooked maize flour, vegetal mixes, pastas, or noodles, texturized vegetal proteins, and soya flour) tripled during the 1975–79 period from 62,000 to 196,000 tons (Uribe Mosquera 1980, 1983). The Technological Research Institute (IIT) Pan-financed research and technical assistance, and the PAN-related World Bank Agroindustrial Credit channeled through Colombia's central bank were the main driving forces behind such an achievement, though other research centers and sources of finance also participated.

PAN was born during the Lopez Michelsen administration (1974–78), as a formal component of the National Development Plan. The latter characterized Colombia as a dualistic society, with a modern sector highly responsive to macroeconomic measures and with a labor-intensive traditional or informal sector that, though it had been losing ground steadily due to long-standing policy discrimination, was essentially dynamic in nature and remained of considerable importance to the national economy. This was especially the case from the standpoint of popular employment and consumption. If properly assisted by the government, that informal sector could be energized anew and help attain some of the key social goals stated for the country, such as productive employment and income redistribution. In order to prove effective, however, such assistance must not only undo policy discrimination, but it must take the form of direct state investment, real-income transfers, extension, and training. Such a description closely fit the original policy statement of PAN and DRI as well as that of other policies and programs that also aimed at the poorer, informal segment of Colombian society.

Designed and approved in 1975, PAN and DRI began experimentally in 1976 and reached a significant scale of implementation in 1978, when they were officially extended by the incoming Turbay Ayala administration (1978–82). The latter also ordered their 1981 expansion, even as it discontinued a number of key interventions. Finally, in 1982, except for a very few components, PAN was swiftly terminated in all but name by the government of President Belisario Betancour. Among those phased out, coupon food distribution and the food system strategy of which it was a part, and the nutrition education component were especially noteworthy. Other programs pertaining to health and sanitation were continued after 1982 but solely or chiefly within a sectoral rather than an integrated framework. Still others were simply downscaled and renamed so that they could continue within DRI.

PAN's fate, to be sure, was hardly extraordinary when seen in a political context. No new government is content with merely following in the footsteps of its predecessor—it is bound to put some distance between the former's actions and its own, between the situation it inherited and that which it can genuinely acknowledge, for good or for bad, as resulting from its own policies and performance. The refusal to assume responsibility for the past or to give the former rulers credit for the present is simply a matter of good politics. In countries such as Colombia, where presidents change every four years and are forbidden by the constitution from succeeding themselves, development priorities and programs are likely to shift.

In addition, Colombia's regional and community-level government is essentially political in nature. PAN largely ignored it below the regional level—and, in so doing, probably made a mistake. DRI carefully cultivated it by, for instance, systematically inviting mayors and councilmen to participate actively in its municipal committees. To the best of the author's recollection, no regional or national politician ever attacked PAN (some community-level politicians occasionally did, almost always in the larger cities). Many did assail DRI, usually for its limited and necessarily selective coverage of the country, for example, for excluding either their respective region or areas of electoral importance to their political party or group. The same kind of criticism was never leveled at PAN, whose multisectoral coverage, while much broader than DRI's, was also geographically limited.[3] In plain words, PAN was never a political issue, while DRI not only sought greater political exposure but succeeded in turning it to political advantage. When PAN was being dismantled sotto voce, the political community never blinked: apart from not being informed by the government, it was probably not sufficiently concerned to find out by itself, let alone try and do something about it.

The Central Setting of PAN and DRI Coordination

The National Planning Department (DNP), which coordinated PAN and DRI, and the cabinet-level National Council for Economic and Social Policy (CONPES), chaired by the president of the republic, are the only two bodies formally invested with global planning and policy-making responsibilities in the development field, though, in practice, the Ministry of Finance has a lot to say. The DNP drafts the National Development Plan for CONPES's consideration before its submission to Congress as an official government project. The DNP's clearance is required for all public-sector investment appropriations, prior to their inclusion by the Ministry of Finance into the year's draft budget and prior to the budget's approval by Congress. In addition, DNP officials sit on the board of directors of most decentralized public enterprises at the national and regional level, and the DNP has all of Colombia's Regional Development Corporations under its direct command. These and other top-level functions lead to the ubiquitous involvement of CONPES and DNP in Colombia's development process. No program requiring interagency coordination on a significant scale and a clear overall priority is likely to succeed without their support. That was precisely the reason why the general administration of PAN and DRI was entrusted to the DNP rather than to any other government agency and why their coordination was formally placed under the aegis of CONPES.

Initially, the corresponding organizational strategy seemed to work well enough—to the extent the same individual actors who either conceived and designed PAN and DRI or were instrumental in their adoption remained in charge. With time, however, and particularly after the Turbay Ayala admin-

3. Some of PAN's interventions were truly nationwide, e.g., mass-media education, water-quality control, school feeding, and ICBF's mother-child direct feeding. So was PAN's policy dimension. However, the full package of community services applied initially to only 11 *departamentos* (out of 23) where 60 percent of the population lived. The 1981 expansion extended it to 21, i.e., most of Colombia.

istration took over in 1978 and most of the people in high position changed, DNP's support wavered. PAN and DRI departed not only from Colombia's long tradition of indicative, rather than directive, planning programs but also from the specific institutional role therein of the DNP. Their abrupt territorial expansion in 1981 exacerbated that feeling by compelling the DNP to get involved in innumerable operational aspects on a regional and sometimes even more disaggregate level. PAN's unusual combination of community-level interventions and of strategies and actions of a more aggregate nature struck the new DNP administration as unwieldy—or worse. As a result, PAN's food-policy dimension and national mass-media education program were both dismantled, the step being accompanied by a number of complementary actions. Their loss, in turn, weakened PAN's capacity to reach out to public opinion and other sources of potential support, including food suppliers. Also, PAN was increasingly reduced to what its opponents regarded it to be: a number of sectoral actions, which each implementing agency could well carry out by itself, with one extraneous component—coupon food distribution.

The Aggressive Development Planning Style of PAN and DRI

In Colombia, development priorities crystallize centrally, through CONPES, but their de facto observance then rests with each individual sector and is largely a matter of institutional self-discipline on the national, regional (*departamento*, district), and community (*municipio*) levels. The sectoral ministries and the decentralized agencies under their formal command are to be found on the national level. The regional and community levels are represented by branches or representative offices of a number of ministries and decentralized agencies, sometimes pertaining to the same sector and occasionally committed to highly interdependent tasks across sectors.

The National Planning Department is formally invested with the "coordination, evaluation, and direction" of the entire development process and with follow-up responsibility, but it is understood that the latter may not normally interfere with established hierarchical channels within each sector. As a result, the process is mostly exercised on a national level, through formal communication channels with sectoral ministries and agency headquarters as well as through the participation of official DNP delegates on the boards of directors of decentralized agencies. The kind of integration that takes place in CONPES is not replicated at the regional or the community level, nor does the DNP's watchdog role usually extend to those levels, except in indirect fashion or insofar as it may be taken up under local interagency agreement by a Regional Development Corporation under the DNP's command. The task of enforcing development priorities thus remains correspondingly elusive and subject to the oft-noted internal and external constraints associated with the bureaucratic pluralism of Colombian institutional life.

The substantive changes brought about by PAN and DRI can be contrasted with the institutional pathway traditionally followed in Colombian planning and with the peculiar Cuban style of development planning.[4] In the latter, the planning body (National Planning Board of Junta, JUCEPLAN) is at center-stage on both the national and the regional (provincial) levels, where it provides sectoral agencies (here referred to under the same names as in the traditional Colombian planning case) with the priorities and targets for them to fulfill. On a community level—and sometimes higher up, for greater coordination, enforcement, and control—JUCEPLAN's orientations are taken up by such vertically structured mass organizations as the Committee for the Defense of the Revolution (CDR), the Organization of Women, and the National Association of Small Peasants (ANAP). Sectoral channels from one level to another do exist but for coordination only; for most practical purposes, JUCEPLAN and the mass organizations centralize sectoral communication and channel it up and down.

Finally, there is the composite style of development-planning of PAN and DRI. It is an identifiable mix of the former models, with the DNP taking its coordinating role within CONPES two steps further down the institutional scale: first, to the National Food and Nutrition Council (CNAN) or its DRI counterpart, the National DRI Committee, and then, on a regional level, to the Regional PAN or DRI Committees. The final step—to the community level— was almost exclusively controlled by DRI, in the form of so-called municipal committees, which the local agents of Colombia's agricultural bank (Caja Agraria) customarily coordinated on behalf of the program. Members of the community were eventually elected to participate in both municipal and regional committees. PAN tried to use preexistent community-level coordination groups to the same end, in the National Health System and the agricultural sector.

A central communication channel was thereby created, which ran parallel to, but could not supersede, established sectoral channels. Together with the national, regional, and (sometimes) community-level committees, where a formal commitment was requested of the sectoral implementing agencies for concerted programming, budgeting, implementation, and evaluation purposes, the existence of a central channel helped to put sufficient pressure on them to achieve the kind of genuine integration that multisectoral schemes such as PAN and DRI obviously required. Such a pressure, in turn, would prove helpful

---

4. The comparison centers on the interaction and respective role of central and sectoral channels in the implementation and enforcement of national development priorities already in force. The comparison eschews the discussion of how these priorities were defined and, therefore, of the choice between so-called bottom-to-top and top-to-bottom planning processes—a matter not unrelated and of interest in its own right, on grounds somewhat different from those of concern here. All the same, it is worth bearing in mind that an efficient communication channel, once opened, can use both upward and downward communication and thus transmit feedback from below, if allowed to do so.

either to the respective implementing agency to gain sought-after support from headquarters, or to the headquarters to gain effective compliance from the regional implementation agency as well as political or budget support from higher up.

Failing that kind of association, someone was bound to lose a degree of bureaucratic power or freedom that he or she previously enjoyed, and could easily perceive PAN or DRI as a grating and undue interference. At some agencies, the needed conciliation never materialized and a continual irritant resulted, which could reach venomous proportions and inordinately affect the sectoral perception (and acceptance) of PAN or DRI. Expectedly, this phenomenon tended to concentrate in agencies in which low morale, lagging efficiency, a communication breakdown between the national and local levels, or other serious internal constraints already prevailed.[5] However, because such problems so often came to light due to PAN and DRI's organizational "shortcuts," the impression was sometimes conveyed that the fault lay with the corresponding interference, that is, with the new, aggressive, and unfamiliar style of development-planning rather than with the agencies themselves.

In the end, institutional friction with implementing agencies proved most damaging to PAN and DRI. It brought about pressures for their breakdown along sectoral components and was instrumental in both PAN's doom and the transfer of overall responsibility for DRI to a strictly sectoral framework, under the Ministry of Agriculture. It also kept some of the sectoral participants from looking at what they did within PAN or DRI in a truly multisectoral fashion. They continued to see these activities as exclusively their domain and to regard as PAN's or DRI's only those which could not be assigned a single sectoral label. This was more often the case with PAN than with DRI, since the latter is basically a well-managed and carefully designed rural development program, while the former included such novel schemes as food coupons, local pilot projects in food security, and a mass-media component that no sectoral agency could claim as its own.

The Sectoral Impact of PAN and DRI

As if to add insult to injury, the contribution of PAN and DRI to the investment budget of sectoral ministries, including those for health and agriculture, was not a net addition resource. It implied a partial substitution of previous independent monies toward PAN or DRI.

The above analysis was not lost on the people in charge at the Ministries of Health and Agriculture, and ICBF, among others, and may have helped to tip

5. More agencies could be so characterized in DRI than in PAN. None, however, exemplified this situation better than PAN's ICBF, the main recipient of food aid and formerly the leading institution in the field of nutrition.

the balance against PAN and DRI. In retrospect, however, three considerations ought to have qualified this judgment. The first involved the chilling deficit in the public investment budget from 1978 onward. The competition for scarce budget resources inevitably pits short- and long-term priorities against each other. The National Planning Department's strong concern for the latter was enough, traditionally, to insure a place for them in the development strategy. As the deficit grew larger, however, the Ministry of Finance was increasingly called upon to decide on the nature and extent of the sources of finance for any given item. In the process, it effectively redefined development priorities—to the detriment of the allegedly "soft" priorities of the social sector, including PAN. Second, the PAN or DRI budget not only tied up budget resources, but a large proportion of it was for operating expenses. Though never labeled as PAN's or DRI's, those were formally regarded as counterpart funds in the loan agreements (variously signed with the World Bank, USAID, IDB, and others) that aimed at guaranteeing their stability and continuity under changing political conditions. This particularly applied (in a ratio of 8 to 1) to primary health care.

Third, PAN and DRI not only strengthened the overall priority granted to a sector but also impelled a fundamental reordering of intrasector priorities. Thus, DRI (like PAN's "small-plot" or "kitchen-plot" program) aimed at winning a greater priority for small and even part-time farmers within the agricultural sector. It no doubt succeeded, as witnessed by the significant (10 percent) share of agricultural sector credit wrested for small DRI producers by 1980, as compared with a formerly negligible participation level. Likewise, PAN strove to make primary health care, rural water supply, and nutrition into three of the clearest priorities within the National Health System—an undeniably successful approach.[6] While the Ministry of Health fully agreed with such a goal, it nonetheless required the kind of firm outside prodding on all levels mentioned earlier. The attempt to reorder intrasectoral priorities also extended to ISBF-administered interpersonal education (with a degree of success) and direct-feeding programs (to little avail). Among the latter's many serious and persistent flaws, which PAN unsuccessfully sought to remedy, was a strong tendency to focus attention on people living close to health posts and feeding centers. However, the poorest households are highly unlikely to be found in these areas. Enduring and damaging bitterness ensued from PAN's involvement in both ICBF programs.

The sectoral impact of PAN was hurt by its gradual retrenchment over

6. By 1981, some 3 million people, or half the national coverage, had access to primary health care within PAN. Forty percent of the half million rural households with access to aqueduct water got it through PAN. Food-quality control across the nation, through laboratory networking (with most of the investment paid for by PAN, from World Bank funds), was initiated by the National Health System. Finally, the NHS had earlier served as the main vehicle for PAN's nutrition education campaign on child diarrhea (1978) and breast-feeding (1979–80).

time. With its beneficiaries significantly poorer and far less organized and politically assertive than DRI's, and with little communication with the political class, PAN lacked a power base of its own and depended on the central government's support. What political commitment there was waned as the administration changed in 1978. When the government then turned restrictive (starting in 1979–80), PAN was in effect reduced to a diminished status. This followed mainly from the loss of key dimensions and components, though other forms of discrimination, that is, in the disbursement of budget monies, were also involved. In turn, the misperceptions of PAN ironically became self-vindicating: as they led to its progressive downgrading, what was left lacked the cohesion and scope of the original whole and could be more easily criticized. PAN was also unable to maintain the goodwill of its occasional business supporters (especially from agroindustry) and of public opinion or to get the attention of the political community.

In the end, for supporters and opponents alike—whether beneficiaries and sectoral implementing agencies, central planner, private suppliers, or third parties—PAN was found to have shed so many of its former clothes that it was close to strategic nakedness. What PAN had contributed in the past was forgotten. What it could contribute in the future seemed ever more limited, and the entire arrangement appeared to be somewhat artificial, with the food-coupon program no longer quite enough to tie the package together. The notion accordingly developed that putting an end to coupons would suffice to terminate the arrangement, with all other components painlessly reverting to the sole responsibility of their respective sectors and with no obvious or demonstrable sectoral cost accruing in the short term. That, indeed, is what happened in late 1982.

Conclusion

Why was PAN dismantled despite its reported extension, efficiency, and success? The analysis identifies a good many important reasons. Five reasons are particularly noteworthy:

1. *The Colombian political system.* With a four-year presidency and no reelection, development priorities are seldom sustained over time in the absence of a strong political commitment. It was clearly there during the 1974–78 administration that created PAN, diminished with its 1978–82 successor, and disappeared altogether under the 1982–86 government.
2. *Sectoral hostility.* Sectoral agencies (in health, agriculture, education, public works, etc.) have a long history of jealously guarding their practical autonomy. PAN's (and DRI's) peculiar brand of "directive" planning (at the hands of Colombia's National Planning Department) infringed upon such autonomy, even though the respective (sectoral) implementing agencies were not rewarded with any enduring increase in budget resources.

While DRI picked up more fights overall, the battle between PAN and ICBF was more bitter, damaging, and protracted.

3. *Technical bureaucracy.* PAN and DRI were under the direct responsibility of DNP—perhaps the single most technical and powerful agency of the central government. While the DNP's commitment lasted, they benefited from such a central setting. As it waned, however, both PAN and DRI were faced with increasing uncertainty. They conflicted with DNP's own idea of development and planning and further compounded its doubts through a jolting territorial expansion ordered from above in 1981.

4. *Divestments.* PAN was weakened by successive divestments. As it lost more components, some of them strategically important, it was left with a national food and nutrition strategy that could be more easily criticized. In the end, PAN was perceived as merely superimposing one component (coupons) on top of others that sectoral agencies implemented and could carry on by themselves.

5. *The political priority of nutrition.* PAN's beneficiaries were among the poorest in Colombia and had little political voice, and, for that matter, PAN did not try to organize or integrate them into the political process. As a result, PAN had no constituency of its own, though, for some time, it did enjoy the support of agroindustrialists and other groups. Available data on malnutrition were at times so confusing and conflicting as to puzzle decision-makers and turn their attention away from food and nutrition to other, more traditional development approaches. As for public opinion, it was only briefly aware of PAN's existence—while its nationwide mass-media education campaigns were on the air. Public information on the nutrition problem, on the other hand, generated criticisms of ineffectual government programs rather than the belief that nutrition deserved a higher priority and greater support.

Of the conclusions listed above, the first three and the last one point to the inapplicability of the "integrated nutrition planning" approach to the Colombian context, because of both the difficulty inherent in maintaining the priority over time and the conflicts inevitably caused by the associated peculiar organizational framework. Finally, PAN's divestment is an illustration of the process whereby the prevailing forces of the political economy actively resist and hack at the integrated nutrition "intruder" until, largely bereft of its original content, it can more easily fall prey to the country's periodic winds of change.

5 The Political Economy of the Food Stamp Program in the United States

MARGARET S. ANDREWS AND
KATHERINE L. CLANCY

Among the advanced industrial countries, the use of food stamps to alleviate poverty is unique to the United States. Food stamps, which are vouchers that can be exchanged for food in designated retail stores, were first instituted at the close of the Great Depression as a means of simultaneously increasing the food purchasing power of the poor and raising the income of farmers. Despite the connection with agriculture, funding for food stamps waxed and waned in the early years of implementation in accordance with the theory that relief programs for the poor are responses to social unrest. However, sustained growth of the Food Stamp Program during the 1970s and 1980s and its conversion into a major form of income maintenance cannot be explained by such a theory.

This chapter examines the history of food stamps in the United States in a political economy framework that incorporates structural changes in government and market, and social institutions and ideologies. These large patterns of change explain developments in the use of food stamps in the United States that cannot be explained by more narrowly based examinations of legislative bargaining and pressure group politics. Because the dynamic pattern of change has tended to transform food stamps from a food transfer into an income transfer, special attention is paid to the evidence that has been collected about the effectiveness of food stamps in improving levels of food consumption and nutrition. This evidence is used to reflect on possible future directions for food assistance.

This chapter was originally written as a paper presented at the Workshop on the Political Economy of Nutritional Improvement, jointly sponsored by the International Food Policy Research Institute (IFPRI) and the United Nations University (UNU), held June 10–13, 1985, in Berkeley Springs, West Virginia. The authors have benefited greatly from the helpful comments and advice of Ken Farrell, Rob Fersh, Robert Greenstein, William Hoagland, John Kramer, Chris Leman, Glenn Nelson, Janet Poppendieck, Ben Senauer, Bard Shollenberger, Marcie Simon, and participants at the IFPRI/UNU Workshop. The authors' names are listed alphabetically and no difference in relative contribution is implied. Any opinions expressed in this paper are those of the authors alone.

Social Unrest and Relief Programs for the Poor

Piven and Cloward (1971) argue that governments have historically been reluctant to take on the responsibility for permanently providing for the needs of any segment of the population. Because of the work ethic in Western democracies, public institutions have tended to expand their involvement in relief programs for the poor only during periods of social unrest associated with market fluctuations and rapid technological changes that displace large numbers of people from the labor market. Work requirements have frequently been invoked for those receiving relief, and when labor market conditions improve, sources of public relief have disappeared. Furthermore, relief programs resulting from social unrest have not followed a pattern of progressive liberalization but rather an episodic pattern in which relief rolls expand and then contract in a manner that allows the relief system to maintain civil order in times of economic hardship, enforce work, and preserve the work ethic.

Before the 1930s, the availability of relief for the poor in the United States was limited and based on community and local institutions.[1] However, as the Great Depression took hold, demands for expanded relief exceeded community resources and the fiscal capacity of state and local governments. In 1933, the federal government enacted the Federal Emergency Relief Act (FERA)—a measure that allocated funds to the states for cash relief for the unemployed. In 1935, the focus shifted from cash to work relief with legislation that created the Works Progress Administration (WPA). Limited federal cash relief was continued under the Social Security Act, which instituted provisions for social insurance and specific programs of aid for the aged, disabled, and families with dependent children.

With rising employment after the recession of 1937–38, funding for WPA was reduced. In 1939, the program was changed to prevent any worker from retaining employment under WPA for more than eighteen months. Funding was completely terminated during World War II. Although the provisions for categorical aid under the Social Security Act continued to be available after the war (if not always uniformly enforced by state administrators), the cessation of federally funded relief for the working poor was taken by Piven and Cloward (1971) as evidence that the U.S. experience in the 1930s conformed to the general pattern outlined above.

Food Assistance in the 1930s

The history of food assistance in the 1930s followed a similar pattern. Poppendieck (1986) has analyzed that history in the context of the "paradox of

---

1. Previous social programs sponsored by the federal government were limited to veterans' compensation and military pensions, federal employee retirement programs, and workmen's compensation. See March (1981), pp. 5–18.

want in the midst of plenty." This paradox first became a national issue in the late 1920s when the federal government began to amass agricultural surpluses through the U.S. Farm Board at the same time that reports of hunger among the poor and the unemployed were increasing. The irony of this situation generated public sentiment so strong that in 1932, part of the surplus federal wheat held by the Farm Board was eventually released to state and local relief agencies despite opposition by the Hoover administration. Under the Roosevelt administration, public outrage (this time over the slaughtering of piglets in August 1933, carried out under the farm price support provisions of the Agricultural Adjustment Act [AAA]) again precipitated federal action to make food surpluses available to those in need. In October 1933, the Federal Surplus Relief Corporation (FSRC), later renamed the Federal Surplus Commodities Corporation (FSCC), was formed to purchase surplus commodities for distribution to those receiving cash relief under FERA. When federal cash relief was converted into work relief under the WPA in 1935, the responsibility for food distribution was shifted to the U.S. Department of Agriculture (USDA).

Under USDA administration, food assistance became more directly associated with the goals of surplus commodity removal. In 1935, section 32 of the amended AAA provided additional funding for food distribution through federal customs receipts. Yet, food assistance did not expand rapidly. Difficulties arose, in part, because the droughts of 1934 and 1936 reduced surpluses but also because cautious USDA administrators did not use all the available funds for fear of disrupting agricultural markets.[2] The limitations of FSCC procedures for providing food assistance became evident during the recession of 1937–38, precipitating various organizational changes.

Among these changes was an experimental food stamp program first instituted in Rochester, New York, in May 1939. By 1941, four million people and more than half of the counties in the United States were participating (Berry 1984; Fishbein 1977). The program was popular among merchants, administrators, and clients. Nevertheless, as food surplus turned into scarcities during the war, this food stamp program, like the WPA, was terminated.

In assessing the experience of food assistance in the 1930s, Poppendieck (1986) believes that the linkage of food assistance with farm surplus within the USDA did not serve to sustain availability of food benefits. So long as surpluses persisted, the programs were funded, but when changing economic conditions eliminated the surpluses, food assistance programs suffered cutbacks. Moreover, because relief administrators were generally committed to the ideal of

---

2. Some of the administrative bottlenecks that reduced the amounts and usefulness of food assistance were (1) the practice of shipping commodities to areas where they were uncommon, in order not to compete with local farmers; (2) the limited range of commodities distributed; (3) the "over-and-above" policy that restricted personal food allotments of each commodity to prevent leakage of donated foods into the market; and (4) tremendous disparities between regions according to the practices of local relief agencies.

cash relief, they failed to recognize potential benefits to their clients that could have been gained by a more active institutional pressure on USDA to promote food assistance.

Enactment of the 1964 Food Stamp Program

Food assistance through direct commodity distribution by the USDA's Agricultural Marketing Service continued at reduced levels after the war ended. It expanded somewhat after 1953, when USDA agreed to pay the costs of shipment to the states, but the program did not operate in eleven states and in seven others was limited to 10 percent of public assistance rolls (Berry 1984). One of the major problems of the commodity program was that only a small number of the more than twenty approved commodities was usually available for distribution, which lowered the nutritional value of the package (Latham 1971; De Bello 1980).

As the problem of agricultural surpluses reappeared in the 1950s, programs such as the National School Lunch Program enacted in 1946 and the Food for Peace Program (PL-480) that began in 1954 were promoted as outlets for the surplus commodities. Legislation to reinstate a food stamp program was debated in every Congress in the 1950s, but no legislation was passed. USDA had the power to reinstitute a food stamp program through section 32 of the 1935 AAA, but chose not to do so because food stamps were not viewed as a cost-effective alternative for dealing with surpluses.

Hunger became an issue again in the 1960 presidential campaign, and President Kennedy directed the secretary of agriculture to establish a pilot food stamp project in May 1961 (Berry 1984; Kotz 1969) and to increase the amount of surplus distribution. Evaluations of the pilot food stamp projects were positive and showed that the market had been expanded for agricultural products, retail sales of food had increased, and the dietary quality of recipients had been improved (USDA 1962).

Despite the positive evaluation, passage of the Food Stamp Act of 1964 proved difficult because of hostility to the program in the House Agriculture Committee. The program that was eventually enacted required counties to choose between commodity distribution and food stamp programs. Eligibility was limited to households receiving public assistance or those below the income and asset eligibility levels set by each state. Variations in relief eligibility standards among the states continued, and many states or counties were slow to institute the program (Berry 1984).

In those counties that chose to switch their food assistance from direct distribution to food stamps, the number of households receiving food assistance declined. Unlike participants in the commodity distribution program, recipients of food assistance under the Food Stamp Program had to pay for their stamps. The coupon allotment increased with income on a sliding scale, as did the amount of money a family paid for its stamps, so that recipients would buy their stamps for about the cost of what they usually spent on food (Berry 1984). This meant that the same size family with a higher income received a much greater value of stamps but paid more for them. In many instances, the purchase price was beyond the financial means of the neediest families.

The combination of small appropriations for food stamps, the large number of people who dropped out of food assistance programs when food stamps were introduced in a county, and lack of interest in or active hostility toward the program on the part of some local welfare departments prevented the Food Stamp Program from making any substantial improvement in the hunger situation in the early years of its operation. In April 1967, hunger was again "rediscovered" in America through hearings of the Senate Subcommittee on Employment, Manpower and Poverty in Mississippi (Kotz 1969). Yet, despite growing manifestations of public concern, legislative activity in the late 1960s produced no immediate reforms.

The hunger issue did not disappear, however, and in 1969, President Nixon addressed the problem in his inaugural speech. The reluctance of Congress to act on proposals to improve food assistance led to very extensive administrative changes. In late 1969, Secretary of Agriculture Hardin set a national standard for benefit levels based on the cost of the economy food plan (a low-cost, nutritionally adequate diet), decreased the purchase price of stamps so that no family would pay more than 30 percent of its income for food stamps, and made food stamps free for the lowest income group. These changes led to rapid expansion and outreach of the program. In 1970, these administrative changes were translated into law, and national standards of eligibility were also legislated.

The Role of Social Unrest in the Food Stamp Program

Like previous episodes of expansion in relief for the poor, the early history of the Food Stamp Program can be related to the social unrest of the 1960s. Although originating legislation that passed in 1964 did not respond directly to any particular social uprising, it was rooted in growing perceptions of the seriousness of poverty. The pressures of popular protest were most directly apparent in the program expansion. For example, Reynolds (1980) shows by means of internal documents from the Johnson administration that specific actions were suggested to expand food distribution in areas plagued by urban rioting and that in 1965, food stamp programs were particularly emphasized in riot-torn localities in Watts and Philadelphia.

A number of events, such as the publication of *Hunger USA*, the airing of the CBS-produced television documentary "Hunger in America," the Poor People's March, the White House Conference on Food, Nutrition and Health in 1969, and the establishment of the Senate Select Committee on Hunger and Human Needs, placed the issue of hunger near the top of the political agenda in the late 1960s. A major demand of the Poor People's Campaign during their

1968 encampment in Washington, D.C., was for USDA to enact the reforms recommended by the Citizen's Board of Inquiry (as reported in *Hunger USA*), including free stamps for the poorest families and reduced-price stamps for all program participants. As the campaign wore on, food stamp reform became the paramount demand (Kotz 1969). These incidents of social unrest by poor people and the efforts of hunger activists focused national attention on the hunger issue. The major expansion in program benefits enacted administratively in 1969 by Secretary Hardin has been attributed to the intense public pressure of the late 1960s (Berry 1982; Kotz 1969).

The Food Stamp Program as Welfare Reform

Although social unrest appears to have been a factor in the growth in the Food Stamp Program during the 1960s, it does not appear to have accounted for the program's continued growth in the 1970s. That expansion, in fact, represents the kind of progressive liberalization that Piven and Cloward (1971) found absent in the earlier episodes of public relief they examined. Not only did participation in the program expand rapidly in the decade, but the Food Stamp Program became in many ways a major welfare program with some resemblance to a guaranteed annual income.

At the time of enactment of the 1964 Food Stamp Act, the direct link with surplus commodity distribution had already been broken.[3] As the new program evolved, the dynamics of change transformed it from a surplus-removal into an income-maintenance program (Berry 1978). The imposition of a nationwide benefit standard and the adoption of uniform national eligibility criteria provided a minimum level of income to any U.S. citizen, irrespective of work status or family structure. The national benefit level compensated for variations in locally administered welfare programs (e.g., AFDC), and the marginal benefit reduction (30 percent) encouraged additional work effort and made the program attractive for the working poor. Because of these changes, Nathan (1980) credits the Food Stamp Program (along with other in-kind transfer programs) with having achieved, in an incremental and indirect manner, the major goals of the Family Assistance Plan for guaranteed income that the Nixon Administration had unsuccessfully pressed for.

Program Growth in the 1970s

The reformed Food Stamp Program rapidly grew to a major income maintenance program in the 1970s. In 1969, participation was 2.9 million, with expenditures of $240 million. By 1974, participation had grown to 12.9 million

---

3. In contrast with the New Deal program, food stamps under the 1964 act no longer had to be applied specifically to the purchase of commodities declared to be in surplus.

persons, and outlays reached $2.8 billion. During the recession of 1975, one-fifth of U.S. citizens were eligible for the Food Stamp Program at some point during the year (Fishbein 1977). Participation was over 20 million by the end of the 1970s.

The program grew in this decade even though the links with the farm surplus problem became even more tenuous after 1973. Agricultural stocks held by the Commodity Credit Corporation were greatly reduced in the early 1970s, and direct commodity distribution was phased out in the 1973 Agriculture and Consumer Protection Act. Yet the Food Stamp Program was not cut back in this period of short supply. Instead, the USDA was mandated to institute a Food Stamp Program in every U.S. county (including those in Puerto Rico) by the end of 1974 and to encourage participation through outreach efforts.

Food inflation (which at the time required semiannual indexation in program benefits) and the severity of the recession in 1974–75 further fueled the program's expansion. The Ford administration proposed administrative actions to reduce program expenditures by introducing a change that would have required recipients to pay a flat 30 percent of their net income for stamps. Other Ford administration proposals would have dropped many of the working poor from the program and set up a strong work registration requirement. Despite growing public disapproval of the size of the program, and after great debate about fraud, abuse, income eligibility, and the eligibility of strikers and students, no changes were enacted. Litigation by the Food Research and Action Center and other hunger advocates (Berry 1982) emerged as an important factor in sustaining the program.

The appointment of Robert Bergland, a staunch supporter of food stamps when he served in the House of Representatives, as secretary of agriculture marked a change in administrative attitude toward the program. Bergland supported a particularly controversial proposal to eliminate the purchase requirement for food stamps. This change, enacted in 1977, was meant to encourage participation among eligible households that had previously not chosen to participate because of the purchase requirement. Participation increased by 3.4 million within a year after the new provisions went into effect, exceeding projected estimates.

The Role of Special Interests

To understand the political economy of the Food Stamp Program, it is important to address the question of why incremental changes transformed the program from an agricultural surplus measure into a major welfare program that provides, through an in-kind transfer, a minimum level of guaranteed income. Furthermore, why were these incremental changes possible when direct initiatives to enact programs of guaranteed income failed?

Although the development of an income maintenance system based on in-kind benefits is frequently maligned by policymakers on the basis of administrative inefficiency, inequity, and social stigma to client groups (Steiner 1971), one explanation for why such a system developed in the United States relates to the inductive nature of U.S. policy-making. Leman (1980) argues that the relative openness of U.S. policy-making actually invites considerable influence by special-interest groups and various political coalitions in the making of domestic policies. In-kind transfer programs are particularly vulnerable to brokering by special-interest groups because such programs not only benefit the recipients of the transfer but also the providers of the in-kind benefits. Although there is always a diversity of opinion among members of any interest group, in general, the special interests directly involved in the provision of medical care, housing, and food have a stake in the growth of targeted welfare benefits.

Congressional logrolling between agricultural interests and food stamp advocates has been a factor in food and agricultural legislation enacted in the past two decades. Although farm-interest groups have not been active proponents of the Food Stamp Program, they have repeatedly engaged in vote trading in order to obtain favorable action on a particular piece of farm legislation. One of the most widely cited instances of logrolling occurred in 1964 during the legislative process that enacted the program. When the House Rules Committee appeared to be delaying the consideration of the Food Stamp Act, Congresswoman Leonor Sullivan (D-Missouri), a member of the Banking Committee, responded by blocking discussion of a tobacco-research bill. She then enforced an informal logroll by linking the House vote on a wheat-cotton price support program with the food stamp vote (Ripley 1969).

Other instances of logrolling included legislative maneuvers related to the 1973 Agriculture and Consumer Protection Act, whereby representatives of union interests, who wanted food stamps to continue to be available to strikers, traded votes with representatives of cotton producers, who wanted an exception to the $20,000 limitation on payments under the agricultural support programs (Ferejohn 1983). It has also been suggested that there was a logroll involved in the passing of the 1977 Agriculture and Food Act, when House Agriculture Committee Chairman Foley softened his opposition to eliminating the purchase requirement for food stamps in exchange for a more liberal treatment of target prices and loan rates (Penn 1980).

These types of food stamp–farm program trades have been epitomized as the "political glue" that has held the farm program in place for the past decade (Bonnen 1984). However, they do not completely address the set of questions regarding the Food Stamp Program's relation to welfare. Food stamp advocates have been able to use their leverage with farm interests to win incremental reforms through this bargaining process. Yet this type of interest-group trade-off cannot explain the major liberalization of the program in 1969. As mentioned above, those program changes were motivated by a more widely based popular sentiment that demanded government action on the hunger issue.

A Structural Explanation

Rather than by focusing on the instrumentalities of the policy process, an alternative explanation can be advanced by looking at changes in the Food Stamp Program in the context of the structural developments in the major political, economic, and social institutions of the U.S. political economy. The structural perspective emphasizes contradictions between the market system and the liberal democratic state. The market practices of a capitalist economy structure control over economic goods according to property rights, whereas within the institutions of liberal democracy, rights to participate in the political process are vested in individuals.[4]

In concrete situations that allow equal participation in both markets and politics, conflicts between the two systems are relatively insignificant. However, in the United States, historical developments of the late nineteenth century brought progressively more economic concentration and increased government penetration into the regulation of market affairs, raising the level of conflict between democratic and market ideologies (Brewster 1970). In the turmoil of the Great Depression, farmers, the poor, and the unemployed turned to the political realm for institutional measures to redress the economic hardships they found in the market. Many of the resulting institutions were temporary (e.g., the Works Progress Administration and the original food stamp program), but others survived to constitute a permanent change in the role of the federal government in income maintenance of individual citizens.

It is true that those programs that tended to survive did not provide an alternative to labor market participation for social groups judged to be employable (except for short-term unemployment insurance). But, nonetheless, the permanence of the Social Security Act, providing social insurance and economic support for the aged, disabled, and families with dependent children (AFDC), and of other programs, such as those of the Agricultural Adjustment Act (AAA), represented a shift in federal government involvement in ensuring the economic viability of individual citizens and redistributing the allocation of income generated in the market.

The growth of the Food Stamp Program in the 1960s and 1970s can be explained in the context of this larger pattern of structural change. Paarlberg (1981) marks the 1960s as the beginning of the third agenda of U.S. food

4. A related explanation of the public preference for in-kind transfers is that the in-kind transfer is the optimal outcome of the utility maximization problem that jointly considers the utility functions of donor and recipient. See Thurow (1974). However, this explanation also does not fully address the issue of why public allocations for food assistance increased so dramatically in the 1970s.

policy, in which the rural and urban poor, minority groups, and consumers increased their involvement in setting farm and food policy.[5] However, this third agenda was not a unique phenomenon for agricultural policy but part of a larger pattern of institutional change that made it easier to place popular demands for more secure economic access to a decent standard of living on the political agenda.

To understand this pattern, it is useful to review the role of the civil rights movement in focusing attention on inequities in the distribution of American democratic rights and in expanding the democratic process. In the 1954 Brown decision, the Supreme Court rejected the principle of "separate but equal": the principle that had sustained racial discrimination in the South since the late nineteenth century. Between 1957 and 1965, four civil rights bills were enacted that extended political rights to formerly disenfranchised Southern blacks and eventually, with the Voting Rights Act of 1965, provided for federal government intervention to enforce those rights. The change was fostered to some extent by widespread mobilization of organizations such as the Student Nonviolent Coordinating Committee (SNCC) and the Congress of Racial Equality (CORE), which challenged segregation in public facilities with sit-ins, "freedom rides," and the nonviolent civil disobedience strategies of the Southern Christian Leadership Conference (SCLC) led by Martin Luther King, Jr. Violent defiance of provisions of the federal civil rights legislation by white elites in the South proved embarrassing in international circles, particularly as the U.S. position in the cold war demanded that the country maintain an image of hegemonic defender of democracy and freedom (Piven and Cloward 1977).

The turmoil over civil rights led to other changes in American political institutions above and beyond the wider enfranchisement of blacks. Within the Democratic Party, the strife over civil rights was particularly disruptive because it undermined the New Deal coalition between industrial representatives and southern elites. Bensel (1984) cites the sectional split in the Democratic Party over civil rights issues as a major factor in the attacks on the seniority system that ensued and eventually led to a greater democratization of decision making in the House of Representatives and a dissipation of the power of traditional standing committees. Further reforms in the primary election process and in election campaign financing procedures are a part of the changes that have led to what Bonnen (1984) characterizes as a shift from representative to participatory democracy in the U.S. political economy.

In this context of greater democratization, it was not only food stamp expenditures but also expenditures on other categorical grant programs that

5. The first agenda identified by Paarlberg was dominated by the populist social activism of relatively small farmers and it extended from the mid-nineteenth century through the Depression, while the second agenda, lasting from the 1930s through the 1950s, was set by the "iron triangle" power base of large commercial farmers, bureaucrats involved in programs that served them, and legislators on the agriculture committees.

increased in this period. Constant dollar expenditures on all income-maintenance programs increased fivefold over the 1960–1980 period, and 80 percent
of the increase can be attributed to food, housing, and medical programs
(Weicher 1984).

While these programs provide an alternative to market wage earnings for
the poor, they do not do so under the principle of a guaranteed annual income—
a concept that strongly conflicts with the ideology of market distribution by
property rights. Rather, the subsistence earnings provided by the government
appear to be ideologically based on respect for the individual's natural right to
housing, food, and medical care. With regard to food, Poppendieck (1985)
attributes the public's strong indignation at wasteful disposal of food to deeply
held beliefs about the primacy of the need for food and about emotional identi-
fications of food with parental care and protection. These feelings sustain
public support for programs to make food available to the needy.

To summarize, the growth of the Food Stamp Program is part of a larger
transformation in the U.S. political economy that has resulted from the exercise
of democratic political rights. The extension of popular economic demands into
the political sphere has fundamentally altered the role of the U.S. government
with respect to income distribution. Further democratization of the political
process after the 1960s intensified demands for economic redistribution. However, the economic gains of the poorest segments of the U.S. population did not
come through the widespread acceptance of the "political right" of all citizens
to be guaranteed a minimum level of income by the federal government.
Rather, the income gains have come via in-kind transfers of the basic needs of
food, housing, and medical care. In a certain sense, this structural transformation of the U.S. political economy also involves a modification of institutional
responsibilities for nurturance, with the government assuming functions that
have traditionally been fulfilled by family and community networks.

Effects of the Food Stamp Transfer on Nutrition

Because such a large component of income maintenance takes the form of
food stamps, increased interest has been shown in the effectiveness of food
stamp benefits in improving the nutritional status of low-income populations.
Although findings of the evaluations of pilot programs in 1962 had shown
substantial nutritional impact, subsequent county-level studies had inconclu-
sive results (Madden and Yoder 1972; Lane 1978). After the 1971 program
liberalization, a number of evaluative studies appeared that attempted to measure and explain both the food expenditure and diet quality effects[6] of the

---

6. Many researchers have used the term *nutrition status* to describe what is in fact only a
dietary quality measure. At this time, there is only one report on the clinical or biochemical
nutritional status of adult food stamp recipients (Davis et al. 1985).

program. In some cases, studies tried to distinguish between specific effects, because increased expenditures are necessary but not sufficient to increase nutritional effectiveness (Congressional Budget Office 1977).[7] The growth of the program and the 1977 changes led Congress to appropriate funds for national evaluation of many of the feeding programs, food stamps among them. Mathematica (1985) reviewed these studies, and the following is a summary of their report:

1. Before the elimination of the purchase requirement, food stamps had an effect on at-home food expenditures that was approximately four times the effect of money income. The marginal propensity to consume food out of money income ranges from .05 to .14; out of food stamps, 0.1 to 0.8.
2. The only study done after the elimination of the purchase requirement shows that stamps still have double the effect of money on the marginal propensity to consume (.23 vs. .11).
3. In Puerto Rico, where food assistance benefits have been issued in cash since 1982, the marginal propensity to consume food out of cash benefits (.23) is not significantly different from what it was when benefits were distributed as food stamp coupons, and it is 30 percent higher than the marginal propensity to consume food out of ordinary income.

The Food Stamp Program thus appears to be more effective than cash in increasing food expenditures. However, the effects on nutritional quality are less clear. A summary of previous findings, again from the Mathematica report (1985), shows the following:

1. Food Stamp Program participation has positive effects on the availability of most nutrients examined.
2. The program effects are weaker when examining food expenditure effects on nutrient availability versus direct effects of benefits on nutrients.
3. More recent studies have found a stronger nutrient effect than earlier studies.[8]

7. Regarding nutritional adequacy, it is interesting that Windham et al. (1983) have reported that the nutrient density (the ratio of nutrients to kilocalories) of the diet of all income groups in the United States is very similar. Advertising and mass marketing have given similar appetites to people even if the economic system has not given them equal purchasing power.

8. See, for example, studies by Basiotis et al. (1982, 1983), comparing survey data from the 1977–78 and 1979–80 low-income national food consumption samples. The 1979–80 survey data showed that food expenditures and nutrient availability were substantially lower in the bottom income quartile in 1979–80 than they had been in the 1977–78 study period. Yet the food stamp program appeared to be more nutritionally valuable in the later period in terms of the effect of food assistance benefits on dietary quality. Because the purchase requirement was eliminated between these two surveys, it is difficult to isolate the causes of these differences. It could be that program changes attracted lower-income households whose bonus stamps made up a larger percentage of their total food budgets. However, the general indication is that inadequate food supplies resulted in nutritional inadequacies among program participants even as food stamps had become more effective in improving nutritional adequacy.

4. Most studies conclude that other factors, such as education, household size, and location (urban or rural), are more important predictors of nutrient availability than program participation.

Another issue in the evaluation of nutritional effectiveness of the Food Stamp Program relates to program goals. Although the 1964 act promised to enable recipients "to more readily obtain a low-cost nutritionally adequate diet" (7 USC.82013[a]), the coupon allotments were determined on a sliding scale, so that lower income participants paid less for stamps but received fewer benefits. Thought had been given to basing the allotment on the cost of the economy food plan. This plan had been developed by the USDA in 1909 and updated in 1933 "for use when the cost of food must be lower than the average expenditures of low-income families . . . essentially for emergency use" (U.S. Congress 1985). If allotments had been based on this standard, the program would have been much more effective at improving nutritional status of the lowest income groups. But the USDA was concerned with maintaining a "self-help" orientation to the program (Berry 1984), which had the effect of preventing any direct linkage between program benefits and a nutritional standard.

When the documentation of hunger and malnutrition led to liberalization of the program in 1969, the cost of the economy food plan was adopted as the basis for coupon allotments. The preamble of the 1971 act also modified the program's goal to state that food stamps should provide recipients with "an opportunity to obtain a nutritionally adequate diet" (7 USC). The USDA claimed that benefits based on the economy food plan were sufficient for nutritional adequacy because, on average, low-income people spending at the level of the economy food plan could meet recommended dietary allowances. However, in June 1975, the U.S. Court of Appeals handed down a decision in *Rodway v. USDA*, 514F.2d809,820 (DC Cir. 1975) that disagreed with the USDA position. The judges pointed out that the 1971 amendments had identified a major shift in policy, "a shift from supplementing diets of low-income households to guaranteeing those households the opportunity for an adequate diet." The court ruled that basing food stamp levels on the economy food plan did not fulfill Congressional intent.

The USDA response to the *Rodway* decision was to develop another food cost plan, the thrifty food plan, to substitute for the economy food plan. The response of Congress was to change the wording of the preamble to read, "to permit low-income households to obtain a more nutritious diet" (7 USC Sec. 2013[a]). The thrifty food plan, developed in 1975 and revised in 1981, uses information on the nutritional composition of foods and the recommended dietary allowances (RDAs) to define the set of foods that are most nutritionally adequate. The cost of the foods in the plan is constrained to the same dollar amount as the economy food plan, and the food mix is constrained by existing food consumption patterns among low-income people. Although the thrifty food plan does not meet all dietary requirements,[9] the change in the wording of the preamble seemed to preclude a legal challenge to the plan. Nonetheless, in *Butte Community Union v. La Faver,* this plan has also been found nutritionally inadequate (Schneider 1985), thus again raising the issue of the extent to which the Food Stamp Program is intended to be a supplementary program.

In summary, the evaluations of the effectiveness of food stamps demonstrate that the food expenditure effect of food stamps is much stronger than the dietary quality effect, although enhanced nutrient availability is certainly a feature of the program. The stated program goals have changed over time, but the direct linkages between program participation and the maintenance of a certain nutritional standard have not developed. This means that even though food stamp transfers have a positive impact on food expenditures and diet quality, hunger will continue to be raised as an issue in future debates over the adequacy of food assistance through the Food Stamp Program.

Hunger, as a concept, has no consistently applied definition. Many definitions of hunger are, in fact, social definitions—they describe situations in which individuals or households have no food or inadequate food over some period of time. Likewise, the health effects of hunger are not widely agreed upon. Yet, because half of the recipients of food stamps are children, the risk of health effects such as stunted growth, wasting, and failure to thrive, which have been attributed to instances of hunger, is a serious societal problem. Thus, reports of hunger will most likely continue to evoke public concern regarding the effectiveness of food stamp expenditures.

Developments in the 1980s

The 1980s began with expectations of reduced spending on social programs. In April 1981, President Reagan proposed to immediately cut real expenditures on income maintenance programs by one sixth and to reduce them further by 2.5 percent annually beginning in 1982, so that real outlays would have been reduced to 1975 levels by 1985 (Weicher 1984).[10] As for domestic food assistance, the budget proposals would have reduced total program spend-

9. Peterkin, Kerr, and Hama (1982) have reported that only 12 percent of people receiving food stamps in the 1977–78 survey who spent at the level of the thrifty food plan received 100 percent of the RDA for all nutrients. Constraints of cost and typical food-intake patterns have made the thrifty food plan nutritionally inadequate. This has been defended on the grounds that some of the RDAs have wide safety margins and overestimate the needs of some individuals. There, however, is no way of knowing who these might be. Unless all poor people have reduced nutrient requirements (a strong argument can be made for the obverse), it is unquestionable that the thrifty food plan is not adequate for some number of the people using it.

10. These targets for spending cuts include human capital and service program expenditures in addition to the more direct income maintenance programs.

ing between 1981 and 1985 by 25 percent and food stamp spending by 14.6 percent (Hoagland 1984).

Although many provisions of the Reagan program were rejected, Congress did authorize program changes designed to reduce projected Food Stamp Program outlays by 16 percent over the 1982–84 period mainly through limiting eligibility to households with gross incomes under 130 percent of the poverty line, cutting funds for Puerto Rico by 25 percent, and modifying other administrative procedures. In 1982, Congress accepted modest cuts, including stronger penalties for poor quality control by local administrators, but by 1983, few of Reagan's other proposals were accepted by Congress, and the Congressional attitude toward further food stamp cuts was notably less favorable (Hoagland 1984).

Despite the attempts to curb growth in program costs, federal expenditures on food and nutrition assistance between 1980 and 1983 increased in real terms by 7 percent. Much of this increase can be attributed to the severity of the 1981–82 recession. Under normal circumstances, the 1981 legislative changes would have had a more pronounced budgetary impact.[11]

Despite the claim that budget cutbacks in social programs were designed to preserve a basic safety net for those in need, evidence has accumulated that the incidence of poverty increased even after the economic recovery began in November 1982. According to estimates by the Census Bureau, the number of people in the United States living below the poverty line between 1979 and 1983 increased by 35 percent. Even after noncash benefits such as food stamps and Medicaid were accounted for, the increases in poverty were the largest recorded since the reporting of poverty figures began. There was also evidence of a significant redistribution of disposable income from the poorest to the wealthiest families.[12]

Given this background, it is not surprising that hunger became visible again throughout the country, especially in areas with high unemployment. Many studies reported large increases in the numbers of people using emergency rations, soup kitchens, and surplus commodity handouts (Food Research and Action Center 1983; Physician Task Force 1985). In January 1984, the President's Task Force on Food Assistance concluded that measures were needed to address the problem of hunger, including a restoration of the food

11. The Congressional Budget Office estimates that after adjusting for the business cycle-related expenditure changes, Reagan's 1981 cuts in social expenditures reduced the real rate of growth of income maintenance programs by one half (Weicher 1984).

12. A 1984 study by the Urban Institute showed that the tax burden of families at the poverty line had risen since Reagan's tax cuts. The study showed that when taken together with cuts in income maintenance programs, the real disposable income for families in the bottom quintile of the U.S. income distribution decreased by 7.6 percent, while that of the top quintile increased by 8.7 percent (Palmer and Sawhill 1984).

stamp allotment to 100 percent of the cost of the thrifty food plan and a liberalization of eligibility requirements.[13]

The shift in the Reagan strategy in 1985 to seek budget cuts in middle class (rather than low-income) entitlements can be interpreted as an indication that the political constraint on cutting programs for poor people had been reached. Because that constraint was not made evident through widespread political mobilizations by poor people, it is interesting to consider the source of the constraining factor.

With respect to the Food Stamp Program, the hunger issue was instrumental. Organizations such as FRAC, Community Nutrition Institute (CNI), and the newly formed Center on Budget and Policy Priorities (CBPP) maintained public visibility for the food programs and were active in attempts to monitor the rising incidence of hunger as programs serving poor people were cut back (see, e.g., FRAC 1983; CBPP 1984). The efforts of these professional hunger advocates help explain the apparent political constraint on further cutbacks in food stamp funds that is evident in the 1985 budget deliberations.

Another interpretation can be based on constraints imposed by changes in the social structure, predominantly in the composition of families. Despite the cultural and ethnic diversity of family structures in the United States, there have been clearly documented trends toward smaller families, more female-headed households, and declines in the proportion of children living with two parents (Levitan and Belous 1981).

The conjunction of these events has led to the "feminization of poverty."[14] At the same time, changing middle-class values toward the appropriateness of women with young children working outside the home no longer hold poor women with dependent children as the "deserving poor."[15] Despite the fact that 90 percent of women on welfare have worked, the reality of the earnings differential between men and women on the labor market is such that few are able to establish financial independence (Pearce 1984). In 1984, for example, a woman with three children working full-time at the minimum wage would have earned slightly less than $7,000, well below the poverty line cutoff of $10,178.

13. Among the 1981 legislative changes in the Food Stamp Program was a provision to lower the level of the maximum benefit to 99 (rather than 100) percent of the cost of the thrifty food plan. This exacerbated the impact of other factors, such as lags in compensation for inflationary price changes, rounding rules, and state sales taxes that tend to reduce the purchasing power of the thrifty food plan allotment. In some states, these factors lowered the buying power of the allotment by as much as 12 percent (U.S. Congress 1985). Congressional action in 1984 restored the allotment levels to 100 percent of the thrifty food plan.

14. Almost two thirds of the impoverished adults in the United States are women, and 52.2 percent of poor children live in female-headed households (Shortridge 1984). Two-thirds of female-headed households do not receive child support from the father of the children (Levitan and Belous 1981).

15. Work incentives were introduced into the AFDC program in 1967 to discourage "welfare dependence," and the real value of benefits made available through AFDC decreased by 20 percent during the 1970s and by a further 13 percent in the 1980s.

Because women are more likely to earn the minimum wage than men, the economic resources for provision of basic needs for poor, female-headed families are inadequate without continued support through the large, in-kind transfer programs such as the Food Stamp Program.

The extent to which this situation is itself a result of the nature of U.S. welfare policies is an intensely controversial subject. Murray (1984), for example, has argued that the social policies enacted between 1950 and 1980 not only undermined the work ethic, but that the cash and in-kind welfare benefits made available to single mothers have caused the decline in the family. These conclusions have been countered with analyses that show no correlation between changes in the level of welfare benefits and changes in the proportions of households headed by women (e.g., Danziger and Gottschalk 1985) and by arguments that the breakdown in families is more a result of changing attitudes toward divorce, illegitimate children, and the desirability of women's dependence on men in the traditional nuclear family relationship. Irrespective of the cause of this social change, the special needs of female-headed households effectively placed a constraint on the extent to which income maintenance programs can be dismantled.

Conclusions

Within the U.S. economy, the Food Stamp Program has become an essential institution for income maintenance of poor people. We arrive at this conclusion from a broad historical perspective that recognizes significant structural changes in political, social, and economic institutions of the U.S. economy. After twenty-five years of sustained economic growth, the long postwar boom ended in the 1970s. This increased the numbers of people living in poverty. Political institutions also shifted in the 1960s and 1970s to reflect a move toward greater democratization in the political process. Families became smaller and more likely to be female-headed. These structural changes established new parameters that modified the functioning of public assistance.

It is not likely that we would come to the same conclusion if we had limited our analysis to the interactions among competing interest groups. Food assistance in the United States has been associated with the management of farm surplus since the New Deal, and the interplay between farm and food advocates has shaped both food and agricultural policy. Historically, the economic rewards to political organization first favored the exercise of political power by commercial farmers who can obtain large economic gains from organizing to influence policy. But then food advocacy steadily increased to counterbalance the special interests of farmers. There have been instances of vote trading and coalition building, or both, between representatives of these groups, which accounts for certain program changes. Yet instances of major program change, such as the administrative liberalization of the program in

1969, cannot be explained solely by a pluralist, interest-group approach.

A final theme that recurred in our review of the history of the Food Stamp Program was the high level of public support for food-related transfers, particularly in periods when it appears that hunger is coinciding with surplus food production. Over its history, the process of program liberalization converted the Food Stamp Program into a transfer that took on more of the characteristics of income. This was done to encourage participation among eligible nonparticipants, who in some cases were those most in need of nutrition assistance.

It is interesting to note that increased levels of income maintenance through food stamps received continued public support—as opposed to programs for guaranteed income. The direction of program liberalization suggests that benefits would be most acceptable to those in need of food assistance if they were given in cash. This has been successfully done in Puerto Rico, where cash food-assistance benefits increase food expenditures in a manner equivalent to food stamp benefits (Mathematica 1985). It does not seem likely in the near future that the U.S. food stamp program will be "cashed out." However, if concerns about reaching more hungry people become widespread for some reason, it is conceivable that further program liberalization could occur. Although food stamps may then be replaced by cash, our historical review suggests that the level of program funding will likely depend on the extent to which the cash benefits can maintain a credible image as food assistance.

6 Limits to Change in a Postrevolutionary Society: The Rise and Fall of Cheap-Food Policy in Nicaragua

PETER UTTING

Introduction

During the past decade, the concept of food security has been widely promoted as one of the guiding principles of development policy. In many countries, however, food security projects and programs are highly limited in pace and content. This tends to reflect both the lack of political will of Third World governments and their lack of control over patterns of resource use and allocation. Without these two elements it is impossible to bring about the changes in tenancy relations, production, marketing, and income structures that are necessary if genuine food security is to be achieved.

By focusing on the case of Nicaragua after the revolution, we refer to the experience of a country in which there can be little question that the political will existed for bringing about the required structural changes needed to improve the situation of the poor. Also, the potential to control patterns of resource allocation and use was relatively high in Nicaragua, due largely to the nationalization of the banking system and foreign trade immediately following the revolution in 1979 and direct state control of approximately 25 percent of production. Nevertheless, a series of objective political and economic constraints clearly limited the options available to the government vis-à-vis structural change, while the effectiveness of policies geared toward food-security objectives was restricted by other constraints and difficulties in policy design and implementation. As a consequence, the content of food policy changed significantly between 1979 and 1985. This chapter analyzes the determinants of food policy in Nicaragua at two levels: first, in terms of the new political orientation of economic policy following the revolution, as expressed in the

The author would like to thank Solon Barraclough, Valpy Fitzgerald, and Tim Coone for their comments. Extracts from *Economic Reform and Third-World Socialism,* by Peter Utting, are reprinted with permission from The Macmillan Press Ltd. Copyright 1992 by the United Nations Research Institute for Social Development.

mixed-economy and basic-needs approach; and, second, in terms of specific policy changes that occurred during the revolutionary period relating to the rise and fall of cheap-food policy.

The Mixed Economy and Basic Needs Approach

National liberation movements that culminate in successful revolutions have experienced a variety of approaches toward the political orientation of economic and social policies, including, for example, large-scale state control of production and marketing systems (Cuba) or a strategy based on a worker-peasant alliance (China, Vietnam). The course steered by the Sandinista government has incorporated elements of both, but policies affecting food production are more conditioned by the mixed-economy approach in which newly emergent state and cooperative sectors participate along with capitalist and peasant sectors in the structure of resource allocation.

The nature of the participation of diverse sectors in agriculture is explained by Barraclough (1982):

> The Government's strategy is to encourage increased production and productivity in (state, peasant, and entrepreneurial) sectors. Special emphasis is given to the public sector as a source of capital accumulation. Priority is given to the small farming sector as the source of basic foods and of seasonal labor for the large farms. The small producers are encouraged to organize a dynamic cooperative sector that will also produce export crops and invest in improved technologies. . . . The strategy is also to encourage the large and medium private farmers growing export crops to increase their production and invest . . . providing that they recognize the workers' right to unionization . . . [and] minimum wages and meet minimum standards of working conditions.

The term mixed economy is, of course, used to describe numerous economies throughout the world, be they developed, underdeveloped, capitalist, or socialist. In Nicaragua, the mixed economy may be defined in terms of an economy in which diverse forms of property rights coexist. However, patterns of resource allocation and use are to a large extent regulated by the state, which is oriented by a political project responding first and foremost to the basic needs of a broad category of social sectors that comprise the mass of the population (referred to in Nicaragua as the "popular" sectors) rather than to the interest of capital (Gorostiaga 1982).

The mixed economy approach was thus addressed to a basic-needs strategy in which not only the working class and the peasantry but also those employed in the tertiary and urban informal sectors benefited from a series of redistributive policies introduced since 1979. The main policies that characterized the mixed-economy and basic-needs approach until 1985 may be summarized as follows:

1. An agrarian reform policy that transformed the agrarian structure largely on the basis of an initial wave of confiscations of the properties of those directly associated with the Somoza regime. The agrarian reform has not resorted to large-scale expropriations of non-Somocista lands in an effort not to alienate the capitalist sector.
2. Pricing and credit policies as well as input, machinery, and technical services geared toward boosting production of all sectors, be they state enterprises, peasant, cooperative, or capitalist producers.
3. Fiscal and monetary policies that rely heavily on monetary emission rather than large-scale tax increases for specific social groups to finance redistributive policies and programs.
4. The establishment of a new food-distribution system involving the creation of an extensive network of privately owned retail centers located in both urban and rural areas, and rich and poor neighborhoods and communities, selling a range of basic goods at official prices.
5. An indiscriminate subsidy policy and rationing system for certain key products and public services.
6. Broadly based health and education programs as well as infrastructural services that have provided much of the population with access to electricity and drinking water.
7. Policies conducive toward the ongoing participation of transnational corporations in the economy.

The stated goals of Sandinista development policy sought to promote significant structural reforms. Such reforms were prompted by both the ideology of the revolution, based on a strong commitment to the interest of the popular sectors, particularly workers and peasants, and the political organization of these sectors in what are known as "mass organizations," representing workers, youth, women, urban neighborhood dwellers, peasants, and small commercial farmers. However, the nature of these reforms and the pace at which they could be implemented are conditioned by a range of factors. In this sense, the socialist dynamic of the Sandinista revolution was tightly restrained by the rein of reality; reality in this case having four key facets.

First, structural change was conditioned by the specific configuration of social forces that united to overthrow the old regime. Rather than expressing itself as a class war, the Sandinista revolution was a broadly based liberation movement against a specific target—the Somoza dictatorship. The mixed-economy model clearly reflected the active participation of a broad spectrum of social forces, including the bourgeoisie, in the revolutionary movements of 1978 and 1979.

Second, private producers (over 35 hectares) retained effective control of approximately 60 percent of agricultural land. Given the state's own limitations in directly administering production (recognized early in 1980 following the confiscation of Somocista farms), the difficulties of establishing extensive credit, input distribution, and extension services to support peasant production, and the pressing needs of reconstruction of a war-torn economy, it was imperative that the private sector be encouraged to take an active role in the development effort.

Third, there was Nicaragua's position in the world economic market and its dependent relationships with advanced capitalist countries; the nature of structural change; and the extent to which the capitalist sector might be displaced or squeezed. There were clear limits to the extent to which the agroexport sector (where capital has traditionally been concentrated) may be reduced, given its importance for the reproduction of the economy as a whole. As in many other small underdeveloped economies with a restricted internal market, a domestic capital-goods industry was largely nonexistent, and foreign exchange generated by agroexports provided for essential intermediate and capital goods required by agriculture, industry, commerce, and infrastructural development (Fitzgerald 1984). The extent to which the economy could be reoriented toward production for the internal market (or, specifically, toward peasant production) thus encountered severe constraints. Dependency also imposed limits on the effectiveness of economic planning, given that the state exercised no control over import and export prices. In the case of Nicaragua, foreign trade accounted for approximately 40 percent of GDP. In addition, a less-developed country is vulnerable to varying types and degrees of economic, political, or military pressure imposed by a range of international agents, be they foreign governments, transnational corporations, or international finance agencies. The nature of economic policies and the pace and content of structural change is obviously affected by these pressures.

Fourth, structural change will not follow an ideological or policy blueprint but will be highly conditioned by the existing social structure and sociopolitical and economic forces. In the case of Nicaragua, there existed a number of important objective constraints to transforming agriculture along socialist lines. The development of Nicaraguan rural society since the 1950s gave rise to a heterogeneous social structure, integrated by wage laborers, a large sector of seasonal workers with partial access to land, highly differentiated peasant and entrepreneurial sectors, and the traditional large landowners or *latifundistas*. In contrast to other Central American or Andean countries, however, the polarized structure of subsistence peasants and large landowners (minifundia and latifundia) did not predominate. Much of agricultural and industrial production was in the hands of peasants and small entrepreneurs integrated into the market (Baumeister and Neira 1984). This type of social structure was not particularly conducive to a strategy of socialist development based on state enterprises or collectives. Large-scale capitalist production units that might have provided the basis for a program of nationalization, giving the state direct control of agricultural production, were not predominant. The relatively small size of a subsistence peasant sector, the dispersed character of peasant production, and the importance of small commercial farmers conditioned the nature of agrarian reform and cooperative development policy, imposing constraints on the pace of land distribution, the growth of producer cooperatives or collectives, and the possibility of effectively planning rural development. A strong sociopolitical organization representing the landless peasantry and demanding a radical program of land redistribution did not emerge. Following the revolution, three major organizations represented rural interests: large private producers, salaried workers, and small commercial farmers.

Having outlined the nature of the mixed-economy and basic-needs approach that conditioned the general character of food and agricultural policy in Nicaragua, the next section makes an in-depth analysis of some of the more significant changes in food policy that took place during the revolutionary period in relation to cheap-food policy and identifies the principal political and economic forces that intervened to bring about these changes.

The Rise and Fall of Cheap-Food Policy

The main components of cheap-food policy consisted of guaranteed producer prices that were periodically increased for a range of food products, including basic grains, beans, sugar, milk, meat, and vegetable oil; official retail prices set for most basic food products other than fruit, vegetables, cheese, and fish; subsidies on maize, rice, sorghum, beans, sugar, and milk; and large-scale food imports sold cheaply on the internal market via an overvalued exchange rate. Credit, exchange rate, and fiscal policy also aimed at lowering production costs and producer prices by offering ample credit at low rates of interest, cheap imported inputs, and tax exemptions.

To ensure that consumers had effective access to cheap food, significant reforms also took place in the marketing structure, with the establishment of state procurement and wholesale agencies, and an extensive network of official-price stores in both state and private hands. Regional and family quotas were also established for a limited range of basic food products to ensure an equitable distribution of available supply.

Food-pricing policy had three broad objectives: to correct the historical inequalities of a marketing system that left the peasant producer receiving minimal prices for produce sold to middlemen; to minimize the adverse effects for both the small producer and the consumer of major price fluctuations; and to improve the access of the low-income consumer to basic food products through reduced prices.

It should be pointed out that price policy was not used as an instrument to change dietary habits from the point of view of nutritional criteria. Strict nutritional criteria did not play an important part in the definition of food policy. Rather, emphasis was placed on ensuring that sufficient supplies of the basic foods that comprise the local diet were available to as many people as possible, with little evaluation of the nutritional content of the food products involved and little priority assigned to the most vulnerable groups. While certain mal-nourished children and women were incorporated into nutritional programs, receiving, for example, a monthly quota of calorie- and protein-rich foods free of charge, such programs were limited in scope. At the level of food production and investment policy, a similar situation prevailed, with resources being chan-neled toward the production of what the mass of the population normally eat rather than what they should eat from a nutritional point of view. At the level of the media and education, very little attempt was made to change dietary habits. The typical Nicaraguan diet, however, based on beans, rice, and corn (tortilla), neatly combines calorie and protein sources. Although little research has been undertaken to assess changes in consumption and nutrition after the revolution, it is suspected that food policy was instrumental in increasing calorie intake for major sectors of the low-income population and in their improved access to products such as rice, sugar, and vegetable oil, with less significant advances being recorded in other areas.

The way in which pricing policy was conceived clearly reflected the ideological position of the new government and its commitment to improve the standard of living of the so-called popular sectors in general and not specifically the very poor, the malnourished, or any particular social class. The subsidy mechanism was considered crucial to resolving the trade-off of interests be-tween producers and consumers. In the long term, however, it was hoped that technological advances in basic food production and increased productivity would be able to fulfill a similar function. Between 1980 and 1983, there were periodic increases in official producer prices, while consumer prices in most subsidized products were frozen. By 1983, a significant price differential meant that the state marketing agency (ENABAS) was buying basic grains at prices generally between 50 to 100 percent above its selling price. Basic food sub-sidies increased steadily until 1985. In 1984, the main subsidies associated with basic grains, sugar, and milk accounted for 6.3 percent of total government expenditure, 45 percent of all current budgetary transfers, or 3.7 percent of GDP.

In addition to direct consumer subsidies that cheapened the price of do-mestically produced food products, the country resorted to large-scale food imports sold at an overvalued exchange rate. This mechanism would ensure that farmers' costs of production were kept low through an implicit subsidy on imported inputs and capital goods.

Immediately following the revolution, Nicaragua became highly depen-dent on food imports. In order to compensate for the decline in production of various product sectors in agriculture and the food industry and to satisfy increasing demand for staple foods, there was a sharp increase in the imports of a range of staple foods as well as raw materials required by the food industry.

The value of staple-food imports rose more than fivefold between 1978 and 1981, reaching 13 percent of the total import bill.

There also occurred a change in the composition of food imports. Strict priority was given to imports of basic consumer goods as opposed to nonessential food items. Hence the share of total food imports accounted for by basic food products increased from 48 percent in 1978 to 84 percent in 1981. While this characteristic was maintained, there occurred a sharp decline in food imports in 1982, when the import bill for basic food products was halved.

The Economics behind the Food Policy Changes

The decline in food imports represented the first of a series of policy changes that would drastically alter the character of Nicaraguan food policy. Why then did this happen? For certain products, the decline in food imports reflected nothing more than the fact that domestic production was increasing rapidly. This was the case, for example, of two of the basic staples, rice and beans. By 1982, Nicaragua had become self-sufficient in these two commodities, although significant imports of beans were resumed in 1983 and large quantities of rice were imported the following year. In the case of other products, such as chicken, eggs, plantains, and corn, the drop in imports was manifested in shortages on the internal market. Domestic production was unable to satisfy an increasing demand, although production in many product sectors was increasing at an acceptable rate.

The implementation of a series of redistributive policies gave rise to an increased demand for basic food products. The rapid recovery following the revolution of production levels in most product sectors and large-scale imports in 1980 and 1981 markedly increased the supply of a number of basic food products, thereby permitting significant increases in per capita consumption levels.

This tendency was particularly noticeable until 1983. Average per-capita consumption levels for the 1980–82 period increased for eight of eleven basic food products. There was, however, a marked change in 1983, when a series of constraints on domestic supply provoked a decline in consumption levels for a number of basic food products. Although two of the major staples, rice and beans, continued to fare well in 1984, there was a drop in per-capita consumption levels for seven products compared with the 1980–82 period. Despite this decline, consumption levels still exceeded prerevolution levels.

The change in import policy was prompted largely by economic pressures brought to bear by an increasing trade deficit. Immediately following the revolution, Nicaragua acquired a sizeable deficit, which averaged 427 million dollars between 1980 and 1984, a figure more or less equivalent to the total annual value of exports. This situation reflected to a large extent the problem of declining export revenues, due in part to a sharp drop in cotton and beef exports following the revolution, but it was primarily a consequence of the deteriorating terms of trade experienced since 1981, when world prices for all four major exports fell consistently until 1984.

In 1981, the trade deficit had reached 500 million dollars. The following year, 32 percent of export revenues were required to service the external debt (ECLA 1984). It is this general context that explains the pressures brought to bear for reducing the import bill. In 1982, we see a strong austerity drive to reduce imports, which declined by 22 percent and have remained fairly stable ever since. It was not only severe restrictions on the overall availability of foreign currency that prompted the reduction in food imports but, in particular, changes in the composition of imports, reflecting the competition between consumption and investment for scarce foreign exchange. In 1981, there was a sharp increase in investment from 15 percent to 22 percent of GDP. Public investment, particularly in areas associated with agricultural production, social infrastructure, and energy, increased significantly. As a percentage of total value added in agriculture, investments in agriculture, and agroindustry increased from an average of 8 percent during the prerevolutionary years to 24 percent in 1981, with high levels of investment being maintained in subsequent years. The debate that prompted the policy change centered very much on the trade-off between current versus future consumption.

More significant changes in cheap-food policy came in mid-1984, when it was announced that the price differential would be eliminated for basic grains. The state, however, would continue to subsidize ENABAS's administrative and operational costs. At the same time, significant price increases were announced for agricultural and livestock producers in general. With the change in subsidy policy, these were passed on to the consumer. Only in the case of milk and sugar did consumer prices remain stable.

Cheap-food policy was dealt a more serious blow in February 1985, when it was announced that food subsidies would be drastically reduced and eventually eliminated; that the national currency would be devalued by 180 percent; that major increases in producer prices would take effect in an effort to boost food production; and that basic food imports paid for in hard currency would be further reduced. This new policy package led to an increase of 205 percent in the retail price index between May 1984 and May 1985, and up to 362 percent in the case of a basic consumer basket incorporating the most essential food items.

A combination of factors intervened to bring about these policy changes— in particular, budgetary pressures arising from the cost of the war; the ongoing foreign-exchange crisis and the threat of economic blockade; contradictions or negative effects created by monetary and pricing policy; and the imperative to stimulate domestic production through increased prices.

Two factors played a part in the decision that would further reduce food imports paid for in hard currency. On the one hand, export revenues had reached an all-time low for the postrevolutionary period. With the escalation of the war, cattle, coffee, and seafood exports were reduced, as production, infrastructure, and the availability of labor in the war zones were affected. Also, Nicaragua's vulnerability to United States pressure and economic-blockade measures became glaringly apparent with the mining of Nicaraguan ports in 1984. Faced with increasing restrictions on the availability of foreign exchange and the possibility that access to imports of basic goods could be disrupted or cut off, the government decided in 1985 to give high priority to local production of basic food products that would replace imports. In practice, this decision meant curbing even further basic-food imports to liberate foreign exchange for the importation of inputs and capital goods required for basic-food production. This policy decision was reinforced with the imposition by the United States of a total trade embargo on U.S.-Nicaraguan trade, effective from May 1985. At the same time, there was a drive to obtain increased food aid from multilateral aid agencies, the European Economic Community (EEC), Canada, and Eastern Bloc countries to relieve any critical situation that might arise from shortfalls in domestic production.

The decision to eliminate subsidies on several basic products was prompted primarily by concerns regarding the size of the fiscal deficit, seen as one of the major factors behind the increasing monetary supply and inflation rate. The government had used monetary emission as one of the principal mechanisms for redistributing income and financing investments. Alternative options for financing redistribution via taxation were limited for a number of reasons. In the absence of a large middle- or high-income-salaried sector and an adequate accounting system, there were obvious limits to which the state could depend on direct taxation as a major source of income. The more general policy to encourage the entrepreneurial sector to maintain or expand production levels meant in practice minimal levels of taxation or outright tax exemptions for agricultural and other producers. Also, the political alliance with the large technical and professional sector associated with the state and the need to contain the postrevolutionary brain drain implied limits on the extent to which this sector could constitute a significant tax base. Indirect taxation, in fact, constituted the principal revenue source, accounting for over 60 percent of taxation revenue. However, the extent to which the government could depend on this form of taxation was also conditioned for political reasons, given its regressive character.

The fiscal deficit rose sharply in 1983, representing half of total government expenditures and 28 percent of GDP. While the deficit was reduced in real terms in 1984, it came under further pressure in 1985, largely due to increasing defense costs. Between 1981 and 1985, defense expenditures increased from 22 percent to 50 percent of total budget expenditures. Both the need to contain the deficit and to restructure the budget due to the priority assigned to defense prompted a revision in the sectoral allocation of government expenditures. In drawing up the 1985 annual plan, it was decided that top priority would be given to defense, existing standards in health services would be maintained, and the education budget would be frozen, while other social services, certain nonpriority investments, and food subsidies would be reduced.

The decision to reduce food subsidies was also in response to a number of contradictions that had emerged in economic policy. Certain groups of producers and merchants undermined government attempts to boost basic-grain production and improve people's access to cheap food. The rationale or logic of these agents clearly ran counter to that of government policy. Certain producers abandoned production of maize and beans, preferring instead to buy at the cheaper ENABAS prices. This occurred particularly at the level of a group of producers that traditionally had produced food to feed their employees (CIERA 1984). At the same time, the marketing costs of the state wholesaler, ENABAS, were being unnecessarily inflated by the practice of both state and private farms to sell produce at the high price, only to buy it back later at a lower price to feed the work force. While the extent of these practices should not be overstated, they clearly played a role in the policy decision to reduce subsidies. Contradictions also arose in relation to marketing activities, particularly in the capital, Managua, where, for example, street vendors would dedicate much time and energy to buying up cheap goods sold in the official retail outlets to sell in the parallel or black market, where the excess demand for basic consumer goods was translated into much higher prices.

Perhaps the major contradiction that reinforced the need for the change in policy was related to the increasing flow of rural inhabitants into the cities and of industrial workers into trading activities. This was due, in part, to the war situation in the northern and southern areas of the interior but also to the large income differentials between workers and peasants on the one hand, and urban traders on the other. The urban informal sector benefited not only from increasing commercial margins derived from the disequilibrium between demand and supply and limitations on the effectiveness of government price controls but also from a range of social programs—such as improved access to health, education, housing, water, electricity, and cheap food—that proved more effective in the cities. As the economic crisis intensified, workers and peasants alike were increasingly attracted to informal-sector employment in the cities, particularly in Managua. For the government, this trend was especially worrying. Economically, it meant that shortages of productive laborers in agriculture and industry were becoming more acute. Politically, it meant that the two fundamental classes upon which and for which the revolution had been built were disintegrating.

The Intervention of Political Factors

Political factors were to play an important role in determining the timing of the policy changes. The announcement of reductions in subsidies and substantial increases in consumer prices in July 1984 was unusual, not just because the decision represented a departure from previous policy but because the announcement took place just four months before a presidential and legislative election. That the government was prepared to make these decisions at such a delicate time reflected both the critical situation of the economy and the degree of public confidence in the government.

The political aftermath of the 1984 policy changes would, in fact, pave the way for the more radical measures to be taken in 1985. The Sandinista party (FSLN) won convincingly in the November elections despite the fact that opposition parties had used the issue of food prices and shortages as a key plank in their platform. Furthermore, there had been little overt opposition on the part of popular organizations to the price increases. While consumers naturally complained, there was little evidence of strikes or street demonstrations à la Santo Domingo, Khartoum, or Guatemala City, even when the state-of-emergency restrictions imposed in 1981 were lifted for the elections. In 1984, as in 1985, the government, supported by much of the media and the leadership of the mass organizations, launched a major publicity drive aimed not only at explaining the rationale behind the policy changes but also at promoting awareness of the need for sacrifice while the country was at war. The effectiveness of this "tightening of the belts" ideology clearly contributed toward minimizing opposition to the measures.

Perhaps more important was the nature of the policy package announced on both occasions. Increases in food prices were just one of a number of changes announced. Other policy measures were taken that were directly intended to benefit the low-income consumer. In 1984, the emphasis had been on curtailing speculation and black-market trading activities by trying to ensure that more food was channeled through what were known as the "secure" retail outlets, consisting primarily of an extensive network of approximately 6,000 local neighborhood stores and 900 workplace commissaries, which sold certain basic goods at official prices (CIERA 1985). Even at the increased official prices, the retail price in these stores would be well below the open market price.

The increase in official prices was not seen by the general public as a major issue. The main concern of the mass organizations was related to the problem of market shortages and rapid price inflation on the parallel market. Hence the principal demand was not for stability in official prices but, rather, for an increased supply of basic goods to the retail network selling at official prices. However, while the leading trade union organizations—Central Sandinista de Trabajadores (CST) and the Asociación de Trabajadores del Campo (ATC)—emphasized the need to strengthen supply channels to the workplace commissaries, the local community organizations (the CDS) demanded the expansion of what was known as the territorial network of peoples' stores, located at the neighborhood level. The 1984 measures accommodated both these demands by expanding the territorial network to a group of six essential consumer goods acquired on a card system that provided for a weekly family quota, while expanding the supply of other basic consumer goods to the workplace.

In 1985, the increases in retail prices coincided with a radically new wage policy that was intended to index salaries to retail prices. Between October 1984 and May 1985, three significant wage increases were announced and incentives were introduced as productivity bonuses. Until May 1985, wages had kept more or less at par with the general retail price index, although real wages had clearly deteriorated when compared with the increased cost of a basic consumer basket composed of the most essential food items.

The new wage policy represented a radical departure from the austere policy that operated until October 1984. At the same time, it was announced that salaried formal-sector workers, and particularly workers in primary and manufacturing sectors, would be given priority in the official distribution system for a range of basic consumer goods affected by shortages. Outside the capital, this would be achieved by expanding retail outlets located in the workplace, while in Managua, three of the eight supermarkets were accessible only to salaried workers in the formal sector. By incorporating compensatory measures that would defend the standard of living of the working class, the nature of the policy package differed substantially from the standard International Monetary Fund recipe for crisis situations faced by many Third World economies.

Pressure exerted by the mass organizations and their participation in the policy decision-making process was crucial in producing this blend of measures. The intervention of these organizations in the policy process assumed various forms. Indirect forms of pressure brought to bear by way of strikes or street demonstrations have not been prominent in Nicaragua. Strikes were formally banned by legislation that introduced a state of emergency in 1981 to deal with the emerging crisis situation of the economy and the war. However, the need to resort to actions such as these had been mitigated by the existence of alternative mechanisms for influencing policy. A number of the mass organizations participated directly both at the executive and legislative levels. Particularly important was the participation of trade union, producer, and consumer associations in national commissions, which acted as policy-review boards in areas associated with production, basic goods supply, prices, and incomes. Until the 1984 elections, the mass organizations were also each assigned a number of seats in the legislative assembly, with the CDS, in fact, having the largest number of seats of all the organizations represented.

The mass organizations also influenced the policy decision-making process given their close ties to both the media and the Sandinista party. In relation to the media, two of the three leading newspapers, numerous radio stations, and the state-controlled television network were important channels for the expression of popular interests. A prominent feature of *Barricada,* the official Sandinista newspaper with the largest circulation in the country, was its defense of popular interests when these were seen to be undermined by certain malpractices in government. The paper frequently carried articles which were critical of bureaucracy, inefficiency, or abuses of power in various ministries, particularly the ministry that oversaw basic-food distribution. The mass organizations constituted the basis of support for the FSLN, and the party was clearly the main avenue for ensuring that policy decisions took account of popular interests.

Membership of the FSLN was instrumental in opening up effective channels of communication between government ministers and vice-ministers on the one hand, and leaders of the mass organizations on the other. These more informal bilateral relations considerably enhanced the extent to which the mass organizations were able to influence the policy process. A number of the leaders of these organizations also participated both in the Sandinista assembly, one of the highest decision-making bodies within the party, and in the new legislative assembly, sitting directly as FSLN representatives.

A major political development of the 1981–1984 period was the emergence of the National Union of Farmers and Ranchers (UNAG) as a powerful mass organization representing primarily agricultural cooperative members and small commercial farmers. Established in 1981, the UNAG claimed a membership of 100,000 in 1985, over half of the country's agricultural producers. From 1984 onward, when commercial farmers assumed a more prominent role within the organization, the UNAG came to press increasingly for the liberalization of the government's grain-pricing policy.

After mid-1984, important changes took place regarding the participation of the CDS—the main organization representing consumer interests—in the food-policy design and review process. This organization had taken an active role in the policy process, influencing the definition of policies relating to food distribution and directly overseeing policy implementation, particularly in urban areas. The CDS played a major role in establishing the guaranty card system in 1982, which was gradually expanded to provide family quotas for a number of essential food and nonfood products. The organization also played a major role in defining which type of retail outlets would constitute the basis of the official retail system. The state had experimented with a variety of outlets of different sizes and locations, some based in residential zones, others in the workplace or in established shopping areas (markets and supermarkets). Control was in the hands of a variety of agents, including the state retail chains, private traders, community organizations, and industrial and agricultural enterprises. Pressure from the CDS, however, influenced policy decisions that eventually gave priority to the expansion of an extensive network of retail outlets known as people's stores, based at the level of the neighborhood community and controlled by the local private store owner. The CDS selected which of the local retailers would distribute the basic goods sold on the guaranty card system. This development was important, for it meant that the state had recognized certain limits to direct intervention at the level of retail distribution. Such activities were considered best left to private retailers who were accepted by and easily accessible to the local population. These agents would work on an associative basis with state wholesale agencies, receiving regular quotas of certain basic consumer goods and selling these at official prices. At the same time, they were free to sell other goods, the prices of which were not regulated.

With the setting up in 1983 of a high-level food-policy review board, the National Supply Commission, the CDS was able to influence the nature of the policy reforms incorporated into the Laws of Consumer Protection, passed in July 1984 (and subsequently reinforced in August 1985). The law increased the number of basic products to be included on the guaranty card system and introduced a series of controls on marketing activities. These included the nationalization of wholesale distribution of eighteen food and manufactured products, restrictions on the territorial movement of basic goods, and stricter control on retail prices sold in the parallel market. Once these measures were taken, however, the commission became less active and was finally disbanded. While the rural and industrial workers' associations continued to participate in the policy process via the more informal relations outlined above, the participation of the CDS declined markedly.

In September 1984, measures opposed by the CDS were introduced to channel a proportion of the total supply of the guaranteed products to the state supermarket chain, where they would be sold at prices just below the open market price. Although the CDS, supported by the newspapers, opposed these measures, the economic logic of government held sway. By setting up this official parallel market, the government was accepting the existence of the parallel black market as a fact of life. It was considered necessary to compete with this market both as a means of appropriating surplus for the state and in order to extract liquidity from the economy. The total quantity of goods channeled to the new official parallel market would, it was argued, represent a very small percentage of total supply and should not affect supplies to the guaranteed-price stores. The CDS, however, did not agree.

Direct channels of communication between the CDS and the Ministry of Internal Trade were broken off when a government reshuffle brought about a change in the top ministry personnel. At the beginning of 1985, the National Planning Council was established as the highest planning authority. The CST and ATC were invited to participate in an important council commission overseeing production, prices, supply, salaries, and employment. The CDS was conspicuously absent from this commission.

The declining participation of the CDS in the policy process was to a certain extent symptomatic of an overall crisis in the grass-roots support of the organization. Throughout 1984 and 1985, active participation of community members in CDS activities, including those associated with overseeing the implementation of food pricing and distribution policy, declined sharply. Much of the urban population had become critical of the organization, which was seen to have divorced itself from real community interests and concerns. In September 1985, the general assembly of the CDS met for several days to evaluate the crisis in their organization, recognizing that the organization's leaders had become separated from the base membership and proposing a new program that would effectively relate to community interests.

The declining participation and strength of the CDS also reflected, and no doubt contributed to, a change in the political orientation of economic policy. This was expressed in a series of measures affecting prices, wages, food imports, taxation levels, and the distribution of basic consumer goods, introduced at the beginning of 1985. These aimed at boosting production and productivity by (1) establishing much higher guaranteed prices for agricultural produce and limited access to dollar incentives for certain agroexport producers; (2) introducing significant wage increases for industrial and agricultural workers and material incentives for increased productivity; and (3) encouraging peasant production by improving the access of the rural household to a range of basic inputs and consumer goods that had become increasingly scarce. Real wages for workers and state-sector employees were also protected—by an agreement signed in February 1985 by the main union confederation (the CST) and the Ministry of Internal Trade (MICOIN), under which workers were given privileged access to consumer goods. As mentioned earlier, three of Managua's eight supermarkets were converted into commissaries where only workers (and family members) with union cards could shop. Such centers were gradually extended to other cities, while in smaller towns and in the countryside, an increased supply of basic goods was delivered to commissaries located in the workplace. In October 1985, the CST acquired further gains when its demands for price reductions on basic manufactures were met—the prices of numerous products sold in the commissaries were reduced by between 15 and 25 percent.

The nature of this policy package was such that increased prices were compensated for by measures that defended the standard of living of the working class and rural producers. However, the urban informal sector, which was the natural constituency of the CDS, received no such benefits. This sector and certain formal service and trading activities were squeezed by the new policies. While large-scale merchants, private importers, and the liberal professions provided a major new tax base, which it was hoped would contribute toward reducing the fiscal deficit, the informal sector was squeezed by commercial controls and restrictions on certain social programs. In combination with the new wage policy, these measures were intended to stem the flow of rural migrants and urban factory workers into trading activities and to curb speculative trading activities (Fitzgerald 1985).

Changes also emerged in relation to the nature of state control over food distribution. Whereas early marketing policy had aimed at increasing state regulation and control of essential consumer goods in general, material and administrative limitations restricted the effectiveness of this policy. For example, controlling procurement and organizing distribution of basic grains among thousands of dispersed rural producers in areas with limited infrastructure proved to be an impossible task. In light of these limitations, a new principle emerged by which the state would attempt to regulate or directly control procurement and distribution of what was considered not only essential but also what, in practice, was controllable. Hence, the marketing policy for beans and corn was liberalized in regions of the interior of the country while the state concentrated its energies on organizing the distribution of a group of agroindustrial and manufactured products, whose procurement could be effectively controlled because production was concentrated in relatively few enterprises.

This new policy package clearly implied a change in the content of the mixed-economy and basic-needs approach outlined earlier, in which food and development policy had been geared toward improving the standard of living of the popular sectors in general. In 1985, we saw a much more explicit prioritization of social sectors in the structure of resource allocation aimed at boosting agricultural and industrial production and protecting the living standards of workers, peasants, and state employees.

Conclusions

The preceding analysis has highlighted a range of political and economic factors that intervened to redefine key aspects of food policy during the postrevolutionary period. These factors may be grouped into four related categories: (1) externally induced pressures; (2) macroeconomic constraints associated with redistributive policies; (3) contradictions at the level of policy implementation; and (4) popular participation and pressure from mass organizations.

Externally Induced Pressures

External dependency conditioned the content of food and development policy and the pace of structural change, given the role of the export sector in the national economy, pressures imposed by foreign governments, international organizations, and transnational corporations, and the effects of price trends on the world market.

The Nicaraguan economy was subject to immense constraints throughout the first half of the 1980s due to declining or stagnant export revenues as prices for the major agroexports, such as coffee, sugar, cotton, and beef, fell on the world market. The upshot of this situation was a large trade deficit that imposed severe pressure on food imports.

In countries such as Nicaragua, where national liberation movements assumed an overtly independent and nonaligned stance, external pressure may manifest itself in a highly aggressive form, involving economic embargo or blockade measures as well as direct or indirect forms of military intervention. The histories of Cuba, Vietnam, Angola, Mozambique, and Nicaragua tell a similar story in this respect. The war inevitably meant that a large share of human resources, the national budget, and production had to be diverted to defense efforts, while productive, infrastructural, and human resources were constantly depleted.

War also required the united response of social forces within the country, thereby reinforcing the principle of a mixed economy that oriented the development process in Nicaragua. Economic-blockade measures had the effect of not only cutting off, delaying, or restricting access to foreign markets, finance, and aid but also reinforcing the principle of self-sufficiency in basic food production, upon which the broader policy of food security was based. As we have seen, tensions and constraints directly related to the war and the trade embargo constituted key determinants of the policy changes outlined above.

Macroeconomic Constraints Associated with Redistributive Policies

Redistributive policies involved large increases in public spending in social services, consumer subsidies, and investment, financed to a large extent through monetary emission. When the costs of the war were added, the fiscal deficit and the money supply increased even further. The money supply also expanded rapidly as a consequence of foreign-exchange losses deriving from policies that subsidized production, consumption, and investment via an overvalued exchange rate that cheapened the cost of imported goods when guaranteed prices for agroexports were set well above the exchange rate. Also, a highly generous credit policy characterized by low interest rates and levels of recuperation increased losses in the government's financial account. The supply response, on the other hand, was insufficient to meet the increased demand, with the resulting inflationary consequences.

As the country initially resorted to large-scale food imports in an attempt to reduce the gap between national production and demand, this in turn generated additional tensions reflected in an increased trade deficit and bottlenecks in dealing with the more complicated marketing circuits involved in international trade. The balance-of-payments deficit was further exacerbated as the country relied on external debt to finance the reconstruction of a war-torn economy and an ambitious investment program, which, it was hoped, would lay the basis for future foreign-exchange savings and increased export revenues. Servicing the external debt reached unmanageable levels, accounting for up to a third of export revenues.

An increasing fiscal and financial account deficit, the growing disequilibrium between demand and supply reflected in an expanding inflation rate, and a worsening balance-of-payments crisis constituted the key macroeconomic constraints that intervened to reorient food policy.

Contradictions at the Level of Policy Implementation

Within a mixed economy, there will be numerous productive and commercial agents unwilling to submit to the logic of the economic plan and its specific policy instruments, particularly those relating to price controls. This will be most apparent in situations of demand and supply disequilibrium that are likely to characterize processes of rapid structural change. Such a situation expresses itself in the form of rapid price rises of basic consumer goods on the parallel or black market. In such situations, we have seen how the objectives of subsidy, pricing, and employment policy can be undermined as people resell goods purchased at official prices and shift from employment in primary or secondary sectors into trading activities.

The changes in cheap-food policy that occurred since 1984 in Nicaragua were in part a response to similar contradictory situations. Effective policy design and implementation must clearly analyze and anticipate the varied responses of numerous social agents that intervene in the food circuit—be it at the level of household, the production unit, or in marketing activities. Also, policies that have the effect of transforming production and marketing relations and of displacing agents must be sure to replace the functions that the latter performed. A characteristic feature of rapid social change is the time lag that often emerges between the disarticulation of the old economic and social structure and the consolidation of the new. Policy design must anticipate this situation and seek to minimize the time lag so as to avoid serious dislocations that affect people's access to food.

Popular Participation and Pressure from Mass Organizations

One of the defining characteristics of the Sandinista revolution was the incorporation of the mass of the population into organizations representing women, youth, agricultural, and industrial workers, consumers at the community level, peasants, and the small agricultural entrepreneurs. Four organizations, representing agricultural producers and workers (UNAG and ATC, respectively), industrial and state sector employees (CST), and consumers (CDS), played an important role in determining the nature of the policy changes we have analyzed.

Popular participation during the revolutionary period enabled important sectors of the population to influence the direction of food policy in Nicaragua. Specifically, we have seen how the intervention of the mass organizations in the policy process affected the nature of policy reforms introduced in 1984 and 1985. Austerity and incentive measures aimed at reducing government deficits and increasing domestic production, respectively, were complemented by other measures that defended the standard of living of important sectors of the population. Changes in the relative strength of these organizations, however, meant that some sectors would be compensated more than others.

In conclusion, the key determinants of food policy in Nicaragua during the postrevolutionary period fell into two broad catagories. On the one hand, they relate to economic constraints of a type faced by developing countries in general—problems relating, for example, to deteriorating terms of trade and a rapidly increasing external debt. On the other hand, these determinants relate to pressures generated by the process of social change that characterizes the Nicaraguan revolution. These pressures are of four broad types: first, redistributive policies that have the effect of increasing demand faster than supply, with consequent inflationary pressures, market shortages, and external dependency on food imports; second, the redefinition of the external dependency relation and, in particular, political realignments with foreign governments that had the effect of restricting access to international finance and the United States markets and of intensifying the counterrevolutionary war; third, the difficulties of transition from a free market to a more planned economy when the state apparatus lacks the capacity to effectively design and implement policies and when market forces undermine policy objectives; and, fourth, new forms of intervention in the policy process of organizations representing the interests of the major social groups that comprise the society.

Political Economy Issues at the Local and Household Levels

7 Bureaucrats and Peasants: The Dynamics of Local-Level Agricultural Bureaucracy in Rural Egypt

RICHARD H. ADAMS, JR.

In recent years, much attention has come to focus on the so-called "forgotten men" of development (Chambers 1966): the local-level bureaucrats charged with implementing national strategies of rural change at the village level. Within the last decade, numerous studies have appeared on the attitudes and performance of local government administrators—nutrition officials, agricultural agents, and health personnel—in a variety of developing countries.

On the whole, two broad themes seem to characterize these studies. The first is the oft-repeated conviction that such officials are biased toward rich peasants.[1] Myrdal (1968) writes that "[local] officials administering development programs require the cooperation of local elites [if they are to achieve successful results]. No wonder then that [the programs they administer] have helped mainly those in the rural population who were already relatively well off." The second theme in this literature emphasizes the incompetence, laziness, and even inconsequentiality of local officials.[2] Lele (1975) claims that the main problem with agricultural extension workers in Africa is that they are "ill paid, ill trained, ill equipped with a technical package and thus very poor in quality. That the farmer often knows more [than the extension agent] . . . has become part of the folklore of extension in developing countries."

Upon reflection, these two themes appear to contain a number of contradictory points. For example, it may be quite possible that local officials are biased towards the rural elite. But how pernicious can this bias be, if these same officials are as lazy and incompetent as some observers suggest? If local bu-

---

1. For Africa, see Thoden van Velzen (1976) and Chambers (1977); for Asia, see Griffin (1974) and Blair (1978).
2. For Africa, see Moris (1972, 1981) and Leonard (1972, 1977); for Asia, see Hunter (1969).

Reprinted, with changes, from *The Journal of Development Studies* 22 (January 1986) by permission of Frank Cass & Co. Ltd.

reaucrats are so poorly trained and equipped, why would any villager—rich or poor—consciously want to work with them?

This study argues that these (and similar) contradictions can be at least partially resolved by paying closer attention to the social, political, and economic dynamics of the environment in which local officials work. It may be true that bureaucrats in a particular village setting are rather inconsequential in terms of promoting new nutritional or agricultural activities. But, as this chapter seeks to demonstrate, the reasons for this inconsequentiality may lie more in environmental factors—either at the national or local level—than in any inherent defect in the officials themselves. For example, in a situation in which the state does not provide local bureaucrats with the proper resources to execute their duties, they may well be more superfluous than productive. Similarly, in a village environment characterized by extreme land or economic scarcity, resource-poor local bureaucrats may not be able to attract the attention of any rural inhabitants. In such a situation, wealthier village elements may choose to consciously ignore local government staff.

This chapter emphasizes the importance of such environmental considerations by drawing on research conducted in district (*markaz*) El-Diblah[3] in Egypt (Minya Governorate)[4] during the 1978–1980 period. Unlike other studies in this volume, the focus of this chapter is not on nutrition officials or nutrition-related programs. Rather, it focuses on the activities of local-level agricultural officials in one specific rural Egyptian locale. Nevertheless, the findings of the study seem broadly applicable to many other Third World situations in which local-level officials are charged with the task of raising the nutritional or health standards of villagers. In a number of developing countries, village-level officials are relatively unimportant; they possess little job motivation and offer only a limited range of goods and services. Their position as public servants is therefore appropriated by a small group of rich peasants who are able and willing to provide poorer village elements with a steady stream of services. In some instances, members of this rich peasant class may choose to work closely with local officials in order to monopolize the resources at their disposal; but in other cases, rich peasants may well choose to ignore resource-poor local officials.

In an effort to elaborate upon these themes in the district El-Diblah, this study is divided into three sections. The first one tries to relate the findings of this local-level study to a larger context by examining the more general environmental factors affecting local-level bureaucratic behavior. In this section, ideas from development administration and political anthropology are used to hy-

3. El-Diblah is a pseudonym, as are the names of all villages and villagers in this study. The names of governorates and national leaders are real.

4. Minya Governorate is located approximately 250 kilometers south of Cairo. Like all governorates in Egypt, Minya Governorate is divided into a number of districts, one of which is district El-Diblah.

pothesize about the character of bureaucratic behavior in different rural settings. The second section attempts to apply these more general principles to an analysis of the nature of the interaction between village officials, rich peasants, and poor peasants in district El-Diblah. The last section summarizes the conclusions of the study.

Environmental Influences on Local-Level Bureaucratic Behavior

In most general terms, it would appear that the activities of local officials are influenced by at least three environmental factors: the nature of state policy; the control powers of bureaucratic institutions; and the character of the local rural elite.[5] We will examine each of these factors in turn.

First, the nature of state policy clearly affects the performance of officials working at the local level. In many developing countries, the local village community is characterized by what Foster (1960, 1965) has called the world of "the limited Good." In this world, "the 'Good' (i.e., land, wealth) exists in limited amounts which cannot be expanded" (Foster 1965). Such a scarcity of resources means that the supplies and the funds necessary to develop the local community must normally be provided by outside sources, usually at the national level. As Bratton (1980) has rightly noted, in most cases "the flow of development resources, such as it is, is predominantly from [the] center to [the] periphery." Local bureaucrats (and communities) have the power to change, but not to initiate, the flow of such resources.

In most situations, both the volume and the timing of such center-to-periphery resource flows are crucial. If, for example, local agricultural officials are to represent an important force in the village community, they must be provided with sufficient seeds, fertilizer, and credit to present to farmers prior to planting. If they do not have such resources, their presence may well become more superfluous than useful.[6]

This point suggests that there may well exist a type of "differentiation of power" among governmental officials working at the village level. Bureaucrats working for well-supplied local-level institutions may be able to command far more authority than their colleagues who are employed by undercapitalized institutions. In any particular village situation, it would be quite difficult to determine in an a priori way which set of bureaucrats (and institutions) are important or powerful, and which are not. This would depend on a wide range of factors, such as the basic government strategy of development (urban or rural-oriented) and the role assigned to different institutions in pursuing that strategy. Some village institutions may be assigned the task of extracting local

5. This list of environmental factors is by no means exhaustive or definitive. Others may well be able to distinguish other equally valid environmental factors that influence the activities of local-level government officials.
6. See, for example, Kees van Donge (1982).

resources (through taxation), while others may be responsible for extending local-level resources (through education).

Second, the ability of local institutions to extract or expand local resources depends on their powers of institutional control. Effective bureaucratic institutions must always be able to set and enforce certain standards of conduct for their employees. According to Weber (1978), a bureaucracy is based on "a clearly established system of super- and sub-ordination in which there is a supervision of the lower offices by the higher ones." Yet in many developing countries, poor salaries, overstaffing, and offers of guaranteed employment all greatly reduce the power of bureaucratic superiors to control the activities of their subordinates.

Such factors often give rise to what might be termed "the exercise of actual arbitrariness" (Weber 1947) on the part of local-level officials. Such arbitrariness allows local officials to place their own personal interests ahead of the more general interests of the state. This not only reduces the ability of local institutions to execute their assigned functions, but it also helps to produce the familiar gap between the government edict and rural reality, which is found in many developing countries. In these areas, what the government claims it will do is not always synonymous with what it actually does do because the bureaucracy exercises only minimum control over its own employees.

Third, the activities of local officials in many developing countries are directly affected by the various powers still exercised by the rural elite. The reasons for this are clear. The pool of landless and near-landless peasants is often so large in many developing areas[7] that there is always a strong demand for a variety of patronage services, including agricultural work opportunities and consumer loans. In these areas, however, local government institutions normally supply few agricultural work opportunities and extend credit only to landowners. At the same time, the officials attached to these institutions are usually not in an economic position to hire workers or to extend credit. According to Lipton (1974), this means that landless and near-landless peasants continue to depend on "the large farmer group, often for land and almost always for security, input purchases, output outlets, consumer credit, intercession with outsiders (especially officials) and jobs to enable them to live. . . . The multiplicity of such ties of dependence of client upon patron constitutes the central feature of almost all pre-capitalist and proto-capitalist rural social structures."

The existence of such ties of dependence in many developing countries suggests an important theoretical point. In areas characterized by a high degree of landlessness, social classes do not appear in a pure Marxist form. Rather,

---

7. According to Esman (1978), in Asia, the proportions of landlessness and near-landlessness in the rural labor force range from 89 percent in Bangladesh to 50 percent in Thailand. In Latin America, the figures range from 90 percent in El Salvador to 50 percent in Costa Rica. Esman (1978) also gives figures on other countries and his definition of near-landlessness.

class relations in such areas tend to remain encapsulated in one dominant type of relationship: the patron-client relationship. Poor peasants who are unable to provide for themselves remain dependent—not on government agencies or local bureaucrats—but on the patronage powers of rich peasants.

On this basis, it would be somewhat erroneous to overemphasize the importance of local-level bureaucrats. These officials may well supervise the flow of state-supplied resources into the villages. Yet, in many cases, the power of these bureaucrats may be more formal than real; environmental factors, such as the urban bias of state policy and the continuing powers of the rural elite,may seriously undermine the powers of local bureaucrats. In such cases, local officials may wield too little control over too few resources to attract the attention of anyone—rich or poor. Local officials may therefore represent only a type of second- or third-order "insider," whose jobs and duties bear no particular relevance to the realities of everyday economic life in the village.

Bureaucrats and Peasants in District El-Diblah

The preceding discussion helps set the more general framework for examining the dynamics of social relations in district El-Diblah. After a brief overview of the basic socioeconomic features in El-Diblah, this section will examine relations between bureaucrats and peasants in terms of the three environmental factors elaborated above: the nature of state policy; the control powers of local institutions; and the character of the local rural elite.

An Overview of District El-Diblah

Located along the Nile River in Upper Egypt,[8] district El-Diblah is a rural administrative area embracing some 155,000 residents. These rural inhabitants live in some 30 villages, small, dusty communities that are linked together by a rudimentary network of narrow unpaved roads. The largest community, and the administrative seat for the area, is the village of El-Diblah. In El-Diblah, as in all of the other outlying villages of the District, simple one- and two-story mud brick houses predominate.

Three main sets of actors exist in district El-Diblah: local government bureaucrats (*muwazzafin*), who have earned a high school or, more rarely, a college degree; rich peasants, who own or rent over 10 feddans[9] of land (2.6 percent of all landholding peasants); and poor peasants (*fellahin*), who own or rent less than one feddan of land (41 percent of all landholding peasants).

8. Since the time of the pharaohs, Egypt has been divided into two broad geographical areas: Upper and Lower Egypt. Upper Egypt now generally refers to the area located upstream of the Nile River from Cairo—that is, the area south of Cairo. Lower Egypt, or the Delta, refers to the large alluvial delta region north of Cairo.
9. A feddan equals 1.038 acres or 0.42 hectares.

Another 41 percent of peasants own or rent between 1 and 3 feddans each.

The approximately 1,400 government bureaucrats in district El-Diblah work in one or another of the welter of government institutions—agricultural cooperatives, health clinics, village councils, and schools—that have been created in the area since the Egyptian Revolution of 1952. The 450 or so rich peasants grow the most lucrative cash crops planted in the area: sugarcane, grapes, and vegetables. To cultivate these crops, the rich peasantry hires workers from among the ranks of the large pool of poor peasants in the area. According to the author's calculations, approximately 64 percent of the total male agricultural work force in district El-Diblah is either landless or near-landless.[10] The bulk of these poor peasants survive by working as agricultural laborers, cultivating the principal cash crops (in addition to the above, cotton) and food crops (wheat, maize, clover) grown in the area.

State Policy and Bureaucrat-Peasant Relations in El-Diblah

It is possible to examine the relations between bureaucrats and peasants by analyzing the Egyptian government's main instrument for directing agricultural change at the local level: the agricultural cooperatives. Staffed by government-appointed bureaucrats, these agricultural cooperatives exist in almost every Egyptian village.

From the standpoint of the state, the principal purpose of the agricultural cooperatives is that of controlling agriculture in order to extract a transferable surplus from peasant producers.[11] The cooperatives provide farmers with their basic agricultural inputs: seeds, fertilizer, and pesticides. They collect payment on these inputs by deducting from the imputed cash value of those cash crops—principally cotton in El-Diblah—that farmers are required to market through cooperative channels. By directing the flow of inputs and outputs to farmers, the agricultural cooperatives in Egypt represent a clever mechanism for taxing the surplus produced by peasant farmers.

The cooperatives exercise their control powers in the following manner. Each agricultural cooperative in Egypt divides the land under its jurisdiction into two or three rotational blocs. In theory, each bloc is then assigned a different crop according to season, with all farmers having land within that bloc being required to grow the assigned crop. In practice, however, farmers have recently been permitted to substitute for the assigned rotational crop with one

---

10. This figure was arrived at as follows: According to population and landholding data obtained in district El-Diblah, approximately 24 percent of the total male agricultural work force in the district is near-landless. While the Egyptian government does not keep data on the incidence of landlessness, estimates made by the author suggest that some 40 percent of the total male agricultural work force in district El-Diblah is landless. For more information on these calculations, see Adams (1986).

11. For more on this point, see Adams (1986).

notable exception: cotton. Since it represents Egypt's main export crop,[12] most farmers are forced to grow cotton according to the assigned rotational cycles. Since 1965, all cotton grown in Egypt has been marketed through the cooperatives. This has enabled the state to indirectly tax the farmers by purchasing cotton at one set of prices and then selling it on the world market at much higher prices. Allowing for handling, ginning, and transportation costs, the government paid the Egyptian farmers only about 60 percent of the export price for cotton during the 1965–1976 period (Cuddihy 1980).[13]

The Egyptian effort to use the cooperative system to control the surplus produced by peasant farmers has a decided effect on the activities of the 29 agricultural cooperatives located in district El-Diblah. Most importantly, it means that cooperative officials in this area spend more of their time making sure that farmers grow certain government-marketed crops than they do in providing these peasants with the means to develop or improve their agricultural productivity. As a result, cooperative officials contribute little to the national development effort.

Part of the problem lies in the state's reluctance to provide cooperative officials with sufficient supplies—seeds, fertilizer, and credit—to execute their duties. The state, for instance, provides cooperative officials in El-Diblah with chemical fertilizer to dispense to farmers on the basis of crop and area to be sown. While these fertilizer allotments are usually adequate for some crops (cotton, wheat), they are generally inadequate for others (maize, sugarcane). This means that there is a flourishing black market for chemical fertilizer. Cooperative officials in this area are able to meet only part of the considerable local-level demand for fertilizer.

In cooperation with the local village banks,[14] cooperative officials in El-Diblah also oversee the flow of agricultural credit to farmers. Given the state's desire to tax rather than develop peasant agriculture, credit is supplied in this area for the cultivation of only three cash crops: cotton, sugarcane, and fruit. Such restrictive credit practices serve to reduce the local-level powers of cooperative officials. In the absence of any government credit to cultivate the main food crops grown in the area (maize, wheat), poor peasants must still frequently turn to wealthier village elements for help. For instance, a small

---

12. Cotton is the most important export crop grown in Egypt. During the 1978–1980 period, cotton and cotton textile exports accounted for between 13 and 16 percent of the total annual value of Egyptian commodity exports. See Scobie (1981).

13. During this period, 1965–1976, similar degrees of price manipulation existed on virtually all other crops (e.g., rice, sugarcane, onions) marketed through Egyptian government channels. See, for example, Cuddihy (1980) and Braun and de Haen (1983).

14. In 1977, the Egyptian government created a network of village banks designed to extend agricultural credit to "worthy" farmers. These banks, however, are still closely linked with the agricultural cooperatives. The village banks extend loans in cash and in kind on the basis of cooperative-supplied data on landownership and cropping patterns.

farmer wishing to plant wheat in November may well have to turn to a village moneylender in order to secure the requisite working capital. Practices such as these suggest that the bureaucrats attached to the agricultural cooperatives have only partially, and not completely, assumed the moneylending functions of the rich peasantry.

The power of cooperative officials is further compromised by the type of control function they perform. In this area, supervising the peasantry takes place from the office, not from the field. There is a strong feeling that cooperative officials are exercising sufficient control over the peasantry if they file enough paperwork with provincial and national officials. Forms on the level of inputs supplied to the peasantry, their cropping patterns, and the amount of land planted in cotton therefore abound.

The problem, however, is that many of these forms bear only a hazy relationship to reality, because cooperative officials are quite reluctant to venture out into the fields to check on their accuracy. This is a reflection of the cultivated "status honor" of these bureaucrats, an exaggerated sense of honor that renders them more vegetative than productive in any developmental sense of the word.

In El-Diblah, the majority of cooperative bureaucrats are recent graduates of the local agricultural high school in the village of El-Diblah. In an area in which illiteracy is still quite widespread,[15] most of these officials believe that their educational achievements entitle them to membership in a rural status elite that is exempt from manual labor. While members of their own family may still toil long hours out in the fields, these bureaucrats sincerely believe that it would be shameful for them to work with their hands in the fields. As one of them said, "How could I ever work out in the fields like a mere peasant? What would my family and friends ever say? I would never hear the end of their laughter."

On those rare occasions when they do venture out into the fields, the cooperative bureaucrats tend to display only a very rudimentary knowledge of practical agricultural matters. Few of them, for instance, know much about such basic agricultural matters as proper crop cultivation, the correct application of fertilizers,and the optimal planting densities for various crops.[16] In this regard, it is instructive to note that a clear majority of farmers interviewed in one agricultural cooperative in El-Diblah said that if they wanted advice on a new agricultural input, they would turn to a relative or a neighbor rather than a cooperative official. In the words of one disgruntled peasant, "The bureaucrats

15. According to the 1976 Egyptian population census, 71 percent of the population in Minya Governorate is illiterate. In the rural district of El-Diblah, this figure probably approaches 80 percent.

16. The lack of practical training given to agricultural officials in developing countries is often cited as an important factor inhibiting the effective operation of small-farmer extension programs. See, for example, Lele (1975).

of the [local] agricultural cooperatives are not here to teach us anything useful. They are here only to make us grow cotton and to fill out various government forms on us."

The Control Powers of Local Institutions and Bureaucrat-Peasant Relations in El-Diblah

As we have seen, the agricultural cooperatives in district El-Diblah are supposed to direct and control the actions of peasant farmers. In practice, however, these institutions frequently lack the power to execute their assigned supervisorial functions. The reasons for this are manifest: these cooperatives are often unable to set and enforce standards of conduct for their own employees. This problem has its roots in the employment practices of the Egyptian government bureaucracy as a whole.

Anxious to avoid massive unemployment of the educated, the Egyptian government has followed a policy of providing each and every high school and college graduate with a government job since the late 1950s. In a country with as weak a private sector as in Egypt, this policy makes sound political sense but egregious economic sense. Since the revolution of 1952, the tremendous expansion of Egyptian educational facilities has created a veritable torrent of graduates that must be absorbed onto the government work rolls: from 1952 to 1972, the number of primary and secondary students tripled, and that of university students quadrupled (World Bank 1978).[17] Every year, a new batch of these young graduates joins Egyptian government institutions, such as the agricultural cooperatives, even though these institutions do not have enough work to keep their original workers occupied.[18]

In El-Diblah, the net effect of these problems can be seen by viewing the daily activities of "Anwar," one of the cooperative officials in the area. As a new cooperative employee, Anwar is supposed to spend most of his time out in the fields, making sure that the peasants in his area are receiving their inputs and that they are growing cotton and other government-mandated crops. In practice, however, Anwar, like most other cooperative bureaucrats, spends only about three months a year out in the fields: two months in the summer, supervising efforts to protect the young cotton crop from pests;[19] and one month in the winter, making annual tallies of the crops grown in his area. During the re-

17. During this period (1952–1972), the total population increase in Egypt was about 62 percent.

18. Disguised unemployment in the entire Egyptian bureaucracy has been estimated at 30 percent (World Bank 1976) and may even be higher.

19. In Egypt, continuous cropping under constant irrigation provides ideal conditions for the development of the cotton leaf worm. Hence, during the summer months, the national government oversees a major effort designed to reduce the incidence of this and other cotton pests. During summer, cooperative officials supervise large gangs of village children who are paid to walk huddled over amidst the young cotton crop, carefully picking off the larvae of the dreaded cotton worm.

mainder of the year, Anwar reports to work at 9 A.M., signs in on the government register, spends an hour or so filling out government forms, and then leaves for the day.

Casual observation on the author's part suggests that such a "no work" pattern of behavior also characterizes many of the other local-level government institutions in district El-Diblah. A visitor to any village bank or village council in the area, for example, will only rarely find a government official actually working. If a bureaucrat is busy, he will probably be engaged in transferring figures from one chart to another. Other government officials, if they have reported to work that day, will be "busy" perusing the newspaper or drinking tea.

It is important to realize that such a pattern of low work motivation is no reflection on the work ethic of Egyptians as a whole. Under the proper circumstances, Egyptian officials can and do work as hard as government bureaucrats in any other country in the world. Yet such a pattern of bureaucratic behavior does point to the considerable problems created by overstaffing, a high rate of disguised unemployment, and government regulations that make it difficult to dismiss an errant employee.

In the one small rural area of El-Diblah, these factors have greatly reduced the utility of local-level officials. The bureaucrats attached to the agricultural cooperatives are like officials without duties, employees without tasks, because their superiors lack the means to adequately supervise their activities. In the words of one peasant, "The [cooperative] officials here do nothing, nothing at all. If the government was to send them all home tomorrow, all we would need would be our seeds and our fertilizer. And, God willing, we would always be able to buy these on the black market."[20]

In district El-Diblah, the low functional utility of cooperative officials encourages what Weber (1947) termed "a wide range for the exercise of actual arbitrariness" on the part of government staff. Such arbitrariness often leads to corruption—that is, to government staff siphoning off supplies that are intended for the public at large. One example of bureaucratic corruption and its concomitant effects on the control powers of local institutions should suffice. Each agricultural cooperative in Egypt has a head warehouseman who is responsible for accepting delivery of government-supplied seeds, fertilizer and pesticide, and for distributing these goods to the peasantry. In at least two of the five cooperatives studied by the author in district El-Diblah, the head warehousemen were notorious thieves. They would accept the government deliveries and then either shortchange the peasants or steal part of the stock for sale on the black market. In some cases, they did this with the assistance of the bureaucratic head of the cooperative, since his help was needed to alter the

20. For a similar reaction by a villager, recorded in the Egyptian journal *al-Tali'a*, see Waterbury (1978).

government books. In other cases, they collaborated with other officials working in the cooperative.

This and similar examples of bureaucratic corruption suggest an important point, namely, that what the cooperative system claims it will do in El-Diblah often bears little resemblance to what it actually does, because the system has practically no control over its own officials. Shrinkage of supplies, work tasks, and funds occurs from Cairo on down to the village level, because bureaucratic superiors are unable to discipline and control the private interests of their subordinates. This drastically reduces the ability of local-level organizations in Egypt to carry out their assigned functions.

The Rural Elite and Bureaucrat-Peasant Relations in El-Diblah

The inconsequentiality of cooperative bureaucrats is as much a function of their limited work motivation as it is a function of their inability to displace the patronage powers exercised by the rich peasantry. In district El-Diblah, the existence of the large pool of landless and near-landless peasants means that there is always a strong demand for a wide variety of patronage services, including agricultural work opportunities and consumer loans. However, the agricultural cooperative system in the area provides very few employment opportunities and extends credit only to landowners and renters who can use land or crops as collateral. At the same time, the bureaucrats attached to the cooperatives and other local-level institutions remain incapable of providing these patronage services themselves. Bureaucratic salaries at all levels of government service are so low[21] that, unless he owns land or a small business on the side, the average bureaucrat is simply not in an economic position to hire workers or to extend credit.

All this means that poor peasants in El-Diblah who are in need of patronage services do not turn to government institutions or to government bureaucrats. Rather, they turn to rich peasants. It is, therefore, these wealthier village elements—and not government officials—who continue to be most consequential at the local village level. According to one informed observer, "The [government] bureaucrats in district El-Diblah tend to come from the smaller, poorer families. Neither they nor the institutions [that they work for] can meet all the daily needs of the poor peasantry. The latter, therefore, continue to depend on the rich peasantry."

In the village of El-Diblah, poor peasants are dependent on a group of approximately 40 rich peasants. All of these rich peasant-patrons own over 10 feddans of land, and a few of them own over 50 feddans. While quite comfortable by modern-day standards, these rich peasants are nowhere near as wealthy

21. During the 1978–80 period, government salaries in district El-Diblah averaged between 20 and 50 Egyptian pounds (U.S. $28 and $71) per month.

as their pre-1952 predecessors,[22] who often owned in excess of 100 feddans of land. In El-Diblah as well as in other Egyptian rural areas, the process of land fragmentation—propelled by the cumulative effects of Egyptian land reform, population growth, and the absence of a rule of primogeniture in Islam—has whittled down even the largest of estates. This means that while rich peasants still provide an important range of patronage services to poor peasants, they no longer possess the monopoly of resources needed to support poor peasants on a permanent basis.

An important shift in the character of patron-client relations has therefore occurred. While the patron-client paradigm may call for each client to have only one intermediate patron at the same time (Moore 1977)—patron monogamy—in the village of El-Diblah, patron monogamy has given way to patron polygamy. The much diminished resources of rural patrons mean that poor peasant clients must now circulate between several different patrons in order to survive.

It is important to recognize that the changed character of patron-client relations in El-Diblah is more the consequence of demographic and economic factors than it is the outcome of any conscious state action. The high rate of population growth on a limited land base,[23] the division of estates upon inheritance, and the opening of employment opportunities abroad[24] have all done more to transform rural patron-client relations than any action by state or local officials.

State and local officials in El-Diblah, in fact, remain relatively distant from the patron-client relations maintained by members of the rich peasantry. This is quite interesting, inasmuch as it runs counter to the model of close bureaucratic–rich peasant ties posited by many authors. Chambers (1977), for example, writes that "[local] officials, as is notorious and has been documented ad nauseam, are locked into relationships with the rural elite. This is especially marked with agricultural extension, but can also apply to other arms of government."

However, local cooperative officials in district El-Diblah are not locked into close relations with the rural elite; in reality, they seem to play the role of the superfluous "third man out." On the one hand, they lack the resources

22. Shortly after the revolution of 1952, the Egyptian government passed a series of land-reform measures designed to reduce the landholdings of the rural aristocracy. The first land-reform act set the maximum limit on landownership at 200 feddans for a single person and 300 feddans for a single family. These limits were later reduced to 50 feddans for a single person and 100 feddans for a single family. As a result of these laws, about 12.5 percent of the total cultivated land in Egypt was redistributed to about 9 percent of the total 1970 rural population (Fadil 1975, 10).

23. Between 1950–54 and 1976–80, the cropped area, which equals the cultivated area multiplied by the cropping intensity, increased by 18.5 percent in Egypt. During the same time period, the total Egyptian population increased by 85.9 percent.

24. According to official government sources, the number of Egyptians working abroad (principally in the Arab oil states), increased from 34,000 in 1973 to approximately 3 million in 1984. For more on the dynamics of international migration in rural Egypt, see Adams (1991).

needed to meet the patronage demands of the poor peasantry. On the other hand, they also lack the supplies and the expertise to attract the attention of the rural elite. They are thus more present than predominant in terms of the local village power structure.

The El-Diblah cooperative officials tend to use the powers they do have to help themselves to the limited amount of resources placed at their disposal. Their administrative malfeasance is based on expediency: the ability to move public resources quickly and quietly into someone's private pocket. Cooperative officials, who are familiar with the daily intricacies of government operation, are thus well placed to pilfer or steal state resources without the assistance of outside groups. They are, as our preceding example with fertilizer suggests, able to siphon off bits and pieces of the state without teaming up with any members of the peasantry, rich or poor.

For the time being, rich peasants seem to accept this state of affairs because the amount of purloined resources is relatively small. Moreover, they can still keep a watchful eye on cooperative officials through the indirect medium of their trusted poor peasant clients. Rich peasants can, for example, arrange to have their indigent relatives or clients "elected" to the cooperative boards that exist in each and every Egyptian agricultural cooperative.[25] These boards are ostensibly designed to assist cooperative officials in dispensing seeds, fertilizer, and credit to peasants. At present, both the powers and the resources at the disposal of these cooperative boards are quite circumscribed. If, however, the resources of these boards and the cooperative system as a whole were to dramatically increase, it is likely that members of the rich pesantry would choose to work much more closely with cooperative officials. Then, and only then, would it be possible to speak of a coalition of bureaucrats and rich peasants in the agricultural cooperatives in district El-Diblah.

Conclusion

In the past, too little attention has been paid to the social, political, and economic dynamics of the environment in which local-level government officials work. As a result, national efforts to improve the agricultural, nutritional, or health standards of villagers have frequently been undercut by the everyday realities of bureaucratic life.

The thrust of the analysis pursued here has been to pinpoint the environmental factors affecting the performance of agricultural officials in one specific rural Egyptian locale. One important merit of this type of study is that it provides a broader framework for examining those environmental factors that affect village officials in a wide variety of settings. In many developing countries, the three environmental factors analyzed here—the nature of state policy,

25. For more on the dynamics of these agricultural cooperative boards, see Adams (1986).

the control powers of bureaucratic institutions, and the character of rural elite—exert a salient influence on the performance of local-level officials. The importance of each of these environmental factors will vary from institution to institution and from country to country. Future research is needed to clarify the salience of each of these environmental factors in different situations.

As we have seen, one of the most important environmental factors affecting the activities of local officials in district El-Diblah is the character of Egyptian government policy. In Egypt, the state uses the agricultural cooperative system more to tax and control the peasantry than to provide the peasants with the means to improve their agricultural productivity. Local-level officials attached to these institutions therefore lack both the resources (fertilizer, credit) and the expertise (practical agricultural skills) needed to make a meaningful contribution to the national development effort.

Lele's (1974) observation that agricultural extension workers in Africa are "ill paid, ill trained . . . and thus very poor in quality" is thus as true in district El-Diblah as anywhere else. In this area, cooperative officials lack the seeds, fertilizer, and credit to attract anyone's attention. At the same time, these bureaucrats also lack the drive and the incentive to go out into the fields to teach the peasantry new agricultural techniques and practices. The bulk of the peasantry would therefore be better off without them.

In El-Diblah, the low utility of cooperative officials is also a function of the limited control powers of the cooperative system as a whole. As a result of government employment practices, agricultural cooperatives in this area are more broad than powerful: they provide "welfare" employment to a wide range of people, but they cannot find enough work to keep all of their employees occupied. Disguised unemployment, goldbricking, and absenteeism are therefore rife. Many of the cooperative (and other local-level) officials could have been removed, and the only change would have been that the local coffee shops would have suffered a decline in business.[26] The inconsequentiality of cooperative officials serves to increase the consequentiality of the rich peasantry. In this area, cooperative officials lack the means and the skills to meet the daily economic needs of the poor peasantry. They must therefore defer to a small group of rich peasants, who are able to provide poorer village elements with a steady stream of patronage services: jobs, loans, and brokerage services with the government. By controlling their own means of subsistence, as well as those of their poor peasant clients, these rich peasants are able to dominate local-level affairs.[27]

It is important to note that such domination occurs without the aid of the type of close bureaucratic–rich peasant ties described by some authors. In El-

26. For a similar conclusion regarding the role of local bureaucrats in Zambia, see Kees van Donge (1982).

27. For more on the way rich peasants in Egypt are able to dominate local-level affairs, see Binder (1978), Waterbury (1983), and Adams (1986).

Diblah, Chambers's (1977) notion of a coalition of bureaucrats and rich peasants does not apply. There is only one dominant social group: rich peasants owning over 10 feddans of land. These wealthy farmers exercise sufficient control over the limited land and economic resources so as to have no pressing need to work closely with cooperative officials. From time to time, a few members of the village elite may turn to cooperative officials for the supply of some agricultural inputs. Yet, given the chronic short supply of such inputs, just as many rich peasants choose to bypass the cooperative system entirely and procure their supplies elsewhere. In no instance are the ties between rich peasants and cooperative bureaucrats strong enough to warrant the use of the term "coalition."

This finding serves to underscore the great diversity of relations that are possible between social actors at the local village level. At one extreme, perhaps, lies our model of a rich peasantry-dominated rural periphery. At another extreme lies the paradigm of a countryside dominated by a coalition of bureaucrats and rich peasants. In between these two extremes undoubtedly lies a veritable plethora of other types of social relations between local bureaucrats, rich peasants, and poor peasants.

More field research is now needed into the various environmental factors affecting relations between bureaucrats and peasants in different rural settings. Such research may well have a very practical output, namely that of improving the ability of government officials to work through different local-level structures in order to implement national programs of agricultural, nutritional, or health improvement. In this era of declining rural economies in Africa and elsewhere, much more attention needs to be paid to providing village officials with the knowledge, means, and support to work more efficiently.

8 Household Behavior and Government Preferences: Compatibility or Conflicts in Efforts to Achieve Goals of Nutrition Programs

PER PINSTRUP-ANDERSEN

The benefits and cost-effectiveness of nutrition-related government programs and policies depend on their design and implementation as well as household response. Governments may design and make available programs and policies, but the household decides whether and to what extent to take advantage of them. If programs and policies are designed and implemented with little or no regard for the preferences of the target household and the economic, social, and cultural constraints within which it makes decisions, the results are likely to be disappointing. This will be reflected in poor program participation, low cost-effectiveness, and waste of public resources. If, on the other hand, program and policy design and implementation are congruent with household preferences and constraints, success in achieving program and policy goals is much more likely.

The potential conflict between government aims and household behavior is frequently ignored in the choice, design, and implementation of nutrition-related programs and policies. As a result, many have failed. The graveyard for unsuccessful nutrition programs would be considerably less crowded had public-sector institutions and individuals paid more attention to program characteristics that would be most acceptable to target households.

When nutrition programs are not utilized by target households to the extent expected by the implementing government agencies, it is often concluded that the poor are irrational and unwilling to make the decisions that would be in their best interest. The arrogance or ignorance regarding household level constraints that lead to such conclusions are not unique to nutrition programs but may be found in many types of "top-down" government intervention.

Since households and the individuals within them have the last word about the extent to which government programs and policies will influence nutrition, their behavior must not be ignored, even in cases where it appears to be contrary

The author is grateful to Alain de Janvry, Bea Rogers, Eileen Kennedy, and Alan Berg for very constructive comments on an earlier draft.

to good nutrition behavior. Households make decisions within many constraints. These constraints are particularly severe for the poor and often include a very limited ability to acquire food and nutrition-related goods and services, and lack of knowledge about the potential benefits of improving nutrition and the nutritional effects of alternative actions.

The poor are generally very efficient in maximizing their well-being, including, but not limited to, the well-being derived from nutritional improvements. Decisions are made regarding budget and time allocation in such a way as to get the most out of available resources as perceived by the household decisionmakers. Efforts originating outside the household to change these decisions without changing the constraints or the relative influence of household members in the decision-making process will be counteracted by the household. Government programs that remove the most severe constraints are likely to be much more successful than those that either ignore the constraints or attempt to circumvent them. Yet, the latter type is widespread.

Why do governments not make greater efforts to assure compatibility between programs and policies, and household behavior? There are three major reasons. First, people designing and implementing programs may be convinced that they know what "good" household behavior is and that any deviance in actual behavior is irrational and should not be taken into account. Second, current knowledge of household behavior is insufficient as a guide for program design and implementation; and third, people and institutions responsible for programs and policies may wish to circumvent decisions by household heads in order to reach selected family members, such as preschoolers and pregnant and lactating women, whose needs they perceive to be inadequately reflected in household decisions. In other words, programs reflect a higher priority on improved nutrition of certain individuals than is indicated in decisions by household heads, and attempts are made by program agencies to alter the intrahousehold allocation of program benefits.

Closely related to the above is the issue of variable behavior among households. Some groups of households have greater opportunities for influencing government action than others. This implies that the poor, who usually have little political power, may be faced with programs shaped largely by the better-off part of the population. If the understanding of the constraints within which the poor function is lacking among the better-off, programs may not be compatible with the needs and preferences of the target group.

The purposes of this chapter are to further examine the factors and relationships that determine the degree of compatibility or conflict between the aims of nutrition-related government programs and policies, and the behavior of target households, and to suggest ways in which the degree of compatibility could be increased to improve human nutrition and the cost-effectiveness of government expenditures for nutrition improvements.

FIGURE 8.1. Schematic overview of factors influencing government programs and policies and the response by households and individuals

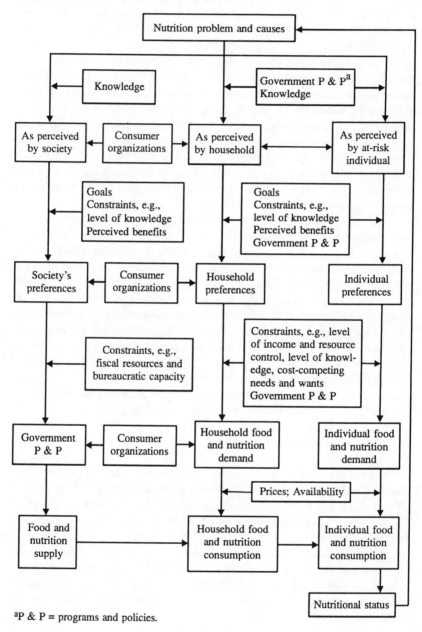

[a]P & P = programs and policies.

An Overview

Many factors and relationships are important in identifying the degree of compatibility or conflict between the aims of programs and policies, and household behavior (figure 8.1). It is postulated that the nutrition problem and its causes may be perceived quite differently by society (as represented by politicians, government institutions, and public sector employees), households (as represented by heads of households), and malnourished individuals. These differences are a potential cause of conflict.

The perception of the problem and its causes together with goals, constraints, and perceived benefits from improved nutrition translate into preferences by society, households, and individuals. Since the above factors are likely to vary between society and households, and possibly between each of these and the individual—unless efforts are made to eliminate such variation through, for example, household organizations—there is little reason for the preferences of the three groups to be identical.

Society's preferences are transformed into programs and policies to the extent permitted by available resources, including fiscal resources and bureaucratic capacity. The household demand for the goods and services provided by the programs depends on the constraints within which the household operates, such as income level, resource control, level of knowledge, and cost of other needs and wants that compete for the household's purchasing power, as well as on household preferences. Household consumption of nutrition-related goods and services is then determined by the extent to which the demand can be fulfilled, that is, by the prices and availability of these goods and services. Government policies and programs may influence household consumption through their impact on demand (knowledge, purchasing power, removal of other constraints) as well as supply (prices and availability). Each of the above factors and relationships are discussed below.

Problem Perception

The nutrition problem and its causes are frequently perceived differently by society, household, and malnourished household members. All three suffer from knowledge constraints. Ideally, knowledge would be shared among the three groups in order to arrive at a common perception. The sharing of knowledge need not imply agreement on how best to resolve the problem, but it can provide a common starting point. Such sharing of knowledge between target households and program designers and implementors is not common, except for a few successful pilot schemes. The success of these schemes depends to a considerable degree on effective two-way communication between households or individual household members and project designers/implementors that permits both groups to improve their perception of the problem and its causes.

Community participation is an effort to foster such interaction.

Most nutrition intervention, however, appears to be based—implicitly or explicitly—on the assumption that society perceives the problem, its causes, and its solutions more correctly than the household with malnourished members. It is therefore assumed that what is needed is one-way communication aimed at bringing the household perception more in line with society's. If these efforts do not succeed, the foundation is laid for conflict between households and society. If agreement is not reached on what the problem is and what it is caused by, it is unlikely that agreement will be reached on what constitutes the best solutions.

The question of which of the three groups—society, household heads, or malnourished individuals—possesses the most correct perception of the problem and its causes varies among cases. Many examples could be cited where government agencies specializing in food-related matters tend to see poor growth in preschoolers as a problem of deficient food intake while health agencies may downplay the role of food, emphasizing primary health care. Households may try to acquire the proper mix of the two while under pressure from one or the other specialized program to focus unduly on one of the components of an appropriate solution. While it is clearly incorrect to assume that society's perception is always closer to the truth than that of households, the opposite is also incorrect. Whether a program is "top-down" or "bottom-up", there is a need for dialogue between households and program designers/implementors to arrive at a common problem perception. Mechanisms to assure two-way communication and effective bargaining between the public sector and households, such as consumer or household organizations, are very important.

Differences in problem perception may also exist within the household. Malnourished household members are frequently those with the least bargaining power, for example, infants and small children, and those with temporary increases in nutritional needs, for example, pregnant and lactating women. They may perceive the problem quite differently from the male head of household. Furthermore, in most cultures, the male household heads are not as close to nutrition-related activities as the adult females and, consequently, perception of the problem may differ widely.

This is part of one of the most intriguing issues in the design of nutrition-related programs and policies: How should the government deal with households in which those members it is trying to reach are not fairly represented in household decisions, and where, as a consequence, household heads attempt to redirect program benefits away from target individuals? In other words, how are conflicts among the preferences of society, households, and individual household members best dealt with in program and policy design and implementation? In principle, the problem is similar to that faced by international aid agencies trying to reach the poor in countries where governments do not place high priority on poverty alleviation and attempt to divert potential benefits of projects away from the target group. Before trying to provide an answer to the question at the household level, it is important to examine the reasons why preferences may differ.

Preferences

Preferences for nutrition-related goods and services may differ between society and the household because: (1) they perceive the problem and its causes differently, as discussed above; (2) their goals differ; (3) the knowledge constraints may be different; (4) their perception of the potential benefits of alleviating the nutrition problem may differ; and (5) the expected relative benefits from various alternative ways of alleviating the problem may differ.

There are indications that society places a higher value on improved nutrition relative to the achievement of other material goals than do households with malnourished members. Although economic theory implies that households gain the largest utility from a particular real-income transfer if the transfer consists of untied cash, food transfers and food-tied income transfers are frequently emphasized by governments. Widespread attempts by public agencies to link real-income transfers to expanded food consumption by target households or selected household members frequently conflict with household preferences and are met with efforts to counteract part of the proposed increase in food consumption by reducing food acquisition from other sources, by reselling transferred food or rights to food-linked income transfers (e.g., food stamps), and by sharing food targeted for selected household members among other members of the household.

A variety of food supplementation programs are targeted to individual household members, such as infants, preschoolers, and pregnant or lactating women. The "leakage" in such programs, that is, the difference between the amount of food transferred and the net addition to the quantity consumed by the target group, is usually large. Such leakage is a result of the sharing of transferred food among household members and a reduction in the quantity of food acquired through other channels. From a review of about two hundred supplementation programs for infants, Beaton and Ghassemi (1979) found that the net addition to the food intakes of the intended beneficiaries was between 20 and 70 percent of the food transfers.

When food transfer programs are targeted to households rather than on particular household members, the sharing with nontarget household members disappears and a lower magnitude of leakage would be expected. However, even in those cases the leakage may be high. Thus, for example, a food supplementation program transferring 850 calories to each of all members of participating households in Bogotá resulted in an average net increase of 150 calories per person, which means a leakage of 82 percent (Mora 1982).

The prevalence of leakage is not surprising. In most cases, the quantity of food that is transferred is less than the quantity consumed prior to the program—it is inframarginal. This implies that households will reduce the quantity of food acquired from other sources to conform to the new level of real income. Thus, unless household preferences in household budget allocations are changed through nutrition education or changes in the relative power of individual household members, for example, men versus women, the effect on nutrition would be expected to be no different from that of a transfer of cash income of the same magnitude.[1] Except for such income effect, and the potential effect of nutrition education and changes in intrahousehold budget control, there is no apparent reason why a food transfer program would make households allocate a larger proportion of its real income to food because the marginal cost (the price of the last unit of food) does not change. If the marginal propensity to consume food is around 0.6—a reasonable magnitude for many households with malnourished members—then it would be expected that 60 percent of any income transfer would be spent on increasing food consumption irrespective of whether the income transfer is in the form of food or cash as long as the transfer is inframarginal.

While the magnitude of leakage in many programs may conform to expectations, the large variation among programs and population groups is a puzzle for which there is little empirical or conceptual explanation. One possible explanation is that some programs transfer more food than what was previously consumed, thus lowering food prices at the margin. However, such programs are rare. Differences in program design that make substitution more difficult in some programs than others (e.g., direct feeding versus take-home rations) may assist in explaining the variations, particularly if direct feeding exceeds food intakes of the particular individual without the program.

As mentioned above, differential impact of the various program types on intrahousehold budget control, linked with differential marginal propensities to consume food among individual household members, as well as differential impact on the demand for women's time may also play a role in explaining the large variations. These and other poorly understood elements of household food-acquisition behavior will be discussed further in the section on research needs.

There are a number of possible explanations for the apparent discrepancy between public and private preference functions. First, economic benefits from improved nutrition may be higher for society than for the individual household. If this is the case, the household budget allocation between food and nonfood will reflect a lower emphasis on food than what is desired by society, and

1. Women may wish to spend more on food and nutrition than men and may have a greater influence over how total household income is spent if a part is embodied in food and nutrition programs. This implies that for a given increase in household income, a larger proportion will be spent on food and nutrition if the income comes from a program rather than cash earnings.

governments will attempt to influence household preference functions toward more food for the malnourished. Although the existence of such economic externalities in nutrition is difficult to prove empirically, the argument has considerable credibility in view of the findings related to the social versus private benefits from public investment in other human-capital formation efforts, such as education. In fact, since poor nutritional status of infants appears to negatively affect cognitive developments and subsequent learning abilities as well as school attendance, economic returns to education may be greatly enhanced through improved nutrition.[2]

Second, better-off population groups generally derive more utility from income transfers aimed at the alleviation of overt human misery, such as extreme and highly visible malnutrition, than from general income transfers where the spending decisions related to the transfers is left in the hands of the recipient households. For this reason, income transfers to the absolute poor may be politically desirable or feasible only if the transfers are earmarked for alleviation of extreme human misery.[3] Poor households, on the other hand, attempt to deal with a number of unfilled basic needs of which malnutrition is but one. Some basic needs, such as transportation to and from work, may not be fully appreciated by the better-off population groups. Furthermore, poor as well as better-off households will attempt to allocate at least some of the available purchasing power to fill demands that society does not deem essential. This refers not only to the frequently cited but poorly documented cases in which a significant proportion of additional income of the poor is spent on beer and soft drinks, but also to the well-documented behavior of substituting higher-cost calories and nutrients for lower-cost ones as incomes increase to gain diet diversity even at very low income and nutritional levels.

Third, governments may attempt to influence household budget allocations toward more food for the malnourished because it is believed that current allocation is not in the best interest of the household as a unit or selected individual household members, for example, infants. As mentioned earlier, a very large part of past and current food transfer programs are targeted to individual household members, such as infants or pregnant and lactating women. While it is clear why such programs are targeted to households with such malnourished individuals, it is not clear why so much effort is spent on trying to reach the individuals within these households, unless there is some concern that household decision-making does not reflect the same desire to reach these individuals as that which motivates governments to maintain the program.

In addition to the possible difference between social and private benefits from improved nutrition, there are at least two reasons why governments may

2. See Mora et al. (1979), Cravioto and DeLicardie (1973), Selowsky and Taylor (1973), and Selowsky (1980) for more discussion of this issue.

3. Further discussion of this matter is presented in Harberger (1979) and Scandizzo and Knudsen (1980).

believe or suspect that household decision-making does not place enough emphasis on expanding food consumption by malnourished household members to maximize the combined utility of all household members. The first is that governments may perceive the household head to be poorly informed. Inadequate knowledge is perceived to lead to suboptimal allocation of food to the malnourished vis-à-vis food allocation to other household members and allocation of real income to nonfoods. Inadequate knowledge on the part of household decision makers has been extensively used by nutritionists to explain why household food acquisition and allocation behavior reflect a lower priority for food and nutrition than that advocated by government nutrition agencies. The result has been a large number of nutrition education programs.

While adequate knowledge undoubtedly has been and still is an important cause of malnutrition, it appears that its overall importance may have been overstated. The need for nutrition education is most pronounced where large changes have occurred in the environment and constraints within which household decisions are made, such as rural to urban migration, shifts from subsistence to cash cropping, and other changes that significantly alter the magnitude and source of household incomes and availability of food or nonfood commodities. However, nutrition education is often promoted in situations where households are unable to respond because of other constraints. Households with severely malnourished members are frequently deprived of other basic necessities as well. Thus, improved nutrition need not be the overriding concern of the heads of such households even when they are well informed about the consequences of nutritional deficiencies.

A second reason why households may allocate less of their real income to improved nutrition is that household food acquisition and allocation behavior is based on the utility function of the decision-maker, which may differ significantly from the utility functions of other household members, for example, inadequate nutrition knowledge or by a deliberate effort to downplay or ignore the needs of the malnourished. In extremely poor households, the question is frequently one of short-term survival and maintenance of an income-earning capacity. In these households, the choice may be one of either allocating enough food to the income-earning household members to maintain their income-earning capacity at the expense of the nutritional status of the economically inactive members, or allocating enough food to the malnourished at the risk of losing income-earning capacity. In such cases, government efforts to reallocate household resources to malnourished household members may conflict with household preferences and, if successful, may endanger the long-run survival of all household members. Attempts to reduce the proportion of incomes that the household head wishes to invest in productive resources instead of consumption present a similar case. Conflict may also occur in cases where households bias the allocation of available food to those children perceived to have the largest probability of surviving rather than to those most in need.

The survival, or at least the nutritional well-being, of household members may be endangered by government programs that replace traditional support systems only to disappear again, leaving the household worse off than before. Lack of trust in government programs is, in fact, an important reason why poor households may not participate if it means giving up existing support systems, even if such systems are part of a feudalistic and exploitative arrangement. Thus, before governments introduce new programs, their potential impact on existing coping mechanisms and local power structures should be assessed.

Fourth, governments may prefer food to cash-income transfer because the perceived or real social cost of food is below private costs. Availability of foreign food aid on concessional terms is a case in point. The fiscal cost of transferring such food is usually perceived by government to be below that of transferring an amount of cash income that reflects the market value of the food.[4] Thus, food transfers are preferred. The existence of government surplus food stocks and attempts to maintain price supports for producers in excess of market prices also tend to push governments toward food rather than cash transfers in an attempt to find additional outlets for surplus food. The United States food stamp program is motivated, at least in part, by such concerns.

Fifth, governments may prefer food to cash transfers because food transfers are easier to target to households with malnourished members or to the malnourished individuals directly. The choice of food commodities and the geographical location of food outlets are examples of targeting procedures in food-related income transfers that are not readily paralleled in cash-transfer programs. The transaction costs to households of circumventing targeting are usually higher for food than for cash transfers. Targeting to individual household members is also perceived by program agencies to be easier in food transfer programs (e.g., direct feeding clinics for infants and preschoolers).

Sixth, government programs and policies may place more emphasis on expanded food intake and improved nutrition than do households either because governments overstate the nutrition problem or because households are unaware of an existing nutrition deficiency. Estimates of the degree of malnutrition in populations are subject to considerable uncertainty, and there is reason to believe that a number of recently published reports overestimate the nutritional problem. If such estimates are used to guide the design of policies and programs, rational household food-acquisition behavior would be expected to oppose the efforts to bias the household preference function toward more food for those believed to be malnourished but who in fact are not. On the other hand, household heads may be accustomed to malnutrition. If most children are malnourished, the problem may not be apparent.

---

4. Although usually perceived as such, the fiscal cost of transferring food need not be lower if the food aid is sold on the domestic market and the revenues, rather than the food, are transferred to the target households.

Finally, the existence of programs and policies that attempt to influence household budget allocations toward expanded food intake by the malnourished may simply be a reflection of the goals and interests of a particular government agency. Although allocations to such agencies are expected to reflect overall government priorities, the design of policies and programs within the agencies need not reflect a balanced approach to the improvement of the welfare of the recipients. Improved nutrition may easily be perceived as superseding all other goals and desires, and when such absolute priority is not expressed by households, an area of conflict develops. Such a situation is not limited to food and nutrition but may be found in other areas, such as housing, health, and education.

Demand, Supply, and Government Programs

Society's preferences are translated into government programs and policies to the extent permitted by the constraints within which the government operates, primarily by the limitations on fiscal resources available for such programs and the bureaucratic capacity for design and implementation. The programs may influence nutrition through their impact on household demand or through the supply of nutrition-related goods and services.

The extent to which household preferences are expressed as actual household demands depends on the severity of the constraints within which the household makes decisions. Among the malnourished, the most severe constraints are usually low levels of income and resource control, costs of needs and wants other than improved nutrition, and, in some cases, insufficient knowledge of how best to achieve nutrition goals within severe income constraints.

The success of government programs in expanding household demand for nutrition-related goods and services depends very much on whether they are successful in alleviating the most limiting constraints. That is why a thorough understanding of existing constraints and ways to remove them is essential to success. The importance of this matter is illustrated in pilot schemes focused on relieving the most severe constraints as perceived by households and thus assuring compatibility between program goals and household demands. When such schemes are scaled up to national programs, their success is often severely diminished. This is due, at least in part, to the disappearance of the intimate understanding of the needs and constraints of the client households.

A focus on household constraints and how they relate to the problem rather than on the problem itself and what households "ought to do about it" moves government action away from a relatively inflexible and narrow nutrition intervention strategy to a more flexible approach with a higher probability of success. Once the constraints are identified, their relationship to the problem understood, and their relative importance estimated, a variety of solutions may be explored. Although the problem may be one of insufficient calorie and protein intake by preschoolers, it cannot be concluded that a food supplementation scheme for preschoolers is the best solution. The problem and the constraints within which it exists should be specified separately from possible solutions and not in terms of a particular solution. This comes naturally to those directly affected (i.e., the malnourished) but not necessarily to those designing and implementing government programs.

Household consumption of food and other nutrition-related goods and services is determined by the demand and supply of these goods and services. The potential impact of government programs on demand was discussed above. They may also influence supply through prices and availability. Untargeted food-price subsidies for unrationed quantities make food available at a lower price with the likely impact of increasing food consumption. New primary-health clinics may make nutrition-related services available in areas where none were before.

As in the case of demand-related interventions, the success of supply-related programs and policies depends on whether they are successful in alleviating the most important constraints. For example, if one of the most limiting constraints on the household is a very heavy demand on women's time, making primary health-care facilities available would probably not be successful if women have to spend a great deal of time in order to obtain the benefits, for example, taking children or themselves to the clinic, waiting for services, etc. Transaction costs for the poor associated with program participation are often underestimated by those who design and implement programs. As a result, increases in the supply of nutrition-related goods and services may not be matched by increased demand. The real cost of time needed to benefit from programs is probably the most underestimated factor. Poor people normally spend a large number of hours per day coping with low productivity in wage labor or self-employment, movement to and from work (frequently on foot), gathering firewood, carrying water, etc. Nevertheless, it is not uncommon to hear arguments such as "one thing the poor have is time" in connection with program design. Failure to focus on constraints may result in failure of the program.

In addition to (1) low levels of income; (2) limited resource control; (3) high food prices; (4) high demand for women's time; and (5) insufficient knowledge, the household response to programs and policies may be influenced by other constraints embodied in (6) intrahousehold budget control; (7) income source and composition (the form in which real income enters the household, e.g., food, food stamps, nutrition services, cash, etc.); (8) the range of goods and services competing for the household budget and their costs; (9) the frequency and fluctuation in household incomes and program benefits; (10) the degree to which incomes are considered transitory or permanent by the household, which may be a reflection of program design and implementation; and

(11) cost and availability of energy sources for food preparation, for example, firewood and kerosene.

Concluding Comments and Research Needs

Governments may improve human nutrition by (1) alleviating existing constraints on household demand for and the supply of nutrition-related goods and services, (2) seeking to alter household preferences through improved information and promotion, and (3) attempting to impose society's goals and preferences where they conflict with household goals and preferences. But what is the appropriate role of government in household acquisition and allocation behavior regarding food and nutrition? Does the government have the ethical right or even the obligation to interfere in household food acquisition and allocation behavior if the rights or needs of the malnourished are not "appropriately" reflected by household decisions? Such government rights are accepted and exercised in many countries with respect to child abuse. Presumably, severe malnutrition that endangers the life of an infant would fall into a similar category. But where is the limit? Where does respect for household sovereignty cease to be reasonable? Clearly, household sovereignty is not violated by providing nutrition education or primary health care, altering food prices relative to the prices of other goods, changing the relative prices of individual food commodity prices, or offering food-linked income transfers. But when attempts are made to limit the program benefits to particular household members, implicit doubts are expressed as to the ability of the household to allocate its limited resources in the most appropriate manner. It might be argued that the sovereignty of the household head is being infringed upon.

Household behavior will attempt to offset the intended targeting in accordance with the household preference function, and leakages will occur. Thus, evaluations on narrow nutritional grounds may show a low cost-effectiveness, and public resources spent on intrahousehold targeting and tying of income transfers to food may be at least partially wasted. Since this issue is likely to be politically sensitive, it is not usually dealt with explicitly in program and policy design. However, explicit consideration along with a focus on identifying and alleviating household-level constraints to improved nutrition might assist in eliminating ineffective design and implementation elements, reduce administrative costs, and increase the cost-effectiveness of food and nutrition policies and programs.

Passing judgment on the ability and interest of household heads to properly represent the nutritional needs of other household members, particularly infants and small children, and the justification for public intervention is beyond the scope of this chapter. But irrespective of such judgment, an improved understanding of household behavior and its interaction with food and nutrition policies and programs would clearly be useful for the design and implementation of future policies and programs. In particular, there is a need for improved knowledge about how participation in program design and implementation and the bargaining power of poor households and weak members within such households can be improved in order to assure future programs that are more relevant to their needs and preferences. The interaction between the poor and the better-off households at the local level and the ability of the former to influence program designs as part of community participation is poorly understood and needs further examination. Given the nature of local power structures (chapters 6 and 7), one cannot assume that community participation results in a strengthening of the bargaining power of the poor.

A number of research needs necessary for such understanding have surfaced throughout this chapter. In summary, research is needed to (1) identify the principal factors and processes determining household food acquisition and allocation behavior regarding nutrition-related goods and services, its interaction with food and nutrition policies and programs and structural changes in the household decisionmaking environment, and potential conflicts with government preferences; (2) estimate the relative importance of each of these factors and processes within specified socioeconomic settings; and (3) develop general principles that may assist in future program and policy design and implementation. In addition to the estimation of traditional demand parameters for population groups of interest, such research should attempt to explain the large variation in the magnitudes of these parameters and in the degree of leakage found across programs and policies for households with similar nutrition problems and across households with malnourished members for similar programs and policies.

Finally, the research should attempt to clarify the role of a series of factors and processes in household food and nutrition acquisition and allocation behavior, including, but not limited to, the following:

1. Intrahousehold budget control and its effect on household food and nutrition acquisition and allocation behavior among various groups of households. Under what circumstances would it be reasonable to expect a difference in the marginal propensity to spend on food between incomes controlled by women and men? Why would such differences occur and what are the principal factors influencing their relative magnitudes? To what extent are these differences associated with the socioeconomic status of the household? Are some household characteristics particularly important in this regard?

2. Interaction between the demand for individual household members' time and nutrition. Under what circumstances would policies and programs be expected to have a significant nutritional impact through their impact on the demand for women's time, and when might lack of time be expected to be a major constraint to the implementation of nutrition-related programs and policies?

3. What are the effects of structural changes in the household decision-making environment, such as rural and urban migration, expansions of the availability of goods that compete for the household budget, and transformation from subsistence or semisubsistence to a cash economy on the demand for nutrition-related goods and services? What are the processes and how do we effectively estimate the effects on nutrition?

4. What are the circumstances under which household food consumption and allocation is influenced by income source in addition to the magnitude of incomes generated by or transferred to households with malnourished members? Are there cases where the marginal propensity to consume food would differ between inframarginal food transfers or food-linked income transfers and untied cash incomes?

5. What are the program and policy characteristics that induce the intended beneficiaries to consider income transfers as transitory rather than permanent income?

6. What are the criteria and behavioral processes determining household decision-making in a situation of extreme poverty in which households are faced with a choice of maintaining the existing income-generating capacity or feeding the malnourished? How do households arrive at the preferred trade-offs?

7. Which household characteristics are most important in determining the effectiveness of the household to bargain for desired programs? How does household organization influence this effectiveness?

PART III

Improving Labor Productivity through Nutritional Improvements: An Expedient Political Justification?

9 The Relationship of Nutrition to Productivity and Well-being of Workers

MICHAEL C. LATHAM

Introduction

There are many ways in which nutrition may affect the productivity and well-being of workers. Energy from food provides the fuel for human work, certain nutrients are essential for the proper functioning of the human body, and the synergism of malnutrition and infections means that nutritional status may influence a variety of infectious diseases and vice versa. Past malnutrition and ill health may negatively influence current functioning and reduce work capacity or dexterity. Poor nutrition in childhood may leave the body stunted, deformed, or weak, prevent the realization of full intellectual potential, and cause permanent sequelae, such as blindness, deformities, or other permanent scars. Diseases that are influenced by nutrition may leave certain organs of the body with a less than optimum level of functioning—for example, tuberculosis may reduce respiratory function, osteomyelitis may result in deformities or lameness, and measles may precipitate xerophthalmia with loss of vision.

While recognizing the importance of the various ways in which nutrition affects productivity, this chapter will concentrate on energy deficits and anemia as causes of lowered productivity and impaired well-being of workers. Discussion will be confined mainly to current deficits, and it will not deal with the lagged effects of energy or iron deficiency earlier in life. The term "workers" refers to all those who provide productive labor and is not confined to those who

I am grateful to many colleagues, some of them graduate students, who have helped me in my thinking and in the conduct of my research on the topic discussed in this chapter. I wish especially to acknowledge the contribution of Dr. Lani Stephenson, Dr. Peter Heywood, Mr. Terry Elliott, Dr. Mark Brooks, Dr. June Wolgemuth, Dr. Andrew Hall, and Dr. D. W. T. Crompton. I am also grateful to Ms. Agathe Pellerin whose review of anemia and work capacity helped provide material and references for this chapter. Finally, I wish to thank Ms. Doreen Doty for her typing of the manuscript and for all her other help.

I also acknowledge with thanks the financial support of the World Bank and the British Overseas Development Ministry for some of the research conducted in Kenya.

are employed away from home for wage employment. The term therefore includes women who are often not considered in discussions of labor productivity because they are labeled as "housewives," even though they may be active in agriculture, gathering fuel, carrying water, and other work.

Other papers have discussed in detail the relationship of nutrition to intellectual development (Cravioto and DeLicardie 1973; Latham 1974) and the synergism between malnutrition and infection (Scrimshaw, Taylor, and Gordon 1968; Latham 1975). Although both of these may also relate to physical fitness and worker productivity, they are not discussed in detail in this chapter.

Of some relevance to the topic under discussion is the suggestion made by Seckler (1982) that "small is healthy," a view that has been espoused in part or in its entirety by others. Some of the differences of opinion are due to the fact that terms such as "health" and "malnutrition" have not been defined by the protagonists in the debate over this politically charged and important matter. I do not accept the view that low anthropometric measurements found in groups of children in developing countries may be "normal" or that "smallness" is generally advantageous. As Gopalan (1983) rightly observes, these kinds of statements play into the hands of those who advocate "triage" and "life-boat ethics."

Our analysis of data from Kenya shows that underprivileged children with poor diets and many infections grow much more poorly than do privileged East African children from similar ethnic backgrounds (Stephenson, Latham, and Jansen 1983). An editorial in the *Lancet* (1984) based in part on our work states that "the poorer growth so commonly observed in the underprivileged is due to social factors—among which the malnutrition-infection complex is of primary importance—rather than to ethnic or geographic differences." Most retardation in growth occurs due to adverse dietary, social, and health conditions before children reach 4 years of age, and often in the period between 4 and 36 months of age. Therefore, Africans, Asians, Latin Americans, and others who are over 4 years of age are often small because of adverse conditions or serious deprivations encountered in their early life, with the corresponding higher risk of mortality or morbidity. A variety of adverse factors over long periods of time prevented proper nutrition at the cellular level. These groups of small people have the permanent scars of past malnutrition or undernutrition. They may not now be wasted or consume grossly inadequate diets.

It should be noted that this discussion refers to groups of persons. There may be individuals who are dwarfed or small due to other causes, including genetic and metabolic reasons, and there is a recognized range of differences in anthropometric measurements for normal people (Stephenson, Latham, and Jansen 1983). Ethnic differences in adult stature are well recognized, but examination of growth data from many countries suggests that in groups of young children in poor societies, much larger differences are due to deprivations than to inheritance.

Of importance also is whether those persons who have survived and are small can actually function as well as those who did not suffer undernutrition and disease in early life, and now have greater stature. Adequate functioning depends on what is expected of individuals in their subsequent life. For certain kinds of work, a strong physique is clearly an advantage, and for many other jobs, good mental functioning is important. Both may be adversely influenced by early malnutrition.

We should agree that smallness is generally the result of an earlier insult and is the permanent scar of early childhood malnutrition. When Seckler (1982) makes smallness a desirable attribute, it is similar to making a virtue of the scarred lungs and reduced breathing capacity of a person who has survived a severe attack of pulmonary tuberculosis.

Smallness in groups of young children provides good evidence of past ill health, suggests a prolonged period of deprivation, and is largely preventable. As we conclude in our monograph (Stephenson, Latham, and Jansen 1983): "It is easy and rather common for privileged people to suggest that underprivileged children especially of a different ethnic group are 'naturally small' or 'better off small' and in this way to obscure the problems of undernutrition, disease, poverty, and deprivation that are the real causes of stunting and smallness."

The Relationship of Energy Deprivation to Work Capacity

Introduction

In most Third World countries, agriculture is still mainly dependent on human labor and the expenditure of large amounts of physical energy by subsistence farmers and by other workers involved in farming. Agricultural mechanization is progressing at a variable pace, and in some countries, animal power is being harnessed to do work previously done by humans. Agricultural mechanization by no means always reduces labor demand. Frequently it may increase the need for human labor; for example, if fields are ploughed with animal or tractor power, then a greater area may be cultivated, leading to greater demands for weeding and harvesting. Outside of agriculture, human labor produces a good deal of the power needed for work in mining, forestry, construction, certain manufacturing processes, and elsewhere. For the poor in developing countries, much human energy (often particularly the energy of women) is expended in fetching water, gathering fuel, and other chores. In rural areas with a paucity of mechanized transport, large amounts of energy are spent by people getting from place to place—where there are no school buses children often walk long distances to school; women walk to buy and sell their produce in the local market; people use energy to attend meetings, seek health care, conduct business of all kinds, and also participate in social, religious, and sporting events.

High levels of productivity demand adequate energy intake and reasonable health for those who labor to produce and harvest crops and are involved in many other labor-intensive, work-related activities. Considerable energy expenditure is also needed to function as part of society, to fulfill obligations and responsibilities to the state, the community, and the family, and for other essential, important, and pleasurable pursuits.

Special consideration must be given to energy availability, which is very variable under different circumstances. Energy is not equally available to all individuals in most societies. Food and energy intake vary between countries and between groups within countries; even for individuals, there may be seasonal, economic, and other factors that influence the amount of energy consumed in a particular week or month. (Daily variation, which has little influence on physical fitness, work capacity, or nutritional status, is not of concern.)

The concept of energy balance is simple to grasp, but its importance for development is seldom considered. A suitable analogy is a bank account. If more funds are expended than deposited, the balance is reduced. If we wish to maintain a steady balance, the money expended in a month must equal the amount placed in the account. In the case of human energy utilization, there are, of course, other factors at play, such as differences in basal metabolic rates and in specific dynamic action. However, compared with other uses of energy, these kinds of differences are relatively small.

The importance of this analogy is that human beings make decisions about expenditure of their money and also about expenditure of their energy. It is my view that most poor persons make rational, sensible decisions concerning their expenditure of both money and energy. Both types of decision-making are extremely complex, and that of energy expenditure has been inadequately studied. But in both cases, the risks of a wrong decision have graver consequences for the poor than for the affluent.

A poor person may have calls on his or her income that are regarded as essential or near essential—these may be for food, rent, transport to work, taxes, essential agricultural inputs, etc. The same individual has essential caloric needs for energy expenditure at rest (basal metabolism) and for certain obligatory activities. The poor person may have relatively little income and energy beyond what is regarded as essential or almost essential. He or she has a choice to make about how best to spend these other funds and energy. In the same way that we can argue about poverty ceilings and levels of income that are essential, we could argue, but seldom do, about energy.

Beaton (1983) has suggested that we should think of energy requirements as "the level of energy intake and expenditure at which balance is established." This statement has sometimes been taken out of context and has also been misquoted. For example, Jonsson (1983) has written:

> Beaton argues that a low energy intake is not dangerous per se and should not be used as the criteria for assessment of the number of undernourished. In-

stead those with negative energy balance, e.g., those using more energy than they receive, should be counted. With this definition the number of malnourished in the world is dramatically reduced. In fact Beaton's thoughtful article does recognize that persons in energy balance may be foregoing desired activities. But this concept, which suggests that only those with current anthropometric evidence of severe or moderate malnutrition are worthy of our concern and of interventions because only they are nutritionally deprived, is gaining credence and is dangerous because it is untrue. It is often used by the same persons who seek to show that "small is healthy," when frequently the smallness they write about is in fact the result of serious malnutrition and disease earlier in life.

Energy balance is not an indicator of an adequate energy intake. To return to the previous analogy, no one would dispute that an extremely poor person may have a bank account that is in balance; each month he spends the same amount that he earns, but he may still be very income-deprived and we regard him or her being below the poverty line. A person may be in energy balance, with caloric intake equaling caloric expenditure, but in fact be greatly reducing his or her activity levels in order to remain in balance. Consciously or unconsciously, he or she may choose to do less work on the farm, reduce household chores, play less with the children, refrain from playing soccer, curtail social and community activities, and, instead, rest and sleep more. Such an individual in energy balance is in a state of energy deprivation. Yet a physical examination of that individual may indicate no evidence of malnutrition.

It is difficult to define with any accuracy the basic needs for income and energy because we cannot objectively state or agree upon the essential monetary or energy needs of an individual and those expenditures that are unnecessary, flippant, or extravagant. If a man chooses to work less hard at his job in order to expend extra energy to play with his children or to go hunting, is that flippant? Does a person without access to an adequate energy intake have the right to reduce his work because he prefers to conserve energy for what he sees as needed social, family, or even pleasurable activities?

In healthy populations, persons who have access to a plentiful or adequate food supply will tend to adjust their calorie intake to their energy expenditure on activities, including work and play.[1] In contrast, people who are underfed will usually adjust their activity to their calorie intake. This hypothesis has never been, and perhaps never can be, properly and ethically tested in a controlled experiment. But it is of great importance, and many data from animal experimentation and indirect evidence from human studies suggest that it is largely true.

1. Obesity represents an exception, but even a person who has gained 22.5 pounds over a period of 10 years has consumed only an average of 20 calories per day above his or her energy needs (this is equivalent to one-quarter slice of bread per day). So even the obese are very close to being in energy balance.

Longhurst (1984) has argued that poor subsistence farmers in Africa may be in a form of "energy trap" because they have to maintain high levels of energy expenditure, especially at some times of the year, leaving little time and energy to accumulate capital. In his research in Nigeria, Longhurst shows that it is the poor, rather than the better-off workers, who have a higher energy expenditure, because they cannot afford to hire labor or purchase energy-saving technology, such as tools or fertilizer, and yet the "energy intake of the poor in terms of their requirements is expected to be lower" than that of the rich.

Longhurst's analysis of data from the village of Dayi in Northern Nigeria seems, in part, to validate the conclusion that at least for this population, the poor are indeed trapped. This concept of an energy trap seems to fit in well with the analogy made above with regard to similarities between energy and income. The concept of a poverty trap is an old one. But Longhurst's work also illustrates that the ramifications of inadequate energy intake have importance beyond simply the male worker, who is often the person studied.

Strauss (1984), also using data from West Africa, has taken annual energy intakes for families in Sierra Leone and has shown that the intake is related to productivity on farms. The higher the levels of food consumption, the higher the productivity of the population in this area, where food deficits were undoubtedly a problem, at least at certain times of the year. In this study, energy intake of individuals was not obtained. Studies of poor families, including male workers with marginal energy intakes, may be used to suggest that there is no energy problem because the men show no clear evidence of malnutrition. But this is a false conclusion. Members of these families may, in fact, be seriously energy deprived.

Physical Fitness

Physical fitness itself is difficult to define. Shepard (1978) reported that a WHO expert committee, after several days of deliberation, was able to define physical fitness as merely "the ability to perform muscular work satisfactorily." But clearly, the capacity of an individual to perform muscular work is influenced by a number of physical, physiological, and environmental factors. A fit person, when compared with an unfit individual, has lower oxygen consumption for a given amount of external work, can obtain a higher maximum oxygen consumption (so called VO_2 max.), and achieves a smaller increase in pulse rate and a more rapid return to resting pulse for submaximal work (Consolazio, Johnson, and Pecora 1963).

There is an extensive literature on the physiology of work and physical fitness that cannot be reviewed here. There are also reasonable, but not accurate, data on the amount of energy that different kinds of individuals expend per minute on different activities, ranging from complete rest to strenuous work. These data are based mainly on measurements of oxygen expenditure in limited numbers of individuals performing these activities. Indirect measurements, such as determinations of heart or pulse rate, have also been used, but these are dependent on correlations made between heart rate and oxygen expenditure. Under field conditions, none of these determinations are easy to conduct on large numbers of individuals, and all methods have difficulties and considerable margins of error.

Measurements of work performance are often of more interest to governments and agencies than are physiological tests of physical fitness. Development economists want to know how diet, nutritional status, and health influence work productivity. Government planners seek advice on which practical interventions—for example, worker feeding, health measures, etc.—are likely to raise work output levels. Economists ask for estimates of the cost of these interventions in relation to the value of the increased work that may be obtained.

However, studies relating health and nutritional status to worker productivity have not been the subject of very extensive investigation, and such studies are difficult and expensive to perform. Much more is known about physical fitness than about labor productivity.

Food Intake and Work Output

When considering the relationship of food intake to work output, it is necessary to make a distinction between the effect of past intake and the effect of current intake of energy and other nutrients. Past deficiencies may have resulted in the individual being smaller than he or she would otherwise be; they may have left the person with some serious or less serious physical disability, ranging from blindness, marked bone deformities, or neurological disability (resulting, for example, from severe deficiencies of vitamin A, vitamin D, or thiamine), to milder conditions, such as impaired vision, pelvic contraction, or lameness due to contractures, as a result of less severe deficiencies of the same nutrients. All of these may affect physical activity and work output.

The most frequently quoted study of experimental energy deprivation is undoubtedly that performed by Keys and his co-workers (1950). This large and carefully conducted study, carried out in Minnesota, provides information not available elsewhere. The team placed 32 male volunteers (all conscientious objectors) on a semistarvation diet for 24 weeks. The mean daily energy consumption of the group was about 3,500 calories prior to the experiment, and at the end of the experiment, they were in energy balance at an intake of 1,800 calories. Adaptation to this much lower intake was achieved in part by reductions in the cost of activity (58 percent), basal metabolic rate or BMR (32 percent), and specific dynamic action (10 percent). The reduction in cost of activity was mainly due to a decrease in spontaneous activity and to the fact that weight loss led to a decrease in the actual cost of each activity. The adaptive change in BMR resulted mainly from the reduction in total body weight, but there was also a 15 to 20 percent drop in BMR per kilogram of body weight. At the end of the study, the men had a significant decrease in total body fat and, thus, in energy stored. Psychological changes were very evident and included marked apathy and a reluctance to engage in overt physical activity. This study is old history, but it is one of the few well-conducted and well-controlled ones. Such a study could probably not be repeated today because of ethical considerations.

The Minnesota Starvation Study documents that men put on a low energy intake (about 1,550 calories) for 24 weeks, lost about 25 percent of their body weight, and could then be kept in energy balance at about 1,800 calories. But although in balance, they clearly were not in a desirable state of well-being. The diet of these individuals is believed to have provided adequate amounts of all nutrients—with the possible exception of vitamin A, which might have been marginal. There are undoubtedly many millions of individuals in developing countries who are also in energy balance at about similar or slightly higher energy intakes—which need to be adjusted to age, size, and sex—whose diets are often deficient in other nutrients and who, unlike the Minnesotans, have other health problems with little medical care. It is justifiable to extrapolate from the Minnesota study and to conclude that these persons, mainly in developing countries, are deprived and that this level of diet affects activity levels, including work, and, when severe, results in psychological changes, including apathy.

Several studies were carried out in Germany during and after World War II. Kraut and Muller (1946) reported on studies linking low energy intakes to food shortages and corresponding low levels of productivity in the Ruhr coal mines; a later study by Keller and Kraut (1959) shows a close parallel between the decline in energy available for work and the productivity per man of steel workers. These and other examples are suggestive of a causal link between energy intake and production. But in the absence of data on other factors that might influence productivity, it is necessary to be cautious in interpreting these results.

Intervention studies can be used to relate energy intake to work output. In this kind of research, extra energy is provided and its effect on work output is then determined. Ideally, such studies should be conducted under circumstances where the subjects of the study are reasonably matched, where there is evidence that all have suboptimal energy intakes, where the quantity of work available is unlimited, where there is an incentive to do the maximum amount of work, and where accurate measures of work output can be made. The studies should be conducted blindly for both the researchers and the subjects, they should be longitudinal, and there should be random allocation to groups or, better still, a crossover design should be employed. These and other conditions that are important for ideal studies have not been met in any published study to date because of the difficulties involved. For example, to blindly provide a substantial caloric supplement to one group and not to the control group is nearly impossible. The amount of food to provide, say 30 percent of an individual's energy requirements, would often be relatively bulky, and it is not easy or feasible to provide a similar quantity of food to a control group and yet not supply substantial amounts of energy. Therefore, less than satisfactory compromises have to be made. Another problem is that nutritionists, physiologists, or physicians carrying out such studies seldom have complete control of the work force or the working environment. Also, human beings who have marked deficiencies in energy intake almost always suffer from deficiencies of other nutrients as well as from other health problems. This complicates the evaluation of the effects of energy deficits alone.

In a study in Kenya, our group conducted an intervention study that satisfied some, but not all, of the criteria outlined for the ideal study. In this investigation (Wolgemuth et al. 1982; Latham 1983), the persons studied were poor rural road workers, mainly farmers who were temporarily employed to do heavy manual labor within five miles of their homes. The intervention study (Brooks, Latham, and Crompton 1979) was carried out in an area of Kenya where we had previously shown that a large percentage of men were undernourished, as judged by having a low percent of weight compared with that expected for their height (termed here low weight-for-height), and where low weight-for-height was significantly related to worker productivity. On these roads, tasks of about equal size were allocated to each worker, and the incentive to work hard was that subjects could return home once the assigned task was completed. Wages did not vary with the work done. Each man got paid the same amount for one day of work. But some men could complete a day's task in four hours, while others took as long as nine hours. It was possible to randomly assign workers to two different intervention groups. But the two interventions, though similar for obvious reasons, were not identical and could be distinguished by the subjects. One group received a "high energy" supplement to provide 1,000 calories per working day and the second group received a "low energy" supplement to provide 200 calories per day. These were experimental diets, not those recommended for a worker feeding program. Both consisted of a thin maize porridge locally called *uji*. The high energy supplement was prepared from maize meal, whole-milk powder, and sugar, and the low energy supplement from maize meal and dried skimmed milk. The volume offered to each person each day was the same for the two groups. The two supplements were similar but not identical in taste. Because of absenteeism and other labor problems, workers received supplements on far fewer than the total days of the study. Despite this and other difficulties, there was a statistically significant 13 percent rise in worker productivity among those receiving the high energy supplement and only a 3 percent, nonsignificant rise in productivity in those receiving the low energy supplement (Wolgemuth et al. 1982; Latham 1983).

Also of interest was the fact that improvements in certain anthropometric measurements—notably arm circumference, skinfold thickness, and weight-for-height—during the study were significantly related to gains in productivity. This suggests that "successful" supplementation resulting in improved nutritional status was associated with increased productivity of these workers.

There have been other studies in which the effect of calorie supplements on worker productivity has been measured, but most of these have also had design problems. The research of Immink and Viteri (1981a, 1981b) was of long duration—it included groups of workers receiving high and low energy supplements and attempted to measure food consumption at home using a dietary recall method. But the workers selected to receive the different levels of supplementation were not randomly assigned to groups, because each group lived and worked in a different location. Thus, although this is one of the better studies, there are problems in interpretation of results because the lack of random assignment inevitably leads to questions of comparability between the two intervention groups.

In much of the research, there are problems in controlling endogenous variables (this is discussed in detail by Strauss in chapter 10). More consideration also needs to be given to the direction of the causality. Most studies conducted by nutritionists and health professionals seek to show that increased consumption will result in a higher level of worker productivity. Much less consideration is given to the question of whether higher labor productivity will lead to a higher level of food consumption.

Nutritional Status and Worker Productivity

Another way to investigate the relationship between energy status and work performance, or productivity, is to determine work output of persons who have differing energy nutritional statuses but whose other differences are minimal. The most frequently used parameter to judge energy status has been a weight, expressed as a percentage of the "expected weight" for a person's height, using some selected anthropometric standards. In this type of study, the standards chosen are of little consequence if two or more groups are being studied, or if the data are analyzed with weight-for-height as a continuous variable. Weight-for-height is used because a person of low weight in relation to height usually has less fat and lower energy reserves. On the other hand, physical fitness itself, in which energy reserves are less important, might be especially related to lean body mass.

In a study investigating the relationship of nutritional and other factors to the productivity of Jamaican sugarcane cutters (Heywood, Latham, and Cook 1974), it was found that those cutters whose weight-for height was below 85 percent of the standard cut significantly less cane per day than those whose weight-for-height was above 95 percent of the standard.

In Kenya in 1978, we conducted a study for the Kenya Ministry of Works and the World Bank to investigate health and nutritional factors that might contribute to low productivity in rural road workers, both in the highlands and coastal lowlands (Brooks, Latham, and Crompton 1979). Our analysis searched for relationships between productivity and a large number of nutritional and common health problems. The two conditions most strongly related to productivity were weight-for-height and hemoglobin levels. A regression analysis of percent weight-for-height versus time needed to complete a task for 220 male road workers showed a highly significant relationship ($p = .0001$), which suggested that men who have low weight-for-height take a significantly longer period of time to complete a task than do men with higher weight-for height. In this study, hemoglobin levels were not a confounding factor.

Other researchers have examined these same kinds of relationships, usually with somewhat similar findings. Spurr, Barac-Nieto, and Maksud (1977) and Spurr, Maksud, and Barac-Nieto (1977) studied "nutritionally normal" sugarcane cutters in Colombia, who worked about 35 percent of their VO_2 max. during the eight hour day. The workers were divided into three groups— "good," "average," and "poor"—according to the tonnage of cane cut per day. There were statistically significant correlations of height, weight, and lean body mass with productivity. In a study of Tanzania, Davies (1973) also studied sugarcane cutters. The workers were divided into high, medium, and low producers based on the tonnage cut. No difference was found in anthropometric measurements in the three groups, but there was a significant correlation between daily productivity and VO_2 max. In these studies, the question of endogenous factors deserves consideration.

The Relationship of Iron Deficiency and Anemia to Work Capacity

Introduction

Hemoglobin is the substance present in the red blood cells that transports oxygen from the lungs to various parts of the body. Physical activity is the factor that is most important in determining the total oxygen consumption of a healthy individual. Anemia is usually defined as a low level of hemoglobin in the blood. It is not surprising then that persons with quite low levels of hemoglobin, or severe anemia, have a reduced capacity to sustain energetic work of long duration. Evidence has accumulated that persons who are moderately iron deficient—but not anemic—may also show symptoms such as lethargy and more frequent infections. It is believed that this is caused by alterations in tissue metabolism due to iron deficiency but is distinct from the effect on the hemoglobin levels in the blood (Beutler 1980).

Anemia caused mainly by iron deficiency is an extremely prevalent condition worldwide, affecting approximately 750 million persons. It is usually more prevalent among the poor than the better-off segments of the population. Groups at special risk are girls and women during the childbearing years and children. But men are also commonly affected, and we found that 41 percent of 367 road workers in coastal Kenya had anemia (Latham et al. 1983). Iron-deficiency anemia may be influenced by low intakes of iron; the types of iron in the diet; factors that influence iron absorption and utilization, such as ascorbic acid (Latham 1984b); abnormal loss of iron from the body due to infections with hookworm or schistosomiasis; and others.

Anemia and Work Capacity

Work capacity is likely to be influenced in the anemic individual by several factors, including the level of hemoglobin in the blood, the strenuousness of the work being done—or the test being used, that is, maximal vs. submaximal— and the ability of subjects to sustain a given work load (Spurr 1983).

Experiments on animals and humans conducted over many years have shown an effect of hemoglobin levels on work or exercise capacity. In a study on African men, Davies (1973) showed a 34 percent decrement in maximum aerobic capacity in anemic subjects compared to control subjects, using sub-maximal measurements. Viteri and Torun (1974) showed a direct relationship between hemoglobin levels and scores on the Harvard Step Test (HST) in Guatemalan sugarcane cutters. When one group of workers was given extra iron, their hemoglobin and HST scores rose, while a group receiving placebo tablets showed no change in hemoglobin or HST scores. In Indonesia, Basta et al. (1979), also using the Harvard Step Test, reported an improvement in HST scores in rubber tappers following iron therapy, even though only 3 out of 400 workers had a hemoglobin level below 9 g/dl. It should be pointed out that although many studies have shown a fall in VO_2 max. in anemic subjects, Davies (1973) and others have reported only small differences between anemic subjects at submaximal work levels and nonanemic controls. But in many of the studies, submaximal work did lead to increased heart rates and a longer period of time for the heart rate to return to normal following the work. It is important to stress the relationship to submaximal work, because most everyday tasks are performed at submaximal levels. What is of special interest, then, is how long an anemic person, compared with a nonanemic person, can sustain a given task. This phenomenon might be termed as endurance or work capacity, but motivation and other factors also play a role. In the end, the anemic person and the employer will be most interested in how much work can be reasonably performed in a normal working day, a term which is often called worker productivity.

Anemia and Productivity

A study in Indonesia (Basta et al. 1979) showed a significantly lower work output for rubber plantation workers with anemia. Iron therapy provided for 60 days resulted in a significant improvement in work output.

A series of studies on health and nutrition factors related to work performance in Kenya also examined the effects of anemia (Brooks, Latham, and Crompton 1979; Latham and Stephenson 1981). These studies showed a significantly lower level of productivity in anemic road workers compared with nonanemic workers. The measurements conducted were of time taken to complete a given task requiring prolonged, heavy physical activity. Take-home pay was not influenced by the speed of work. The incentive for the workers was that once the task was completed, they could go home and receive a full day's wage. In these studies, anemia was believed to be due to several different causes, including dietary iron deficiency and parasitic infections (hookworm, schistosomiasis, and malaria). Unlike other studies, the Kenya studies were followed by a series of interventions designed to determine whether anemia could be easily reduced under field conditions. The interventions included midday worker feeding with two different levels of iron in the snack; provision of medicinal iron each workday; the treatment of hookworm disease and schistosomiasis; and the giving of chloroquine tablets once weekly to prevent malaria. All of these interventions proved feasible, and all had some, though variable, effect on anemia (Latham et al. 1983).

In one of the few studies using female subjects, Gardner et al. (1977) measured maximal work times using a progressive multistage treadmill test. Several other physiological and biochemical tests were performed. The 75 women were from a tea estate in Sri Lanka and had hemoglobin levels ranging from 6.1 to 15 g/dl. The ability to finish the test was used as a measure of work capacity. The results showed that even at hemoglobin levels of 11–12 g/dl, maximum work time was significantly reduced. The more severely anemic subjects had a much greater reduction in work time. The same investigators, in another publication (Edgerton et al. 1979), also studied work output of tea pickers—measured by weight of tea picked—and found a significantly lower amount of tea picked by anemic pickers, compared with nonanemic pickers. The investigators found a significant increase in work output after correction of the anemia. They also reported that some response to iron occurred before there was a change in hemoglobin level. This is an important finding that deserves further study because it supports other research suggesting that iron deficiency itself affects behavior, even before it reduces hemoglobin levels (Beutler 1980).

In summary, it seems that iron deficiency anemia has a negative effect on maximum work capacity in humans and experimental animals, and that it leads to reduced endurance and work productivity in humans at submaximal work loads. Most human studies show that anemic people, especially those in developing countries, are engaged in strenuous occupations and do perform important tasks. But their capacity to endure high energy expenditures for long periods is often compromised by low hemoglobin levels, and in the end, this may seriously affect their work output. Because millions of people, many of whom are required to perform strenuous activities, also have anemia, it is easy to conclude that anemia, like calorie deficiencies, is an important cause of low work output and a detriment to development. Anemia also probably adversely affects activities that are not usually considered to be work but that are an important part of a decent human existence.

Discussion and Conclusions

Most of the research relating nutrition to worker productivity has been conducted on males. This is, in part, due to the fact that "work" has often been defined as paid employment away from home. In many poor, nonindustrialized countries, women do a great deal of agricultural work and are sometimes required to perform more energy-intensive activities than men. Females often work long hours at high levels of energy expenditure, fetching water, gathering fuel, and carrying produce to and from the local market. Beyond these activities, they are responsible for many household chores and child care. There is insufficient evidence on intrafamily food distribution, but, clearly, women are often consuming insufficient food to provide for their energy needs, and adult females frequently have a higher prevalence of anemia than do adult males.

It is suggested that energy deficits for males and females be defined as energy intakes over a period of weeks or months that are insufficient to provide for the wants of an individual. These wants are defined as those activities, both work and otherwise, that a person wishes to engage in. Individuals in energy balance may be energy-deprived, and frequently they are. Energy requirements and energy needs are difficult to define for groups of persons and for individuals because there are so many factors involved.

Healthy human beings with adequate access to food will normally balance their energy intake over a period of months according to their energy expenditures and, therefore, to the activities they perform. In contrast, those with an inadequate access to food and energy will be forced over a period of months to limit their activities according to the food and energy available to them. If they do not do this, they will have to borrow from their energy reserves.

Work in agriculture or as paid employment away from home needs to be regarded as one call, among many, on the energy of individuals. A brief review shows that energy intakes limited over a long period of time eventually lead to a reduction in physical fitness, work capacity, and work productivity. However, even with such deficits, humans are often able to perform strenuous work, but without much endurance. What has been inadequately investigated are the other essential and desired activities that are forgone under these circumstances. There is a need for research to determine how activities are affected at varying energy-deficit levels in different kinds of persons under differing conditions and how these findings relate to development and quality of life.

The evidence that anemia (mainly iron-deficiency anemia) also reduces work capacity and performance is strong, especially in persons with rather low hemoglobin levels. The physiological explanations for this phenomenon are relatively clear. It is more difficult to show that mild anemia has the same effects. Much of public health seeks to reduce risk, and this should be applicable to programs trying to reduce anemia. New findings suggesting poorer performance and the existence of symptoms in those who are iron deficient but who do not have anemia need to be further investigated in terms of the relationship to physical fitness and work performance. Anemia in the developing countries is often influenced by parasitic infections—especially hookworm, schistosomiasis, and malaria. The treatment or control of all three could substantially reduce anemia and improve physical fitness and productivity. Schistosomiasis itself has been shown to be related to lower work productivity (Prescott 1974) and to physical fitness (Stephenson et al. 1985).

There can be no doubt that nutrient intake and nutritional status influence physical fitness as well as work capacity and work output. This relationship exists in housewives, factory workers, and in those engaged in agriculture, be it subsistence peasant farming or agricultural labor for wages. The problem is to define, for groups of individuals, what levels of nutrient intake or what degree of undernutrition, or malnutrition, are likely to have what effects on work output. It is also clear that the sequelae of childhood malnutrition may have long-term, or even permanent, negative effects on the future capacity of individuals for certain kinds of work. Obvious examples are blindness or poor vision resulting from vitamin A deficiency; serious mental impairment from cretinism due to iodine deficiency; skeletal deformities caused by rickets or fluorosis; and dwarfing due to protein-energy malnutrition.

There is greater uncertainty about the effects on work output of moderate deficiencies in energy intake for individuals who do not suffer from serious permanent consequences of earlier malnutrition. It is suggested that the use of energy for work needs to be studied in relation to all other energy needs, including those for metabolism, for activities around the home, child care, recreation, and other purposes.

There is a rather limited number of studies that have measured the productivity of agricultural and other workers based on their nutritional status, and even fewer have attempted to determine productivity changes following nutritional intervention. The results, in general, suggest that improved energy intake and reductions in the extent of anemia will improve productivity. Many of the studies have design problems, and it must be recognized that research of this kind is time-consuming, expensive, and fraught with difficulties. Much of the research to date has problems of endogeneity. Some new methods have been suggested to bridge these problems and to use a more econometric approach in research of this nature (see chapter 10).

The importance of improving nutrition, particularly in the poor segments of society, needs to be better recognized by planners and politicians, because it will have an impact on the growth of children and on the productivity of all those who work. Great strides have been made in the last three decades in increasing the yields of cereal grains, but in many countries, this has not resulted in significantly more food for the poorest families. The "green revolution" needs to be matched by actions that will result in a consumption revolution for poor families. If food needs can be better satisfied, we will see improvement in human resource development, greater work output, and a better quality of life for poor people.

10 The Impact of Improved Nutrition on Labor Productivity and Human-Resource Development: An Economic Perspective

JOHN STRAUSS

Introduction

Isolating the effects of improved nutrition on labor productivity and on health, education, and other human-capital investments is proving to be very difficult. The research to date has concentrated on health-nutrition linkages and has been carried out primarily by nutritionists and medical doctors, although an increasing number of economists have become involved. Two types of evidence have been presented: experimental (or quasi-experimental) and epidemiological. The experimental evidence usually examines the effects of diet supplementation programs on such variables as labor productivity, physical growth, or morbidity. Ex-ante and ex-post comparisons are made, with varying results. Many conclusions are overdrawn, due either to faulty design or faulty analysis. Almost all statistical analyses of nonexperimental data, as well as some analyses of experimental data, consist of correlations between variables that economic analysis suggests are chosen, or at least influenced, by households. Examples include correlations between measured labor productivity and current nutrient intake. Since nutrient intake is influenced by many factors that are also related to productivity (for example, income), these correlations shed little or no light on causality. Unfortunately, they have been widely interpreted as causal in the literature.

It is sometimes possible to infer causality by using appropriate statistical techniques. A small number of studies have attempted to do this, with promising results. When combined with reliable experimental studies, they indicate that current nutrient intake, particularly of calories and iron, as well as body weight can have a positive impact on work productivity, even when workers are above starvation intake levels.

This chapter will review the methodologies used in the empirical literature, explain why the conclusions drawn from them do not always make sense when the economic behavior of individuals and households is considered, and point out corrective measures traditionally used by economists that have only

149

begun to be used to analyze nutrition-productivity-health interactions. Questions of data-collection strategies are also addressed.

Nutrition, Health, and Productivity Interactions in a Household Model

Household Decisions and Nutrition and Health Outcomes

Households produce and consume both marketed and nonmarketed goods and services. Among these are nutritionally related outcomes, such as improved weight-for-age of preschool children, and health outcomes, such as infant birthweight or individual morbidity. These are "produced" by inputs, some of which are chosen by the households. In the case of adult standardized weight (or changes in weight), the outcome, change in weight, reflects an energy imbalance. The degree of energy imbalance in turn depends upon nutrient intake, infection, and activity levels in addition to variables affecting basal metabolic rate, such as age, sex, and weight. Individual nutrient intake, activity levels, and infection incidence result from current household decisions (infection being related to such inputs as nutrient intake, water quality and consumption, activity levels, and medical treatment).

In turn, current nutrient intake, stature (height and weight-for-height), and health may affect worker productivity. If the market recognizes a nutrition-productivity effect, then better nutrition may also result in higher market earnings, by being paid more for a given time unit of work or by being able to work at particularly taxing and well-rewarded activities, or both.

Higher caloric intake may also raise nonmarketed household production in addition to farm or market activities. Viteri (1974) studied two groups of Guatemalan agricultural workers, one of which had received nutritional supplementation for the previous three years. The group receiving no supplements was largely inactive after working hours, while the supplemented group actively pursued household activities. If this resulted from increased nutrient intake, the benefits from higher intakes would be understated by measuring only the effects on worker productivity and earnings.

Economic models predict that household members try to equate marginal benefits (measured in a money metric or in terms of satisfaction) between different activities. While market imperfections may prevent marginal benefits from being completely equated, an increase in nutritional intake should lead individuals to allocate their time to those activities with the highest marginal returns. In consequence, the pattern of time spent in different activities will be directly affected by nutritional intakes as well as health and nutrition outcomes.

Implications of Household Decisions for Estimating the Impact of Nutrition on Productivity

Economic analysis implies that individual food consumption (thus nutrient availability), other health inputs, and time allocation all result from household choices. Among the factors that affect these outcomes are unobserved variables. Causality between better nutrition and measured worker productivity should not necessarily be inferred from observed positive correlations, since both may be "caused" by other observed and unobserved variables. For instance, sugarcane cutters who are more able cutters should have higher measured productivity than less able cutters, holding constant observable factors that may affect productivity, such as height and age. Yet caloric intake may also be higher for the more able cutters if they earn more income. Thus a positive correlation between caloric intake and sugarcane cut per day may simply reveal an income-caloric consumption curve, not necessarily a nutrition-productivity effect.

Caloric intake is a flow variable. Nutritional outcomes, such as weight or height, are stock variables, in that they represent the accumulation of past flows. It might be thought that using lagged values of stock variables such as weight-for-height might avoid the problem of simultaneous determination of variables. However, this is not necessarily the case. Take the example of weight (of weight-for-height) and productivity. Clearly, current weight changes and productivity are both affected by current household choices. Moreover, past weight changes may be correlated with current "random" errors, which affect both current weight changes and productivity, provided that these errors represent in part individual and household-specific variables that persist over time and are unobserved to the analyst but known to the household or individual. Examples include farm management ability, land quality, or inherent (genetic) healthiness. Such variables may be expected to affect the same household or person over a period of time and to have an impact on all household choice variables. For instance, able farmers from a low-income community may show both higher labor productivity and weight-for height than less able farmers. Hence a positive empirical correlation may be entirely spurious.

The case for treating height-for-age as uncorrelated with unobserved factors that affect current decisions is stronger, especially to the extent that adult heights are largely determined by parental investments made when these adults were children. Unobserved factors that the parents took into account may be uncorrelated, or only weakly correlated, with unobserved factors that the children as adults take into account. Counterexamples would result from factors specific to the individual that persisted from childhood to adulthood, for example, inherent healthiness.

Given the foregoing critique, it is of interest to discern the direction and magnitude of the statistical bias (inconsistency) incurred when using statistical methods of analysis, such as ordinary least squares, that do not correct for the simultaneity of variables used in regression analysis. In general, this cannot be done, although if there is only one explanatory variable that is endogenous, then the direction of the bias will depend on the sign of the correlation between the endogenous explanatory variable and the unobserved disturbance term. The magnitude of the bias will depend upon the strength of that correlation (see Appendix). For instance, suppose measured labor productivity were to be regressed on current caloric intake and an exogenous variable, age of the worker. It is quite likely that unobserved characteristics of the worker, such as "ability," are correlated through income with current caloric intake. This would lead to an upward bias in the estimated coefficient of current caloric intake. It would be possible that a positive coefficient might be found even when no effect of caloric intake on productivity existed, simply because of the positive income-calorie variable and the unobserved error term (ability) in the productivity existed, simply because of the positive income-calorie variable and the unobserved error term (ability) in the productivity equation. Unfortunately, the income-calorie intake correlation is likely to be strongest for very low income households, who have members consuming at low intake levels. Yet it is precisely for such individuals that the nutrition-productivity relationship is hypothesized to be the strongest. Thus, when using data for such individuals, the statistical bias is likely to be greatest.

With more than one endogenous explanatory variable, the direction of the bias is more difficult to judge because it will also depend on the correlations between the second endogenous variable and the unobserved disturbance, and between the two observed endogenous variables (see Appendix). Useful generalizations are thus difficult to generate because they depend on what other endogenous variables are used. Nevertheless, biases may still be expected to be present, so results based on such regressions are suspect if they are used to support claims of causality.

Consistent Estimation of a Nutrition-Productivity Effect

For a nutrition-productivity effect to be consistently estimable from non-experimental data, data must be available on variables (instruments) that influence household choices but have no direct influence on labor productivity. One class of variables that proves to be extremely useful are prices that a household faces: prices of foods, nonfoods, nonlabor farm inputs (for farm households), and health inputs. Distance to various program centers is among the price variables for program service inputs. However, to the extent that migration is prevalent and that program service availability helps to determine whether and where to migrate, then distance to community services will also result from household choices and will be an appropriate set of instrumental variables (see Rosenzweig and Wolpin 1984). The empirical importance of this consideration has yet to be demonstrated. Prices faced in the market will, in general, be independent of household choices. Other variables outside the household's control that affect current behavior, but not productivity directly, are candidate instrumental variables. Among these may be characteristics of the parents, such as education, job history, and height. Care has to be taken with stocklike household-level variables, such as assets, because although they may be predetermined, they may well be correlated with unobserved individual and household characteristics that persist over time.

With data on prices and other community variables, effects of these variables can be traced onto current intake and other nutritional variables that would vary in consequence, without productivity varying directly. Then, by statistically examining how production varies when nutrition or health outcomes (as well as other household choice variables) change as a result of variation in exogenous factors, it may be possible to gain some insight into the potential effects of an (imaginary) exogenous change in these choice variables on productivity. This is, of course, the method of instrumental variables.

In order to obtain reasonably precise estimates, it is necessary to have larger samples than usual. In addition, one needs variation in the values of instrumental variables. Since commodity prices vary only over time or over large regions, data should ideally span both. Thus, panel data are potentially quite useful. In a cross section, data will have to be over a large enough area to ensure real price variation (that is, for the same characteristics of a commodity and for identical time periods).

Implications of Household Decisions for Experimental Design

Analysis of experimental data may also be subject to simultaneity bias if explanatory variables are used that have not been controlled for experimentally and that are endogenous to household decision-making. Even without this problem, individual and household choices can contaminate the data through attrition or refusal to participate in the first place. For example, if in a diet supplementation experiment, the workers with lowest caloric intakes drop out, and if the impact on productivity declines drastically with higher intakes, as it is thought to, then only a very weak positive impact may be measured. This problem is appreciated in the experimental literature, though awareness does not always prevent occurrence. For example, Popkin's (1978) study of the effects of iron supplementation on road construction worker productivity in the Bicol region of the Philippines had to be discontinued because of an enormous exodus of workers (119 out of 157), apparently caused by a change in the payment system during the experiments. Even if sample attrition is not a problem, nonrandom assignment to control and treatment groups may be. Several of the experimental studies summarized below suffer from this problem.

Even well-designed experiments that do not suffer from attrition or simultaneity bias may have difficulty measuring the impacts of nutrition on productivity, again due to household choices. Most experiments attempt to measure the impact of diet supplementation (of calories or iron) on average worker productivity. However, the entire diet is typically not controlled, only the portion eaten on the job. Since the supplement may substitute for food consumption at home, the total change in nutrient intake is apt to be considerably less than the amount given in the supplement. Strong evidence of such substitution is found in numerous studies, for instance, in Akin, Guilkey, and Popkin (1983). Substitution may occur between household members as well as for the member in the experiment. In particular, both food consumption and activity levels of other household members will likely be reallocated so as to re-equate the marginal returns of food consumption, time use, health, and other commodities across household members. Change in household welfare will depend upon these reallocations, which have not been measured in any of the experiments to date. The consequence of following only the individual in the experiment rather than the entire household is that the benefits of supplementation are likely to be understated, though by how much it is difficult to judge.

The Appropriate Concept of Productivity and Its Measurement

The question of observability of productivity measures is an important one. The appropriate concept here is marginal, not average, productivity. In the case of market work, under standard economic assumptions, wages will reflect marginal productivity. Since individual wages can be observed and carefully examined, they might shed light on the existence of a nutrition-productivity effect. It is possible, however, for nutrition to raise labor productivity without affecting market wages. This might occur if it were costly, or difficult, for employers to monitor the food consumption of individual workers. If body size, not current intake, is responsible for enhanced productivity, this should be less likely since body size can be easily observed. For nonmarket family labor with no direct remuneration, marginal productivity is not observable but must be inferred indirectly. This poses difficulties, requiring knowledge of the technical relationship between inputs and outputs, that is, information about the production function. For this reason, most studies of nutrition-productivity relationships by nutritionists have used data from industries in which outputs of individual laborers can seemingly be directly observed. Sugarcane cutters and road construction crews have been among the most intensively studied groups. Even in these cases, there are nonlabor inputs into production that need to be measured in order to estimate the marginal productivity of increased current nutrient intake or greater weight-for-height. For example, different sugarcane fields may have differing qualities or have received different levels of preharvest inputs. Unless laborers are randomly assigned to fields, the effect of working on different fields needs to be accounted for when analyzing the data, whether it is experimental or nonexperimental. This issue is not always addressed in the literature. Exceptions are some of the regressions reported by Immink and Viteri (1981a, 1981b), Wolgemuth et al. (1982), and Popkin (1978). Immink and Viteri control for field conditions in explaining the response of average productivity of sugarcane cutters to direct supplementation. Wolgemuth et al. hold road assignment constant while looking at road construction workers' productivity response to diet supplementation, and Popkin holds rain conditions constant when analyzing road construction worker's response to iron supplementation.

A Review of Empirical Evidence on Nutrition-Productivity Linkages

Overview

As stated in chapter 9, reliable empirical evidence on the existence of a nutrition-productivity relationship is not abundant, particularly for individuals above starvation or semistarvation levels of caloric intake. What little useful evidence does exist suggests some positive impact of increased caloric intake, and possibly weight or weight-for-height, on market or farm-labor productivity for such individuals who are at what might be considered low, but certainly not starvation, levels of intake. Iron deficiency alone also seems to have some negative impact on productivity. However, evidence for the above claims is not voluminous, and there are still many issues which remain unexplored. There are a number of studies, both experimental and nonexperimental, that do not find supporting evidence of a nutrition-productivity link. However, most of these studies suffer from some of the difficulties discussed above.

Evidence of a nutrition-productivity link seems much more substantive at starvation or semistarvation levels. The experiments of Keys et al. (1950) at the University of Minnesota show that activity levels drop precipitously when males are subjected to dramatic decreases in caloric intake from moderate intakes (3,500 calories daily) to extremely low ones (1,500 calories daily). While basal metabolic rates dropped, they did not do so sufficiently to offset the fall in nutrient intake. These experiments controlled the total diet of the subjects and randomly assigned them to treatment groups. Thus they would appear to be free of many of the problems discussed earlier. Other starvation experiments may also be free, or relatively so, of confounding effects (Spurr 1983 contains a very useful survey).

One issue that has been raised (see Sukhatme and Morgen 1982) is whether, over a more moderate range of intake changes, basal metabolic rates may adjust enough to avoid having to change activity levels by much in order to reequilibrate energy intake with energy expenditure. If true, this would imply a very weak or nonexistent nutrition-productivity relationship at higher levels of caloric intake. It is argued that this hypothesis suggests a threshold of rather low intake above which it has no effect on productivity. Then the issue becomes how low such a threshold might be. None of the evidence cited below directly tests for such a threshold, although some studies test for a continuously declining impact of calories on productivity as intake rises. Ultimately, of course, it is very difficult to distinguish between a discontinuous threshold and a sufficiently nonlinear continuous effect.[1]

Specific Studies

Wolgemuth et al. (1982) compare gains in productivity by measuring earth moved per hour between a group of workers whose diet was supplemented by 1,000 calories per day and workers with only a 200 calories per day supplementation. The study is unusually careful in randomizing a number of relevant characteristics between groups. For instance, the daily attendance record for the first month of the study and initial productivity measurements were among the variables that were stratified before random assignments to groups. Randomizing over the first variable should have helped avoid selective dropping out of the sample, while the second variable would control for many unobservable individual effects. The study also measured food consumption at home, finding a net increase of 500 calories per day for the highly supplemented group and no net change for the low-level supplemented group. Wolgemuth et al. then compare mean gains in productivity between highly and weakly supplemented groups, finding a 12.5 percent gain in productivity by the highly supplemented group (more for the low-calorie supplementation group), which was statistically significant at about the .075 level. Unfortunately, this result must be qualified because only 47 individuals out of the original 224 are used. This raises the question of the representativeness of the workers included in this comparison.

Basta et al. (1979) compare gains in productivity between two groups of adult male tree tappers and weeders working on rubber plantations in Indonesia, one getting an iron supplement and the other receiving a placebo. Workers were randomly assigned to treatment groups. Basta and his colleagues found an increased productivity among all groups (potentially related to an incentive wage scheme linked to participation in the experiment), with an especially large increase among anemic workers who received iron supplements. Some effort was made to limit the productivity comparisons to workers working on trees of similar quality. However, due to this and other unstated reasons, only half of the original sample of tree tappers were used in the comparison. The impact of this reduced sample (only 77 workers) on the results is unclear.

In a major diet supplementation study done at Instituto de Nutricion de Centro America y Panama (INCAP), Immink and Viteri (1981a, 1981b) compare gains in productivity between sugarcane cutters in one Guatemalan village

---

1. The direct empirical evidence on the Sukhatme-Morgen hypothesis is too scant to be conclusive, involving only a handful of studies with small samples (15 persons, for example). In addition, there is even less evidence on the speed of adjustment. If the transition to a new equilibrium is slow enough, then productivity losses during the transition period could be important.

receiving a high energy supplement and cutters in another village who received a low-energy supplement. Since all workers in each village received the identical supplement, there was no randomization of assignment to treatment groups. Initial measurements indicate a similarity between caloric intake and cutting productivity among all workers, though there may have been differences in field quality or nonlabor inputs between the two villages. The study lasted 28 months, the first 15 of which have been analyzed, which raises the question of differential sample attrition due to migration or other reasons. Caloric intake at home was measured by 24-hour recalls with the result that workers receiving the high-energy supplement were observed to increase their caloric intake over baseline levels, while workers receiving the low supplement did not. In comparing changes of daily cane harvest by the two groups over time, Immink and Viteri find that productivity of both groups rose during the supplementation period. They test differences between the two dummy variable coefficients to see if the rise in the more highly supplemented group was significant, but their tests are incorrect because of serial correlation in the data that they measured but did not correct for. These comparisons are confounded by seasonal patterns in production associated with both villages. This variation is not completely captured by the analyses, although some attempt is made by running separate regressions for each of two seasons. When the sample is split, any differences between the two supplementation dummy coefficients disappear, the major variation over time being captured by village-level variables measuring days worked in the fields and mill capacity. Since the sugar company regulates total labor used, the village-days-worked variable may be taken as exogenous to the worker.

A different type of time-series comparison is made by Kraut and Muller (1946). They report changes in productivity of different groups of German workers when daily food rations were increased. The workers were living in special camps, so their total diet was controlled. In the three cases reported of worker or plant level response, output per worker-hour increased dramatically following an increase in food rations. This must be interpreted cautiously, since it may represent a morale effect (Stiglitz 1984) rather than a nutrition effect. Also, no nonlabor inputs or institutional changes were measured. It is interesting that worker weight generally remained unchanged, the increased caloric intake apparently being fully expended. This is consistent with findings by Viteri (1982). The one case when a short-run weight loss was recorded occurred when a cigarette premium was offered to workers dumping debris out of railway cars for attaining a given level of productivity. Productivity did indeed jump, workers being willing to endure a loss (perhaps temporary) in weight.

The above studies have comparatively fewer problems than most, since they do not look at correlations between two or more household choice variables and infer causality, for instance, between current productivity and current flows or stocks (past flows) of nutrition intakes. The literature attempting to establish nutrition-productivity links is replete with just such regressions (or correlations). As an example, Wolgemuth et al. (1982) report a regression of gains in road construction worker productivity on total caloric intake from supplements and days worked. The total-calories variable has a positive coefficient that is weakly significant (t-statistic of 1.81 with 44 degrees of freedom), while days of labor supply has a negative and highly significant coefficient (t-statistic of -3.93). The authors imply that causation running from labor supply to productivity changes is driving the correlation. While this is certainly possible, it is not the only plausible interpretation, since labor supply can be varied by households, and much recent empirical evidence indicates that labor supply responds to prices (see, for example, Bardhan 1984a; Rosenzweig 1980; Singh, Squire, and Strauss 1986). In this case, if work was paid by the piece, the diet supplement would increase earnings (provided it raised productivity). Labor supply might decline because of an income effect, negating some of the effect on earnings and leading to a negative coefficient on days worked.

Wolgemuth et al. (1982) also report a pure cross-section regression using the presupplementation data. The experimental nature of the data is not used, making it comparable to other analyses using nonexperimental, cross-sectional data. Productivity measurements are regressed on a set of variables including arm circumference and hematological values. Likewise, Popkin (1978) regresses daily productivity of road construction workers in Bicol, Philippines, on hemoglobin levels. Baldwin and Weisbrod (1974) and Weisbrod and Helminiak (1977) regress daily and weekly earnings of plantation workers on St. Lucia on, among other things, dummy variables indicating presence of parasitic infections, such as schistosomiasis. These "explanatory" variables reflect current-period and past-period investments in nutrition and health, as argued above (Baldwin and Weisbrod are aware of these concerns but do nothing to correct the problem). Even with estimates that are probably biased upwards, the two studies find little, if any, effects of infections on earnings. Behrman, Wolfe, and Blau (1985) separately regress male and female earnings of workers in Nicaragua on variables, including one measuring the proportion of a protein standard satisfied by food consumption at the household level and one measuring days of illness. They also estimate probit equations to explain the probability of working in the market, again using the nutrition and health variables. The measure of protein adequacy is found to have an important positive effect on both earnings and the probability of working in the market; however, its meaning is in doubt.

Immink and Viteri (1981a, 1981b) and Immink, Viteri, and Helms (1982) regress the change in sugarcane cut per day (and per hour) on daily energy intake in addition to variables controlling for field conditions and whether the worker was in the high supplementation group. The problem with the energy variable is that it measures total daily intake, not calories from the supplement. Total intake is endogenous because of substitution of food at work for food at home. Even then, they find that the calorie variable has a very low t-statistic, although the statistic is incorrect given the simultaneity problem. They also use energy intake in a regression, trying to explain tonnage of cane cut per day using only the presupplementation data.

In an earlier study, Viteri (1971, 1974) reports that time-motion studies of agricultural field work done by two groups of agricultural workers, one group having a higher caloric intake and having had a supplemented diet for three years, show that the higher-intake group expended more energy per task, completing them in a shorter period of time, and also expended more energy on household activities. But there is no information on inherent differences between the two groups. The groups were not formed randomly, indeed, the supplemented group consisted of workers who were paid higher than average wages, had an adequate current caloric intake, and worked on the same farm, apparently a better managed one. The second group, by contrast, was from one of the poorer areas of Guatemala and had much lower caloric intakes. While the nutrition-productivity explanation is certainly possible, it is by no means the only one. Different field conditions between the two areas might well have led to the difference in timing (though that would not explain different energy expenditures), as might differences in ability or motivation (the samples were extremely small; 19 for the supplemented group and 20 for the unsupplemented group). Given that the higher productivity group had higher earnings, it is not surprising that their caloric intake might be higher.

Studies relating body size to output are also plagued by the problem of simultaneously determined explanatory variables. Martorell and Arroyave (1984) cite six studies that calculate correlations between a measured productivity variable and weight or weight-for-height. These are Davies (1973); Spurr, Barac-Nieto, and Maksud (1977); Immink, Viteri, and Helms (1982); Heywood (1974); Brooks, Latham, and Crompton (1979); Satyanarayana et al. (1977); and Rao (1980). Typically, a sample of workers is taken and productivity measurements made. The sample is then divided by level of productivity, and average group anthropometric measurements are taken and compared. Martorell and Arroyave conclude on the basis of these studies that body size, particularly weight-for-height, seems to be an important predictor of productivity, especially for demanding work tasks. Since these coefficients are probably upwardly biased, it is not clear what to make of them.

Strauss (1986), Deolalikar (1988), and subsequently Sahn and Alderman (1988), have attempted to account both for the endogeneity of explanatory variables subject to household choice and for nonlabor inputs that affect productivity, in estimating the effects of higher current nutrient intake and stature on labor productivity in subsistence family farms. Strauss uses cross-sectional data on farm households in Sierra Leone that practice hoe agriculture, while Deolalikar uses panel household data covering two years from a semiarid region of south India. Both find positive and statistically significant effects of nutrition-related variables, even after accounting for endogeneity. In Strauss' study, current caloric intake is controlled for, while in Deolalikar's case, both calories and weight-for-height are, with weight-for-height having a substantially stronger effect. These studies are not only the first to attempt to control for input simultaneity, but they also seem to be the only studies other than Viteri's (1974) flawed analysis that are trying to measure the impact of better nutrition on productivity of family farm laborers, this despite the overwhelming importance of family semisubsistence farms in agriculture of developing countries. Strauss estimates an agricultural production function while using instrumental variables to control statistically for endogenous inputs. Variables treated as endogenous include not only nutrient intakes and body size (at least weight-for height) but also variable farm inputs, such as hours of family and hired-labor use. Deolalikar estimates both an agricultural production function and a market-wage equation. Because data are available for two years, Deolalikar is able to examine the effect of changes in calorie intake and in weight-for-height on changes in agricultural production and on changes in market wages. Analyzing changes (or first differences) has the advantage of eliminating confounding effects of underlying worker ability and land quality.

The instruments used by these studies fall into three categories: prices, farm assets, and household size and age distribution, with prices and certain household characteristics, such as family size, being excluded from the production function.

Since it is arguable that even quasi-fixed factors, such as capital stock, land cultivated, and family size, are correlated with unobserved variables, such as land quality or management ability, they may be inappropriate instruments. Strauss examines the robustness of his estimates to dropping these variables, using only prices as instruments, and finds his results to be reasonably robust to this specification. Deolalikar finds that the impact of weight-for-height on agricultural output doubles when simultaneity is accounted for in the first difference (changes) model, compared to when it is not. Unfortunately, the data Strauss uses are not ideal for testing the nutrition-productivity hypothesis. Data are only available for current nutrient availability at the household, not individual, level, and no anthropometric measurements were taken, so the effect of body size cannot be estimated separately. The most that can be done under this circumstance is to make differing assumptions concerning how households distribute food among their members and examine the sensitivity of the results to these changes. Strauss does this, finding almost no changes in the results. In Deolalikar's study, by contrast, data are available for individual heights and weights and even individual levels of food consumption.

Strauss models current caloric availability as augmenting hours of family labor into "effective" hours of family labor. He does this by multiplying labor hours by a function that relates units of effective labor time to units of clock time. This function depends upon current nutrient intake at the individual level.

FIGURE 10.1 Estimated efficiency labor function for Sierra Leone farm households

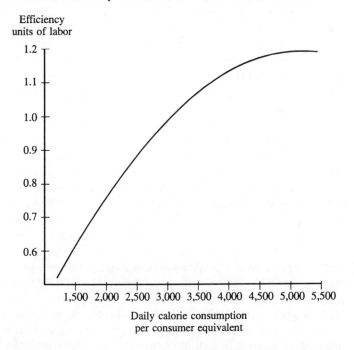

Daily calorie consumption
per consumer equivalent

SOURCE: Strauss 1984.

Strauss finds a high degree of curvature in this function (see figure 10.1), which is approximately quadratic in the range observed in the Sierra Leone data. The estimated efficiency of an hour of work relative to a male consuming 3,000 calories daily is estimated to be 60 percent for a male consuming 1,500 calories per day, and 117 percent at a daily consumption of 4,500 calories. This efficiency function rises steeply to 3,750 calories per day and finally falls after 5,200 calories. It would appear, at least in this sample, that the nutrition-productivity relationship exists even for individuals with relatively high levels (compared to starvation levels) of caloric intake.

Strauss estimates that output increases by nearly .5 percent for every 1 percent increase in calories consumed for low-income workers (who consume 1,500 calories daily). This figure is almost identical to the figure of .5 percent found by Wolgemuth et al. for the Kenyan road construction workers having an average daily intake of 2,000 calories. The estimated impact (or elasticity) drops to .34 for workers consuming 3,000 calories daily, the Sierra Leone sample average.

The potential economic importance of the nutrition-productivity relation is calculated to be high in the Sierra Leone data. The marginal product of a unit of a particular food can be shown to be an estimate of the proportion by which the shadow price of that food is less than the market price. Strauss puts bounds on this figure being between 20 percent and 40 percent for the representative household in the sample (having daily caloric availability per consumer equivalent to 3,060 calories), rising to a very high 75 percent to nearly 100 percent for a very poor household (with daily per consumer equivalent availability of 1,500 calories), and falling to between 15 percent and 18 percent for households with a daily per consumer equivalent availability of 4,500 calories. While these figures are only meant to be illustrative of the order of magnitude potentially involved, given the crudeness of the data, they are nevertheless striking.

Deolalikar finds that a 1 percent increase in average adult weight-for-height would raise the daily value of farm labor's marginal product by almost 2 percent. Approximately the same magnitude effect is found for weight-for-height on daily market-wage rates. The impact of a 1 percent increase in calorie intake on market wages is .2 percent, which is fairly similar to Strauss' estimate for the effect of calories on farm output. The magnitudes of the weight-for-height and calorie elasticities are not directly comparable because to achieve a 1 percent rise in weight-for-height would require greater than a 1 percent increase in calorie intake. Nevertheless, it is clear that weight-for-height and, to a lesser extent, calories may both raise earnings for a given job and enable workers to engage in more taxing, higher-paid jobs in this rural, semiarid Indian sample.

These two studies can be taken as strongly suggestive. They are the first studies to try to grapple with the difficult issue of how to detect nutrition-productivity relationships in the face of household choice, and they show positive results.

Subsequent to the Strauss and Deolalikar studies, Sahn and Alderman (1988) estimated market-wage equations for males and females in rural Sri Lanka, including a household-level calorie-intake variable. They instrument calorie intake with prices, unearned household income, and household demographic variables, and correct their estimates for the potential bias because their sample of market laborers is a nonrandom sample of the rural population. They find a positive, significant at the .01 level, coefficient for calories in the male-wage equation but an insignificant effect for female wages. Their estimates suggest that a 1 percent increase in calorie intake will lead to male wages rising by .2 percent, an increase identical to Deolalikar's estimate. That calories should affect male but not female wages suggests that the tasks undertaken by daily male laborers are different, requiring more energy.

Pitt and Rosenzweig (1985), in a different type of analysis, relate farm profits (net of family labor valuation) and male labor supply of households in Indonesia to sick days of adult family members. They find no statistically significant effects of family illness on profit but do find such an effect on male labor supply. The absence of an effect of illness on profit may reflect recourse to an active labor market, through which family labor can be replaced at a constant wage, and not necessarily absence of a productivity effect. If family and hired labor are perfectly substitutable (in efficiency units) in farm production and if households face a given wage for an efficiency unit of labor, then households demand a certain amount of labor in efficiency units. If household members are sick, laborers can be hired in the market, with the opportunity cost, in terms of efficiency units, being equal between household and hired laborers. Farm profits will therefore remain unchanged. Of course, the potential (or full) income of the household has declined because of the illness, since sick members are unable to work on the days they are bedridden, should they wish to.

A Partial Summary of Studies of Nutrition-Health-Education Linkages

The discussion thus far has concentrated on the limited question of effects of nutrition-related variables on direct labor productivity or earnings. Nutrition also potentially affects time use and such human capital as health (morbidity and mortality) and schooling (both attendance and achievement). Selowsky and Taylor (1973) hypothesized an important impact of better nutrition on the human capital development of children, which directly and through more schooling would raise future productivity. The evidence directly testing this is nonexistent, but certain individual links have been explored, especially between health and nutrition. The literature in this area is vast (see, for instance, Habicht and Butz 1979; Martorell and Ho 1984; Chandra 1982). It is similar to the nutrition-productivity literature in that two types of studies have been conducted: quasi-experimental ("quasi" because complete randomization is usually too difficult to achieve), in which a diet supplement is given to one group, and both treatment and control groups are observed over time, and epidemiological, in which correlations are measured using cross-sectional data. The quasi-experimental literature, for example, the Narangwal nutrition study (Kielmann and Associates 1983) or the INCAP supplementation study (Martorell, Habicht, and Klein 1982), is subject to the same questions raised concerning worker productivity effects (Chernichovsky [1979] makes some of these same criticisms of the health-nutrition literature). In the Narangwal experiment, for example, whole villages were assigned to treatment groups. The control group villages were on the whole poorer, so the fact that their populations show less growth in young children is of uncertain meaning without controlling for differences in economic variables. Likewise, empirical correlations computed from cross-sectional data are plagued by the same problem of household choice, leading to endogenously chosen "explanatory" variables.

A very suggestive study carried out by Chen, Chowdhury, and Huffman (1980) followed preschool children over time in rural Bangladesh. It found that children who were stunted or wasted at the beginning of the study had far higher risks of dying in the subsequent two years than did children who had normal measurements. This correlation for young children between very low nutritional status and subsequent mortality has been long noted (e.g., Beck and van den Berg 1975). However, in this case too, it is not clear what the causal links are, since children with low anthropometry scores at the beginning of the study came from households with less income, less educated parents, poorer housing and water sanitation conditions, and so on.

Not many studies have attempted to link nutrition to human capital development. Moock and Leslie (1982) use data from Nepal, regressing child school enrollment and grade performance on variables such as height-for-age (which for young children is likely to be endogenous), weight-for-height, and hemoglobin levels. Likewise, Popkin and Lim-Ybanez (1982) analyze school test scores of children in Manila using their standardized weight-for-height and hemoglobin levels, and Jamison (1983) examines how the number of grades children are held back in China relates to weight and height-for-age. In a somewhat different study, Kielmann et al. (1983) regress indices of child psychomotor development on birthweight and average weight-for-age over the first nine months of life, finding positive effects that decline as the child gets older.

The problem in interpreting these studies is again that the correlations are between variables influenced by household choices. Schooling attendance (and achievement) as well as current nutrient intakes and stature are outcome variables of processes. For the health and nutrition variables, the processes can be thought of as production functions that relate certain inputs to these outputs. Some of these inputs may also be outputs, such as diarrheal disease affecting child growth and mortality. As was true in the nutrition-productivity literature, correlations between inputs and outputs may simply represent the influence of unmeasured factors on both. For instance, in the psychomotor development regression, there are probably family variables that help determine the degree of stimulation a child gets at home, as well as the food eaten. If these are not being held constant in the regression, the measured "influence" of the average weight (or birthweight) variables may simply convey the influence of those unmeasured variables. While some factors, such as mother's education or income, can be measured and included in a regression, others, such as the inherent "unhealthiness" of the child, cannot.

Far more common than studies of schooling or cognitive outcomes of nutrition are analyses of the determinants of health, nutrient intakes, or body size (see Cochrane, Leslie and O'Hara 1982 for an earlier survey concentrating on the effects of education). In a pioneering study, Levinson (1974) used a sample of children from rural Punjab in India and regressed an average of standardized weight-for-age, height-for-age, and weight-for-height scores on calorie and protein intakes, variables indicating the presence of various diseases, and household income. Estimation used ordinary least squares even though nutrient intakes and disease incidence were treated as dependent variables in other regressions on the same table. He found a positive influence of calorie intake and a negative influence of diarrhea on his measure of anthropometric scores; however, since other variables, such as parental education, may well have affected all three sets of outcomes, the meaning of these partial correlations is unclear.

Heller and Drake (1979) analyze standardized anthropometric scores and morbidity for children living in Candelaria, Colombia. Equations explaining standardized weight-for-height of children are estimated and include many inputs, hence they look like production functions. In particular, illness and diarrheal-disease dummy variables are included, both for current and past periods. Heller and Drake recognize the simultaneity problem for the current disease dummies, using predicted values from a logit equation for disease. However, endogeneity of other inputs is left unaccounted for. Among these are the use of health inputs, such as length of breast-feeding and food expenditures. Also left unaccounted for is sickness duration period (year). As explained earlier, the usual argument of predetermination may be inappropriate here, particularly if parents respond in their input allocations to individual characteristics that change only slowly and are not measured in the data set and thus unknown to the analyst. The same problem exists with Drake and Heller's equations explaining morbidity. Change in relative weight-for-height is treated as endogenous, but variables such as past malnourishment, birthweight, immunizations received, and a dummy indicating whether weaning from the breast occurred suddenly or gradually, are not.

In a related study, Wolfe and Behrman (1982) examine determinants of standardized child weight and height as well as child mortality and average length of breast-feeding, using a sample from urban Nicaragua. Their equations are supposed to represent reduced forms, but they also include variables such as average household caloric intake, length of breast-feeding, and household use of refrigeration, in addition to community characteristics and family background variables. In their study, the only variable that is predicted from a reduced form is the individual wage rate.

Longhurst (1984), examining farm households in Zaria, Nigeria, predicts children's weight-for-height using the child's medical history, immunization record, a dummy for breast-feeding, and birth order. He then notes that economic status variables, such as assets, have little additional explanatory power when medical and demographic variables subject to household choice are held constant. What power these variables would have (assuming they were appropriately defined, which unfortunately they are not in this study) in a reduced-form equation, where the endogenous health and demographic variables are not included, is not clear from Longhurst's results.

Ryan et al. (1984) explain the heights and weights of a sample of rural Indian children, but they condition on the child's own weight and arm circumference in the height equation (or height and arm circumference in the weight equation) his or her energy and protein consumption, evidence of morbidity signs, family size, and the labor market participation of the mother. Ryan et al.

find a negative but insignificant association with mother's education, which is hardly surprising given their controls.

Martorell, Leslie, and Moock (1984) attempt to estimate a production function for anthropometric measurements and hemoglobin levels for children in Nepal. Regressors include types of foods eaten in the past week, value of crop output, and morbidity outcome variables, all endogenous to household choices.

Several more recent studies are not subject to the criticisms made in this chapter. These studies also look at the determinants of nutritional and health outcomes but either use instrumental variables techniques of analysis (if they are estimating nutrition/production functions) or estimate reduced-form equations while being careful not to include variables subject to household choice in the analyses. Rosenzweig and Schultz (1983) estimate a production function for birthweight using a very large (nearly 10,000) national probability sample for the United States. They did not examine the effects of maternal nutrition but, rather, the delay in seeking medical care from a doctor, whether the mother smoked while pregnant, birth order, and mother's age at birth. All are treated as choice variables with instruments including individual characteristics, such as education of the baby's parents, race, income, and community characteristics, ranging from availability of health services to variables representing regional economic activity. The production-function estimates show important differences between coefficients when input endogeneity is accounted for versus when it is not. In particular, the estimated effect on birthweight of visiting a doctor earlier in pregnancy is found to rise tenfold when instrumental variables are used to correct for mothers deciding when to first see a doctor. This is not surprising, since promptness in first visiting a doctor is probably positively correlated with potentially low birthweight, a hypothesis substantiated by Rosenzweig and Schultz's analysis. If not corrected for, this would lead to an underestimate of the impact of early doctor visits.

In a different study, Pitt and Rosenzweig (1985) estimate household-level morbidity production functions in which consumption of different foods is explicitly investigated. Prices of foods, some household assets, and community health characteristics are used as instruments. The food consumption data are at the household, not the individual, level, which is the reason for aggregating morbidity across household members. This is not ideal but nevertheless suggestive. The estimates show that a 10 percent increase from sample mean values in the consumption of fish, fruit, and vegetables reduces the probability of illness by 9, 3 and 6 percent, respectively, whereas a 10 percent increase in the consumption of sugar increases the probability of illness by almost 12 percent.

In addition to estimating the health/production function, Pitt and Rosenzweig estimate a reduced-form equation that provides a direct link between prices and health. This shows that a 10 percent reduction from mean values in the prices of vegetables and vegetable oil will decrease the probability of the household head being sick by 4 and 9 percent, respectively, whereas the same reduction in the price of sugar will increase the probability of illness by 20 percent, albeit from a low base. Presumably, the price effects result from changes in nutrient intake that result from the price changes.

Two other studies that use instrumental-variables techniques are Chernichovsky et al. (1983) and Blau (1984), who estimate structural equations for weight and height, respectively. Chernichovsky used data from the Narangwal experiment, while Blau used survey data from Nicaragua. Their instruments include socioeconomic variables, such as land cultivated, which do not directly affect body size. The Indian data show a positive effect of caloric intake on child weight after controlling for age and sex, while the Nicaraguan data highlight that larger families tend to have smaller children.

Horton (1986) estimated a reduced-form equation for child height, using data from the Bicol province in the Philippines. She finds positive effects of parental education and household wealth as well as of certain community investments, such as having piped water available in the community. The education effects control for parental heights, which should help account for unobserved family background factors that education could be proxying for. In a different study using the same data, Barrera (1988) shows the special importance of maternal education in affecting child height, also controlling for mother's height. He further finds that the impact of maternal education is greatest for children under two years old, which makes sense since these children are at the greatest nutritional risk. Barrera also looks at the interaction between community health investments and maternal education. Better community sanitation turns out to aid the children of less-educated mothers more than children of better-educated mothers, while being close to medical facilities is more beneficial to children of better-educated mothers. This suggests that community sanitation programs substitute for maternal education, while health facilities provide information that benefits those who can better process it (i.e., those having more education).

Behrman and Wolfe (1987) and Wolfe and Behrman (1987) correct many of the shortcomings of their earlier study of Nicaraguan children. They estimate reduced-form equations for height and weight, dropping variables such as breast-feeding duration, which are arguably chosen by parents. In the first study, they use data on education of the mother's parents, while in the second study, they control for the education of the mother's sibling. They find that the positive effect of maternal education disappears after controlling for education of either the mother or sibling of the child's mother. They interpret this to mean that family background characteristics, usually unobserved, and not education, are making the critical difference. However, for rural Ivory Coast and for Bicol, Philippines, Strauss (forthcoming) and Horton (1988), respectively, find that maternal education retains its positive effect even if one controls for both mother's height and unobserved household variables by use of a household-level dummy variable or household fixed-effects estimator (which Wolfe and Behrman [1987] use as well). Both Strauss and Horton are able to control for unobserved household effects because there are households with more than one young child in their respective samples. This procedure is equivalent to analyzing differences between heights of children in the same household and helps remove a major source of endogeneity of household choice variables. The procedure allows Horton to look at the effect of the child's birth order and to find that higher-order children are shorter, but by less if their mothers are better educated. Strauss, who also uses a household random-effects estimator (which accounts for correlation between children of the same household), finds strong effects of community water supply, endemic diseases in the community (particularly malaria), and the quality of community health services.

Finally, Thomas, Strauss, and Henriques (1987) examine child height, weight-for-height, and child mortality, using a very large sample from Brazil. They find very strong effects of parental education also controlling for parental heights, with mother's education having its largest impact for children less than two years old, which is similar to Barrera's finding. Household income is also positively related to both anthropometric and mortality outcomes, but its effect is comparatively small. Across regions, they find that the impact of both education and income is greatest in the northeast, the poorest area of the country. They also find that mother's height has an independent, positive effect on child mortality, even after controlling for parental education and household income. While mother's height is partly proxying other family-background variables, it does suggest a causal connection that has previously been examined only in bivariate relationships (see Chen, Chowdhury, and Huffman 1980, and Martorell et al. 1981).

Conclusions

This chapter has pointed out the great difficulties in interpreting much of the existing evidence concerning the magnitude and directions of interactions between nutrition, productivity, and other human capital development. While most of the concerns relate to the nonexperimental evidence, even experiments exhibit some of these flaws. Yet there is a small body of more reliable evidence that does suggest that higher current nutrient intake and perhaps larger body size (reflecting past intake) do enhance labor productivity when nutrient intakes are low, and for activities that use little capital. A few of these studies have been experimental, although, more recently, the beginnings of an econometric approach to analyzing survey data has emerged.

To date, the evidence has concentrated on what economists call a pure worker effect—that is, output rises as nutrition improves, holding other inputs constant. To the extent that better nutrition and health, both in the past and present, enhance decision-making capabilities (the allocation of inputs), the existing results will understate the economic impact of better nutrition. There is clear evidence (for example, Jamison and Lau 1982) that education raises farm profits, particularly when farmers face major changes. To the extent that better childhood nutrition raises both the likelihood and the outcomes of schooling, as hypothesized by Selowsky and Taylor (1973), the payoffs could be higher. However, there seems to be no reliable evidence on this question yet. Likewise, there is no convincing evidence concerning potential effects of better nutrition on the allocation and productivity of adult activities performed in the home, particularly of females. There is, however, a growing amount of reliable studies that point to the importance of parental education, especially maternal, in raising the heights and weights of young children. Although the magnitudes may sometimes be overstated because of the difficulty in measuring other family-background characteristics that may also affect children's nutritional status, the direction is clear. Exactly how the education effect works is not yet well established.

APPENDIX
An Example of Simultaneity Bias

Consider the following simple example. Let the production or earnings function be represented by

$$Q = \beta_0 + N\beta_1 + X\beta_2 + \epsilon,$$

where Q = output (earnings) or log thereof, N = nutrient intake, and X = a vector of other inputs. The β's are unknown parameters to be estimated, and ϵ is the unobserved disturbance. Decompose the disturbance into two components, one (v) specific to the observation, which represents firm (individual), specific characteristics affecting production (earnings), and the other (u), which represents pure randomness, not specific to an individual observation. As suggested in the text, the individual-specific component might include management ability or land quality. It is critical that it consist of variables known to the household but not to the analyst, while the pure noise component is unobserved by both the household and the analyst.

In this setup, nutrient intake is considered to be a household choice variable, while the vector of other inputs may or may not be. It is then possible to solve for the household's choice of nutrients in terms of all of the exogenous variables the household faces, including the individual-specific error term, which the household knows, but not including the pure noise, not known to the household. Doing this, we can express N as

$$N = \tau_0 + Z\tau_1 + V\tau_v + e,$$

where Z represents all the observed variables taken as given by the household (such as prices and community characteristics, which may include all or a subset of X), and e is a random disturbance representing variables both unknown to the household and the analyst. The elements of X that are endogenous may be similarly expressed.

To simplify the algebra, assume that X is a scalar. If ordinary least-squares method is used to estimate the production (earnings) function, the estimate of β_1 can be expressed as

$$\beta_1 = \beta_1 + \frac{S_{xx} \sum_i (N_i - \bar{N}) \epsilon_i - S_{nx} \sum_i (X_i - \bar{X})\epsilon_i}{S_{xx}S_{nn} - S_{nx}^2},$$

where the i's subscript observations $i = 1, \ldots, T$, the bars represent sample averages, and $S_{xx} = \sum_i (X_i - \bar{X})^2$, with S_{nn} and S_{nx} similarly defined. If the non-nutrient variable, X, is not a household choice variable, it will be uncorrelated with both V_i and u_i, that is, with ϵ_i. Nutrients, however, will be correlated with ϵ_i since the unobserved component v_i will influence the households' choice of N. Moreover, the correlation will very probably be positive, since households with higher output (earnings), holding measured inputs constant, will have higher incomes, some of which will be consumed as food. Since S_{xx} and $S_{xx}S_{nn} - S_{nx}^2$ (and their probability limits) are necessarily positive, one can obtain

$$\text{plim } \beta_1 = \beta_1 + \frac{\bar{S}_{xx}}{\bar{S}_{xx}\bar{S}_{nn} - \bar{S}_{nx}^2} \tau_v \sigma_v^2 > \beta_1,$$

where $\bar{S}_{xx} = \lim_{T \to \infty} \frac{1}{T} S_{xx}$ (which is assumed to exist and be finite), σ_v^2 is the variance of v_i, and τ_v is the coefficient of v_i in the nutrient intake equation and is positive, as argued above.

Now consider the case where X is endogenous. It, too, can be expressed as a function of the Z variables and v. In this case, the probability limit of β_1 has another term, which is proportionate to the product of the correlation of nutrients and X, $\bar{S}_{nx}$, and the correlation between X and v. The signs of these correlations will obviously depend on exactly which variables are used as X. Therefore, no generalizations are possible except to note that the bias (inconsistency) can be reduced (or enhanced) when other endogenous variables are included in the equation.

PART IV

Implications for the Design of Programs, Policies, and Research Needs

11 From Nutrition Planning to Nutrition Management: The Politics of Action

JOHN OSGOOD FIELD

Politics is relevant to nutritional improvement in two respects. Contextually, the international order of power and wealth influences the flow of resources among states, just as the political economy of specific countries is manifest in type of regime, strategies of development, and the distribution of benefits among different groups in society.[1] Functionally, the various policies of government crystallize goals, define programs, and set in motion processes of implementation that bring the state into contact with target groups in society.[2] The politics of context highlights features of the larger system that shape nutritional outcomes and pose opportunities and constraints when efforts are made to improve nutrition. The politics of action consists of these efforts.

This chapter focuses on the latter. The issue before us is how to incorporate political sensitivity into program design and, in so doing, to integrate political calculations with the economics of choice. Such an immense topic is simplified here by focusing on a single theme: the critical importance of management in harnessing political capital, steering nutrition policies and programs through the inevitable maze of government institutions, maintaining momentum as programs are activated in society, and cultivating positive responsiveness among intended beneficiaries.

The argument for adopting a management perspective rests on three propositions. First, management is the key to activating political commitment and amassing and sustaining available energy in support of nutrition programs. Without effective management, these programs are likely to fail inside of

---

1. See the large literature on imperialism, dependency theory, the North-South dialogue, and the new international economic order. Important studies of political economy include Ilchman and Uphoff (1971), Lappe and Collins (1977), and de Janvry (1981). With regard to nutrition, see Field (1983b). See also the intriguing literature on modernization and marginalization, some of which posits a direct link to malnutrition, e.g., Wisner (1980–81), Fleuret and Fleuret (1980), and Packard (1984).

2. See Hirschman (1967), Pressman and Wildavsky (1973), Korten (1980), Warwick (1982), and Rondinelli (1983); concerning nutrition, see Field and Levinson (1975), Field (1977, 1983a, 1985), Winikoff (1978), Pines (1982), and Pyle (1985).

government before they have had a chance to succeed in society.

Second, management is the sine qua non of effective implementation. Management relates program design to organizational capabilities and environmental realities. It is a vital factor in coordinating administrative action and generating understanding, trust, and participation in society. Management, in effect, is the functional embodiment of the "hiding hand" (creative adaptation) so essential to ultimate success.[3]

Third, management is the operational bridge between program strategies, structures, and processes. It is the essential instrument for attaining congruence in situations where incongruity is both common and devastating in its implications. Management is especially important in the scaling-up process because, in the conversion from small to large and from private to public, these three parameters of program success tend to diverge unless willfully held together.

The role of manager is a political role. Managers may influence economic decision-making by raising pertinent considerations outside the normal purview of economic analysis, but their more consequential function is to help economic and other technical expertise to survive and prosper in the real world. When confronting protein-calorie malnutrition, good management, more often than not, is the key to success. Its absence is a principal cause of failure.

The importance of management is addressed from three vantage points. First are the types of people whose influence is likely to make a difference in establishing nutrition programs, energizing them, sustaining them, and making them work. Second is the approach taken to implementation itself, particularly with regard to the relationship between planning and carrying out nutrition programs. The third point concerns the organizational coherence of nutrition programs: the extent to which strategies, structures, and processes are consonant with one another and with salient characteristics of the environment. We shall consider each in turn after a brief review of nutrition as a political issue.

Nutrition as a Political Issue

Nutrition is advantaged in policy space because it is relatively noncontentious—nobody is against good nutrition, and nobody favors malnutrition. Indeed, nutrition programs have the aura of being a social good from which everyone benefits, even though the actual beneficiaries are rarely more than a small subset of society. There is a symbolic value to nutrition as well. Politicians can curry favor with it or, alternatively, use malnutrition as a cudgel

---

3. The "principle of the hiding hand" is an insight advanced by Hirschman (1967). The hiding hand refers to the adaptations made by astute project managers in the face of unexpected opportunities and constraints. It is the salvation made possible by creative problem solving when programs experience difficulties that otherwise would dispose them to premature abandonment.

against their opponents in power.[4] National honor may be asserted or besmirched on the strength of how well-fed people seem to be.

Unfortunately, nutrition's assets as a political issue are outweighed by four deficiencies. The first is lack of salience. Nutrition is difficult to activate in government, and once activated, it is difficult to sustain as a priority commitment. More than most issues, nutrition requires constant energization.

Second, nutrition suffers from poor advocacy. People close to nutrition are seldom close to politics, while the capacity of the malnourished to make demands is as limited as their inclination to make them is sporadic (see Field and Levinson 1975). Advocacy arguments linking nutrition to national development lack credibility in the eyes of those inclined to view malnutrition more as a reflection of underdevelopment than as a barrier to development.[5]

Third, nutrition lacks policy definition and guidance. Even when governments adopt a nutrition policy, it is not clear exactly what they should do. Nor is it always clear how nutrition intersects with established programs in health, agriculture, education, employment generation, and the development of infrastructure. When in the 1970s multisectoral nutrition planning sought to harness, coordinate, and in effect subordinate different ministries behind nutrition goals, the results fell far short of expectations. Even today, in a period of intrasectoral initiatives, nutrition must still find its niche lest it continue to collide with other policies and programs.

Finally, there is the dilemma of knowing how much political commitment to nutrition exists in a government and how much of what appears to be there is real and of enduring significance. Nutrition is extremely susceptible to grandstand gestures and tokenism. Assessing commitment is rendered all the more difficult by nutrition's heavy reliance on international funding and technical assistance.

In sum, nutrition's high problematique[6] makes it a difficult issue to activate and organize. It may well take a hidden political agenda to make nutrition attractive to the leaders of poor countries or, at the very least, a good game plan, such as UNICEF's "GOBI-FFF" and Save the Children's "CBIRD methodology," to command attention and inspire confidence.[7] In any event, once the politics of purpose has anointed nutrition, the politics of process takes over. Here is where the management of nutrition becomes critical. The following three sections explain why.

4. Franklin D. Roosevelt, in his first inaugural address, discerned "one third of a nation ill-nourished, ill-clad, and ill-housed." Later he made explicit reference to hunger in his Four Freedoms. Other leaders who have invoked malnutrition or hunger include Lenin, Mao, Fidel Castro, and Ferdinand Marcos.

5. For example, see Wilford's (1975) reply to Belli (1971).

6. The notion of policy problematique is developed in Cleaves (1980).

7. GOBI-FFF stands for growth monitoring, oral rehydration therapy, breastfeeding, and immunization, and female education, family spacing, and food supplements (see Grant 1982). CBIRD is an acronym for community-based integrated rural (or responsive) development (see Save the Children 1980).

Who Is Important to Nutrition Policy and Why

Two types of people are vitally important to nutrition policy: top political leaders and a small but select number of senior administrators. These are the people who crystallize issues and authorize action. Operationally, the most important persons are those charged with managing nutrition policy within and across sectoral and federal jurisdictions.[8]

The principal role of political leadership at the national level—typically the president or prime minister—is to bestow grace on an issue, heighten its salience in both policy space and the public mind, adorn it with compelling language and imagery connoting vision as well as urgency, compassion as well as realpolitik, and send signals to relevant government institutions that this is an issue whose time has come. A corollary role is to sustain the issue over time by repeated identification with it.

If the national political leadership does not embrace the malnutrition problem and lend the charisma of office and person to press for a solution, little of consequence is likely to happen. It is very difficult for others to energize nutrition if the chief executive remains aloof. The probable outcome is dedicated professional effort resulting in marginal achievement, with nutrition left underfunded and undersupported in the administrative system.

Of course, even if the political leadership does embrace nutrition, there is no guarantee that effective action will ensue. Political commitment (or at least the appearance of it) is a necessary but in itself insufficient condition for launching a national nutrition policy. Granted that funding and organizational capacity are important as well, political sponsorship is essential to there even being a reasonably serious nutrition initiative, especially one that involves different sectors.[9] Similarly, if political sponsorship is confined to initial articulation that is allowed to lapse, what is started will have little prospect of maintaining, much less building, momentum.[10] Nutrition is the kind of policy issue that needs booster rockets to stay on the desired trajectory. Political commitment is not a sometime thing insofar as nutrition is concerned; it must be activated and exploited by professionals for the duration.[11]

Also vitally important are the most senior officials—the minister and his principal deputies—in ministries of agriculture and health, along with their counterparts at the provincial or state level. Agriculture and health are the two most prominent sectors so far as malnutrition is concerned—agriculture be-

8. This section is modeled, in part, on Warwick (1982).

9. As Field and Levinson (1975) wrote, "the question of political commitment is basic. With it, much can be done. Without it, nutrition activities are likely to be constrained by policy tokenism—another pilot project or general survey, a new crumb to the social sector, and so on."

10. This was the fate of Project Poshak in India (Gopaldas 1975; Pyle 1980).

11. See Pyle (1985) for the best analysis of political commitment regarding health and nutrition since Winikoff (1978) and Pines (1982).

cause of its direct relevance to the consumption side of malnutrition, and health because of its direct relevance to the morbidity side. Moreover, when political leaders express concern about malnutrition, it is usually the upper echelon in one or the other of these ministries, or both, who activate that concern by defining specific new initiatives responsive to it. In the absence of a strong mandate from the political leadership, senior officials in agriculture and health are the only persons in a position to energize the issue in a manner leading to action. There is a lesser generator, however, one that is difficult to sustain in the face of inertial forces and contrary purposes and priorities entrenched in the bureaucracy, especially when senior officials can expect only short tenure in their positions.

Senior officials in agriculture and health are also responsible for locating nutrition in the larger pantheon of ministry concerns, objectives, priorities, and programs. Ministries of agriculture, for example, must reconcile nutrition with ongoing preoccupations concerning the production, pricing, and marketing of food and nonfood crops. Ministries of health have to coordinate nutrition in the broader agenda of primary health care and maternal and child health care (MCH) services, which are themselves but a subset of the ministry's responsibilities. In each case, the need for integration is paramount if what is done in the name of nutrition is not to be countered by what is and is not being done on other fronts. In each case, too, the potential for conflict is considerable; left to fend for themselves, nutrition initiatives often clash with established objectives and procedures, with nutrition routines subverted and their effectiveness neutralized unless their introduction is well managed.[12]

In short, the reason why senior officials are important is not that they invariably perform their strategic role but the opposite, the fact that so often they do not. Yet they are the only ones who can perform it. Their inclination and ability to do so are important intervening variables linking political commitment to administrative action, powerfully conditioning the effort made and the results likely to be achieved. Nutrition activities that are added to established policies and programs but neither reconciled nor coordinated with them are extremely vulnerable.

The essential ingredient for success is strong issue management, which is itself a function of the energy breathed into nutrition by political leaders. So, too, is the tendency to create new institutions that become responsible for activating nutrition and that, ostensibly at least, influence how line ministries conduct their affairs.[13] Political leaders who invest prominently in nutrition often want trusted lieutenants at the helm and new stewardship mechanisms capable of moving the established bureaucracy. A critical function of the nutri-

12. The third section contains several illustrations of this point; see also Field, Burkhardt, and Ropes (1981).

13. A good example is the National Nutrition Council and the Nutrition Center of the Philippines.

tion manager then becomes that of marshaling the political resources made available to him, converting political sponsorship into influence of his own, and keeping political interest in and identification with nutrition alive over time. The shrewd nutrition manager exploits political patronage for his ends. He extracts legitimacy and power and he expends political capital to further nutrition goals.[14] Nutrition policy without nutrition management is mere rhetoric.

Three other types of people are circumstantially important to nutrition: middle- and lower-level operatives in administrative systems, opinion leaders in society, and clients.

Lesser officialdom—for example, agricultural extension officers, district health officers, clinic doctors, and village health workers—influence nutrition programs in terms of how they carry out their responsibilities and how they relate to target groups. The more discretion they have, the more important they are. On the other hand, the more removed an operative is from the center of initiative, the less likely he or she is to understand the purposes and rationale behind a program and the more likely he or she is to seek refuge in procedure.[15] The most important implementors of all—those who provide services to beneficiaries—often betray ambivalence toward the people they serve, especially when the providers are well-educated urban males and the clients are poorly educated rural females.[16] Nutrition programs have been compromised by clinic doctors unhappy with having to distribute food and keep new records (Allen and Koval 1982; Field, Burkhardt, and Ropes 1981). Nutrition suffers when it is presented to implementors as yet another responsibility (Allen and Koval 1982; Field, Burkhardt, and Ropes 1981; Underwood 1978). Incomprehension and lack of salience invite nominal compliance, routine behavior, even evasion. Add to these proclivities systemic breakdowns in coordination, supply, and supervision; interagency competition and intraagency factionalism; leadership instability and constant reassignment of personnel at all levels—and goal displacement becomes highly probable even when nobody actually opposes the policies or programs in question. In absorbing and deflecting energy, bureaucracies erode commitment as well.[17]

Opinion leaders are less important in nutrition than in most policy areas. In contrast to family planning, nutrition is not likely to offend nationalist intellectuals, clergy, and husbands (Warwick 1982). It must be rather rare for nutrition

14. Several prominent individuals have played this role with skill, among them Florentino Solon.

15. This is a problem of large bureaucratic systems that tend to routinize behavior. For two examples from India, see Heginbotham (1975) and Pyle (1985).

16. As noted by Esman and Montgomery (1980), "end-of-the-line field workers . . . are rarely motivated to break the cognitive, social, and physical barriers that separate them from the special publics" they serve. Problems of training, motivation, supervision, and support are most severe among those assigned to work with the poor in remote areas.

17. Goal displacement is analyzed in Merton (1949) and well illustrated in Banerji (1973), Heginbotham (1975), and Pyle (1985).

to elicit visceral animus, the usual problem being failure to generate any interest at all. Nevertheless, opinion leaders do exert a more subtle influence at times. They are well positioned to determine whether a concoction such as instant corn soy meal is really a food; whether commodities made available are for children, cronies, or animals; whether it is proper for young girls to receive training in order to provide health services in the community; and whether the government's clinics, extension services, and work schemes are to be accepted or not. Nutrition per se rarely stirs the passions, but opinion leaders will judge the merit of nutrition interventions on the strength of who provides them, how, and with what implications for local society (see Field 1977). Nurse midwives and other indigenous practitioners, in particular, may bad-mouth nutrition when it is offered through modern health services that threaten their status and livelihood.

Clients, like opinion leaders, are circumstantially important to nutrition, especially when program planners and implementors treat them as passive receptacles to be manipulated at will (Warwick 1982; Gwatkin 1979a; Vicziany 1982-83). Such treatment is usually a serious mistake. Target groups must see value in what is being taught or offered; they must trust and have confidence in the provider; and they must be willing to accept the opportunity costs of participation. By virtue of being dispersed, inarticulate, and unorganized, the beneficiaries of nutrition programs are extremely difficult to mobilize. Indeed, there is reason to believe that "persons living in a culture of subsistence respond poorly to a program organized around clinics and bureaucratized methods of service delivery" (Warwick 1982,81; see also Korten 1980; Maru 1981; Steinmo 1982; Field 1983a; Pyle 1985).

Again unlike family planning, nutrition does not engender personal fear and cultural rejection. Even so, food habits resist change. Food is a powerful cultural referent, and ill health is variously defined and explained. Sustained participation in a program requires positive choice repeatedly exercised. Willingness on the part of poor people to adopt new attitudes and behaviors concerning food, health, hygiene, and child-rearing practices is inevitably influenced by a congeries of objective conditions and subjective dispositions. Nutrition agents preoccupied with the flow of services and neglectful of the need to cultivate clients risk leaving demand unresponsive to supply.[18] When this happens, other things might not, such as people contributing resources of their own—money, food, labor—toward the attainment of program goals.[19]

In sum, the priority that a government gives to nutrition is determined

18. Social programs require greater demand mobilization than economic programs because they often need noneconomic incentives to motivate beneficiaries (Paul 1982). Precisely because most nutrition programs lack clear economic benefits, they must be promoted among those for whom they are intended. When client responsiveness is not cultivated, establishing and sustaining contact becomes difficult.

19. These themes are addressed in greater detail in Field (1985). For an analysis of successful client mobilization, see Field (1983a) and Pyle (1985).

principally by the posture taken by the political leadership and, to a lesser extent, by the initiative of senior officials in agriculture and health. Channeling political commitment into a well-conceived program of action is the responsibility of whoever is chosen to manage nutrition within the government. That person might be a minister or chief lieutenant, or he might be a personal representative of the head of state who holds no portfolio of his own.[20] The total number of initiators and program designers and managers is likely to be quite small. The relevant consideration is who they are, what authority they have, and what resources they command.[21]

If these are the people who set the tone and define the course, middle- and lower-level operatives perform the essential tasks. How well they do depends as much on the signals received, incentives provided, and resources made available as on technical competence. Poor understanding at this level and goal displacement born of job frustration compound deficiencies in management at higher levels. Moreover, when the system is confused or otherwise unable to function instrumentally and with sensitivity toward clients, responsiveness in society will be low. Unfortunately, these are common problems in government-administered nutrition programs. Effective management is at least a partial solution.

Implementation: The Weak Link

Well-planned programs that are conceptually sound and technically appropriate often fail in practice because little thought is given to problems of implementation.[22] Nowhere is this more apparent than in nutrition programs, although implementation is a weak link in much of the social sector from health care to agricultural extension. Implementation is subject to neglect by econo-

20. In larger countries, such as India and Indonesia, where policy initiatives are usually tested out at the state or provincial level before being expanded, the major actors in the process of reconciliation are often senior officials at the operative subnational level.

21. National planners—not mentioned here—have limited political influence, no operational authority, and only an indirect relationship to how funds are spent (Caiden and Wildavsky 1974). The same is true of scientists, scholars, and other experts. These types of people are advocates of policy and then, at most, servants of authority. The role of international assistance is more complex because of the different forms that it takes, the money involved, and the technologies made available. International assistance is an important catalyst and lubricant; it offers legitimacy as well as expertise, and it backstops as well as bankrolls. Programs of private voluntary organizations (PVOs) often fill vacuums and serve as demonstration models. As important as these contributions are, they count for little if a government is not prepared to embrace the issues involved.

22. This section is adapted from Field (1985), a review of the implementation literature with nutrition policy concerns in mind. This literature warns against complexity in program design, long time frames, and insensitive treatment of clients. It also takes issue with "machine theory" and its assumptions of plan and control, rationality and order, unitary authority, and many planning models. As an alternative, its emphasizes transactions featuring bargaining and exchange, conscious experimentation, learning and adaptation. See, in particular, Pressman and Wildavsky (1973), Warwick (1979, 1982), and Rondinelli (1983).

mists, who tend to focus on planning and evaluation, and to mechanical treatment by technical experts, whose inclination is to equate implementation with the application of their expertise. Few analysts look at delivery systems independently of what they deliver; most concentrate on the technologies and formal properties of an intervention.

There are several reasons why implementation is a useful organizing concept. It focuses on activity, not rhetoric. Accordingly, it deals with public policy where policy really counts, in terms of what is being attempted, how a given system has been organized to accomplish the stated objectives, and what is actually happening as a result. Implementation also shifts attention from the capital to the countryside, from the locus of initial decision to the environment of subsequent action. It is among the better rubrics for assessing the capacity of the political center to exercise its will on what is often a vast and diverse periphery (Huntington 1968; Migdal 1977; Shils 1975). Moreover, implementation draws attention to how different groups in society respond to governmental initiatives, and it highlights patterns of interaction between state and society that powerfully condition the success of public policy.

There are additional reasons for focusing on implementation. In countries with weak legislatures, limited traditions of interest group activity, and unstable political parties, the policy-adoption process frequently conveys the appearance of easy consensus and high commitment. Official pronouncements articulate an unchallenged national will, while planning commissions allocate resources "rationally" and "authoritatively." All that remains is for the bureaucracy to do as it is told within the constraints of the budget and its own functional capacity.

In most instances, the appearances are deceptive. Issues not considered or deflected in the policy-adoption process typically surface during implementation. Consensus is strained by the need to work out details, activate and coordinate different actors in the system, and ensure the regular and orderly flow of resources as the sine qua non of effective and sustained action. As the process unfolds, it becomes evident that not everyone in a position of authority agrees with the policy or accords it the same high priority. Previously latent opposition is aroused. Ministerial requirements must be reconciled and subnational officials must be harnessed. Often the public must be educated and even cajoled. Many things go wrong when the energizing impulses from the apex lose force when alternative and contrary definitions of purpose intrude, when resources are spread too thin, and when the tasks to be performed exceed the system's competence to perform them. When, on top of breakdowns within the system, one's intended beneficiaries respond to well-intentioned policy with hostility or indifference, that policy's problematique is increased all the more.

Implementation is clearly an important part of the policy process. Not only does it represent the activation of intent; unless conceptualized properly and then managed with skill, it functions as a source of delay, distortion, and derailment. To ignore implementation is to leave policy unprotected and at the mercy of hostile forces. To address it is to improve the likelihood that these forces can be held at bay or maneuvered around, thereby enhancing the prospects of success.

Considering implementation is especially worthwhile in nutrition, health, and related policy contexts infused with the complexities of popular will, motivation, beliefs, and behavior. Despite recent reforms, nutrition policy has been notoriously inattentive to the "black box" between planning and evaluation—much of which is implementation—while operational analyses of nutrition programs are few and of very uneven quality (see Scrimshaw and Wallerstein 1982; Pyle 1980, 1985; Field, Burkhardt, and Ropes 1981; Field 1983a). Moreover, nutrition programs typically exhibit a host of features that accentuate difficulties in implementation, such as reaching the preschool children of poor families on a sustained basis, relying on low-level operatives for initiating and maintaining contact with them, and resolving logistical problems of supply and delivery, particularly when the shelf life of foods and medicines is a factor. The topic of implementation is, therefore, a natural one for nutrition. To ignore it is to risk the persistence of unnecessary error, missed opportunities, and thwarted learning.

It is abundantly clear from the implementation literature that multisectoral nutrition planning, which dominated thinking and constituted the approach to alleviating malnutrition recommended during much of the 1970s, had little prospect of working. It proudly displayed all the programmatic features so devastating to effective implementation: ambitious goals, long chains of causality, organization charts comprising numerous actors, and multiple decision points (Pressman and Wildavsky 1973). The process of multisectoral nutrition-planning was conceptually elaborate and organizationally complex. It entailed long time frames and placed a premium on interministerial coordination. By reifying the planning exercise itself, it emphasized—in effect—central guidance and control over implementation. The emphasis on expertise left nutrition planning largely insensitive to clients, treating them as objects to be manipulated for their own good (Hakim and Solimano 1976; and Field 1977).

Additional liabilities abounded. Multisectoral nutrition planning often recommended complicated methodologies, novel technologies, and innovative but untested organizational forms (for example, nutrition planning institutes and cells). In the face of limited information and formidable logistics, it sought to engineer significant behavioral change and to predict impact. Operationally, the multisectoral approach to nutrition planning encouraged patterns of association incompatible with the compartmentalized structure of government (Field 1977; Pines 1982). It also aspired to predetermine the course of action along the lines of the discredited plan and control model of implementation, and, in so doing, it placed extraordinary loads on very weak institutions.[23]

In sum, multisectoral nutrition planning contradicted every lesson contained in the implementation literature.[24] As Pines (1982, 284) notes in his own review of the lessons of experience, "the leap from multisectoral analysis to multisectoral intervention, never a logical necessity, made nutrition planning seem more complex than was required." He goes on to mention that multisectoral institutions were even less necessary. And yet the approach was honorably and enthusiastically advanced with hardly a murmur of dissent until it ran squarely into the stonewall of reality.[25]

Today, most initiatives in the name of nutrition are occurring within the health and agriculture sectors, sometimes complemented by private voluntary organizations (PVOs). Nutrition is less a guiding principle—less still a rallying cry—than it used to be. Rather, it is something to be represented within established sectors, not planned for separately (Pines 1982). There continue to be discrete nutrition interventions, as there always have been; however, these have increasingly become components of primary health care and broader rural and agricultural development projects.

This retreat from multisectoral nutrition planning goes a long way toward meeting the concerns of the implementation literature. Nutrition interventions have become more simple, direct, organizationally coherent, and compatible with the rest of the policy agenda than was the case only a few years ago. Nevertheless, the warnings of the literature remain salient. Simplicity in design and operational requirements is a virtue, complexity a curse. If good planning is the key to identifying targets of opportunity, adaptability in implementation is the key to eventual success. Programs that treat their intended beneficiaries as mere receptacles or as objects of manipulation are unlikely to stimulate the understanding, trust, and support essential to sustained utilization.

Most important of all are sensitivity to contextual parameters and willingness to learn in the process of doing. Experimentation is a necessity when, in Rondinelli's words, "problems are not well-articulated, elements or charac-

23. See the discussion of operational capabilities in Field and Levinson (1975).

24. It also ignored the findings and theoretical inferences of the literature relating demographic outcomes—especially infant mortality and birth rates—to strategies of development (e.g., Kocher 1973; Rich 1973; Ratcliffe 1977). The result is that multisectoral nutrition planning exhibited insensitivity to contextual factors critical to success (Hakim and Solimano 1976; Field 1977, 1983b; Pines 1982), while offering little more than a standard set of specific interventions that were advanced indiscriminately—and naively—as serious responses to the malnutrition problem.

25. For early expressions of doubt concerning the feasibility of multisectoral nutrition planning, see Hakim and Solimano (1976) and Field (1977). McLaren (1977) equated it with "holistic daydreaming." Sadly, neither these authors nor any other nutrition planning experts seem to have been aware of the rich literature on planning and decision-making available at the time, which would have tempered expectations concerning what the multisectoral approach was likely to accomplish (e.g., Lindblom 1959; Waterston 1965; Chambers 1974; Caiden and Wildavsky 1974).

teristics of a problem have not been clearly identified, alternative courses of action have not been widely explored and their impacts cannot be easily anticipated" (Rondinelli 1983, 91). These are the usual conditions facing the nutrition policy profession, and they call for an implementation style that is incremental, flexible, and experimental.

Herein lies the rationale for the small-scale demonstration and pilot projects that characterize the health and nutrition fields in low-income countries. The need to test new technologies and combinations of services has long been considered essential to the determination of cost-effective approaches that might then inform public policy on a larger scale (Scrimshaw et al. 1967; Gopaldas 1975; Kielmann and Associates 1983). Ironically, the rationale for experimentation may actually increase as nutrition programs expand from their initial trial base. When the replication and expansion of nutrition interventions entail significant changes in scale, setting, stewardship, and scope of effort, as is usually the case, the character of the intervention changes as well. These four parameters of program success are as consequential as the formal inputs and technologies employed, and are addressed more fully in the next section.

The need for experimentation in nutrition programs does not end at the pilot or demonstration stage. It persists and may even be accentuated in large-scale programs, whether or not they originate from small-scale efforts. Establishing scientific validity is not the same as demonstrating operational feasibility. The former can be done at any level; the latter must be done at every level in which important features of the policy environment change. The now common call for an adaptive approach to development administration is every bit as cogent in national nutrition programs as it is in localized pilot projects. What a shame it would be if trial-run creativity in the new generation of nutrition initiatives results in mindless formula adoption as scaling-up or emulation of experience elsewhere is attempted. That would be yet another victory for machine theory, unnecessary and harmful in its consequences.

In sum, implementation is the real "soft underbelly" (Field 1977) of nutrition policy, as it is, in varying degrees, of other social sector efforts in which the process affects the outcome. In nutrition, the plan and control model based on the machine theory of implementation is a proven failure, and few "hiding hands" have come to the rescue. In nutrition, the "what to do"—often sensible— has been confounded by the "how to do it" range of concerns, which technicians seldom ponder in any depth. The danger is that, unless work on implementation is encouraged, the capacity of evaluation to detect failure is likely to outpace the ability of implementation to cause success (Wildavsky 1979).

Managing Congruence

Nutrition programs, like programs in general, possess five attributes that give them identity and condition their prospects for success: (1) goals or objectives; (2) strategies for attaining them; (3) structures that activate the strategies; (4) technologies employed in doing so; and (5) processes by which the appointed structures use the technologies and otherwise conduct their business on a regular basis.[26] Nutrition experts tend to focus their attention on the technologies available to attain the objectives being pursued; less attention is given to the operational parameters of strategy, structure, and process. Development administration theory now asserts the fundamental importance of these three parameters in fulfilling the promise offered by technical inputs and in realizing program objectives (Korten 1980; Paul 1982; Pyle 1985).

The basic argument is simple: the strategic use of manpower and material in the pursuit of development goals should be as consistent as possible with organizational structure and characteristic processes. Development administration theory posits the need for congruence among the strategic, structural, and process attributes of a program both in relation to one another and in relation to the environment into which the program is introduced. According to Paul (1982,124):

> There is a mutually dependent relationship among strategic, structural, and process interventions. Structures are intended to differentiate and integrate the tasks of organizations in a manner that is consistent with their strategy and environment. They need to be reinforced by organizational processes which give signals and influence the behavior of members so that the integration being sought is facilitated.

What Paul terms "strategic management" is the deliberate forging of congruence among these characteristics. Along with political commitment and the necessary economic resources, strategic management is a requirement of program success.[27]

These are salient considerations for the nutrition field, indeed for any field in which new strategies are activated through old structures whose procedures sometimes turn out to be inappropriate to the new strategies. Nutrition programs featuring the integrated delivery of food supplements, education, and primary health care require adaptive organizations with strong logistical networks and an effective capacity to engage and mobilize intended beneficiaries at the base of society. When these tasks are but part of a larger agenda that includes growth monitoring, oral rehydration therapy, immunizations, and family planning—as in UNICEF's GOBI-FFF strategy—the demands on organization and process are even greater. They are greater still when the client population is large, diverse, scattered, hierarchically layered, and parochial.

26. Also important are cultural attributes disposing to various patterns of behavior in administrative systems. See Heginbotham (1975) for a case in point. In the analysis that follows, culture is subsumed under process.

27. Korten's (1980) emphasis on learning in development administration entails forging a "fit" between program design, beneficiary needs, and the capacities of the assisting organization. "Fit" and "congruence" are parallel concepts. See also Hyden (1983).

"It is not unusual," notes Paul (1982, 194), "to find innovative and complex strategies being superimposed on weak and rigid structures." Multisectoral nutrition planning ran afoul of this problem a decade ago. More recent efforts to redirect rural extension to meet the needs of a large number of small farmers, as opposed to a relatively small number of large farmers, have taxed the capabilities of established extension services and called for altered procedures difficult to devise (Chambers 1974; Lele 1975; Heginbotham 1975; Leonard 1977; Johnston and Clark 1982). New initiatives in primary health care heralded at the Alma Ata conference in 1978 are proving especially troublesome for many formal health systems to implement effectively.[28] The new strategy calls for penetration of the countryside, active mobilization of women and children, the learning of new routines by clinic staff, and even recruitment of a new cadre of village health workers. Not surprisingly, physician-dominated health systems have found it easier to embrace the ideals of primary health care than to reorient their long-standing dispositions and procedures.

Specific nutrition-oriented components of the primary health care (PHC) strategy are especially vulnerable when existing health systems take on new tasks and try to perform them within established processes. For example, how many ministries of health actually handle food supplementation well? How many provide understandable and usable health/nutrition education to groups of mothers on a regular basis? How many have developed routines for the periodic monitoring of child growth in areas served by clinics? And how many have combined all three activities into an integrated, operationally coherent program linked to immunizations, oral rehydration therapy, and other preventive and curative responsibilities? The number must be minuscule, if only because these are extremely difficult things to do, especially over large areas and in the absence of strategic management and extensive training of personnel.

In effect, the new strategies in nutrition and health call for new processes and mindsets, particularly when they are implemented by agencies nurtured on a different agenda—for example, doctor-provided, clinic-based health care. Three examples from my own work overseas illustrate the incongruities that are likely to arise in the transition.

Example 1

Several years ago I was on a team visiting a very poor country where senior health officials showed us a large wall map of the country dotted with colorful pins representing health centers. Our hosts were proud of the fact that their network of clinics had attained 84 percent jurisdictional coverage of the population. They informed us that they were aiming for 100 percent coverage in the new five-year plan. We later learned that only about 10 percent of the rural

---

28. Maru (1981); Field, Burkhardt, and Ropes (1981); Steinmo (1982); and Pyle (1985) offer lucid illustrations.

population used the clinics despite their impressive dissemination. Being concerned with malnutrition, we wanted to think about ways of strengthening actual contact with the vulnerable groups and provision of services to them. Our hosts were unenthusiastic. They defined their mandate in terms of physical expansion. One doctor was outright Churchillian: "Give us the tools [money for new clinics, medicines, and staff], and we will finish the job." How rural malnutrition would be ameliorated by building new structures was not specified. Before our departure from the country, one counterpart explained that evaluating performance in terms of expansion was much safer than, and by implication preferable to, holding people responsible for impacting something as intractable as malnutrition. When the emphasis on primary health care is expressed in the building and staffing of rural clinics without simultaneous rethinking of how to engage target groups, the incongruities between strategy, structure, and process can undermine the entire effort.

Example 2

In another low-income country, the ministry of health recently adopted much of the new strategy of primary health care: growth monitoring, supplementary feeding, nutrition education, oral rehydration therapy, immunizations, and family planning. Several problems persist, however, reflecting past thinking and practice. None of these activities is coordinated with one another; each is an extra responsibility for an already overburdened staff left largely to cope on its own. Procedure continues to emphasize the role of the doctor and to deemphasize the role played by less formally trained practitioners, while the training of physicians continues to emphasize Western curative medicine, including specialization. Little attempt has been made to reach out from an impressive network of clinics into the villages they serve; health care remains clinical and passive. As a senior health official declared to me; "Our responsibility is to provide services; it is for the people to decide whether to use them." Thus, while many of the components of the PHC strategy are nominally on the agenda, most are being poorly performed, if performed at all. Organization and process have yet to catch up with the strategy.

Example 3

In a third low-income country where PHC has been embraced, my colleagues and I asked the doctors in charge of rural clinics to think about omissions or deficiencies in their training in light of their present responsibilities. This question elicited two responses with near uniformity over several pretests: "We were never instructed how to manage a health center," and "We were never taught how to relate to rural people." The doctors were acutely aware of the difference between their training and their duties (in effect, the difference between medicine and health care). Impressed, I took this "wisdom of the periphery" to the Ministry of Health, only to have an undersecretary dismiss the issue flatly. "The actual problem," he advised me, "is that our doctors are not adequately trained technically. They have fallen behind the standards of contemporary medicine as practiced in the West. Our principal task is to bring them back to snuff. The rest will sort itself out." Once again, a new priority to primary health care and new initiatives in MCH services are being contradicted by old dispositions and practices, including the mystique of expertise.

Experiences like these have led many to extol the vital role of village health workers. Such workers are agents of contact and mobilization as well as of service and referral. And yet the very fashionability of village health workers underlines the difficulties of reconciling new approaches with established procedures. Village health workers can be very effective when they are well-trained, supervised, and supported; all too often they are merely bureaucratized.[29]

Moreover, innovation at the base of the system is likely to be neutralized if not reinforced by adaptations in thinking and behavior at higher levels. As Korten notes, it is not sufficient merely to append village-level workers at the bottom of an existing structure that itself remains unchanged. Unless higher organizational levels are adapted to the new strategy implied by the introduction of village workers, the latter will "find themselves required to conform to inappropriate procedures and dependent on unresponsive support systems which leave them unable to accomplish the tasks expected of them" (Korten 1980, 499). Reconciling established structures and processes to new strategies, actors, and tasks may be a generic problem in government, but it has special implications for the effectiveness of nutrition programs grounded in the delivery of services, however they are provided.[30]

When strategy and structure are incompatible, one solution is to create new structures. Structures that are ill-disposed to carry out the declared strategy will distort the processes required by that strategy. Unfortunately, creating new structures is extremely difficult in health care delivery; the usual approach is to use the existing system and hope that new tasks will be the cutting edge for more general reform (Field, Burkhardt, and Ropes 1981).

A second solution is to alter the strategy. In the new generation of nutrition and health interventions, however, both the technologies available and the

29. See Esman and Montgomery (1980) and Pyle (1985). To Jelliffe's characterization of village health workers as "skinny Hercules" (pers. com.) can now be added Johnston and Clark's (1982) reference to their "overloaded impotence."

30. A critique by C. Gopalan, India's eminent nutritionist, quoted in Paul (1982), is germane. "We are also beginning to learn that nutrition and other welfare programs among poor communities cannot succeed if they are carried out as highly centralized operations. There must be effective decentralization not only with respect to responsibility for implementation, but also with regard to decisionmaking. The Nutrition Program over which we have spent millions of rupees largely failed for this reason. The pattern of the program must be tailored and adapted to suit local needs and must be based on the felt needs of the community."

strategies for applying them are so intertwined that the former are unlikely to work if the latter are diluted. The challenge is to implement new strategies effectively by adapting old structures to new tasks and by developing new processes supportive of them (see Paul 1982; Korten 1980). Nutrition programs conceived by experts and then parachuted onto unsuspecting populations are not necessarily doomed to failure, but they are asking for trouble if they rigidly adhere to organizational orthodoxy.

The final hurdle concerns the scaling-up process itself. Most of the best examples of effective nutrition programs are small experimental projects managed by private persons or organizations (Gwatkin, Wilcox, and Wray 1980; Field 1983a; Pyle 1985). As scale expands from small to large and as stewardship shifts from private to public, issues of design, replicability, and institutional learning arise that go to the heart of strategy-structure-process congruence.

Intervention Design

Demonstration and pilot projects are not the same; neither are their implications for larger programs. The two differ in both design and purpose. Confusing them leads to false expectations followed by disappointment.[31]

Demonstration projects are intended to show that something can be done in an environment or that a given goal—for example, reducing infant mortality—can be attained by virtue of doing certain things in certain ways. Accordingly, the inputs and operational characteristics of demonstration projects are often exceptional and extremely difficult to replicate on an expanded scale.[32] By contrast, a pilot project represents the humble beginnings of what is to be a larger program in which the input ingredients and operational characteristics—including management quality and style— remain much the same as the effort unfolds. A pilot project is supposed to be a complete or near-complete microcosm of the macroprogram, the only significant difference being scale. Demonstration projects, on the other hand, typically feature such distinctive managerial, manpower, logistical, and process attributes that replication is seldom even possible. Nevertheless, when the model of a demonstration project is blindly assumed to be appropriate for a large-scale program, these attributes usually assert themselves with devastating effect. Indeed, a basic problem with many so-called pilot projects is that they are "pilot" in technology only and "demonstration" in all or most of their other parameters. The more that this is so, the greater the problem of scaling-up.[33]

---

31. Portions of the discussion to follow have been adapted from Field (1985).

32. To illustrate, eight of the ten health/nutrition projects whose accomplishments are highlighted in Gwatkin, Wilcox, and Wray (1980) were essentially research projects carefully designed and administered by scholars.

33. Rondinelli's (1983) discussion of demonstration projects emphasizes advocacy more than establishing potential. Johnston and Clark (1982) attribute the tendency to treat pilot projects as tests of development policy hypotheses as a case of misguided "physics envy."

For pilot projects to be useful as policy experiments, they must be realistic in their operational characteristics. This means that the total approach—the "who," "how," and "what"—must be transferable (Sussman 1980). Two tendencies common to nutrition programs make this difficult. One is the need to show results. The more important it is to achieve impact or to test the capacity of an experimental intervention to obtain the desired results, the more likely it is that the experiment will resemble a demonstration project. The case is similar with the second tendency common to nutrition programs, the high probability of their encountering organizational, logistical, and motivational difficulties. The more they do, the greater the likelihood that managers will introduce special coping mechanisms in order to keep the experiment on track; and the more this happens, the lower the likelihood that the experiment will function as originally intended. Once again, the pilot project becomes a demonstration project.

What Is Replicable, What Is Not

Typically, demonstration projects are not replicable for the reasons noted. With pilot projects, it depends. The strategies of pilot projects are replicable, pilot structures very much less so.

Here, too, the process of scaling-up has profound implications. When replication means expansion, as it does in moving from prototype to program, two critical parameters change: scale and setting. The level of effort increases enormously with expansion, with extensivity replacing or being added to intensivity. Material requirements and personnel recruitment are affected, as are organization and management. All become more complex and demanding. Similarly, the relationship between a program and its clients is subject to change as the number of people to be served increases. When expansion entails moving into new ecological, economic, and cultural environments, the variety of people and their circumstances also change.

In short, replicability in the form of expansion must include structural differentiation capable of matching new logistical requirements, the diversity of beneficiaries, and related management concerns. Pilot projects may be a powerful device to design and test new service concepts, but the structural requirements of replicating a service on a significantly larger scale cannot be learned from the pilot's limited experience (Paul 1982). This is a telling point of importance to nutrition experts who would like to see successful pilots blossom into regional and national programs.

Institutional Learning

When stewardship shifts in the scaling-up process, as from voluntary agency to government, a major parameter that is prone to accentuate strategy-structure-process incongruities changes (see Pyle 1985). One reason is that these three operational components tend to be developed together and in relation to one another. When a different organization with its own procedures adopts a strategy proven effective by others, it must accommodate itself to the functional requirements of that strategy. To adopt means to adapt or fail.

Unfortunately, government emulation of PVO programs in health, nutrition, and community development is usually restricted to their formal properties: the types of intervention and the specific technologies, categories of workers, even the organization chart. Rarely does emulation extend to management style and process variables, and rarely does it produce comparable results (Sussman 1980; Pyle 1985).

Among the reasons for breakdown are shifts in scale, setting, stewardship, and scope of effort. The stewardship factor is not simply that different organizations function differently, granted that voluntary agencies and governments tend to function very differently indeed (Field 1983a). An additional consideration has to do with learning. Successful PVO interventions entail a significant amount of learning and adaptation over time, and they are set up with this approach to problem-solving in mind. Planners, managers, and learners tend to be the same people (in government, they tend to be different people). Moreover, the lessons learned go beyond formal properties to include management, process, and motivational features. In effect, the feedback loops are complete, and the process is integrated.

The problem with a shift in stewardship is that the emulating organization has little experience with the new strategy and less understanding of why it works so impressively. It adopts the blueprint but neglects the operational lessons that are essential to success. Korten (1980, 499) captures the dilemma well:

> The effectiveness of a given program design is at least as dependent on the presence of an organization with a well-developed capacity to make it work as it is on the specifics of the design itself. This is an important reason why pilot project results produced by one organization are seldom replicated by another.

It is also a reason why research projects in the field yield findings that are difficult to translate into effective program design. Again from Korten (1980, 499):

> Unfortunately, their resemblance to the early field experiences on which major successful programs have been built ends there. Carried out as research studies, they are typically under the direction of a special research team, possibly from a university or research institute, and are carried out apart from the direct operational control of any operating agency that might apply their findings on a larger scale. After a predetermined time, the project team is disbanded and its leaders return to the university to analyze and publish their data on the presumption that the final blueprint was the key to whatever results were obtained. *What remains is an idea reduced to paper* [emphasis added] while the operating organization—the vibrant social organism which encompassed the skills, com-

mitment, knowledge, and systems required to give the idea life and adapt it to local circumstances as required—has been discarded.

Shades of the three-village study in Guatemala, Narangwal, Imesi, Kavar, Etimesgut, even Poshak, and so many other celebrated field trials of nutrition and health interventions! When learning is divorced from management, it is indeed "reduced to paper," and management suffers.[34]

Considerations of intervention design, replicability, and institutional learning reveal how fraught with difficulty the scaling-up process is. They also reveal how rare genuine pilot projects are. Moving from small to large alters many essential characteristics. Shifting stewardship from private to public confounds matters further. When all is said and done, the French proverb really holds in reverse: the more one tries to keep things the same, the more different they actually are. Successful adaptation requires strategic management.

Conclusion

Now that nutrition policy is no longer dependent on grand conceptual designs and ambitious multisectoral combinations, it is time for the emphasis on nutrition planning to yield in favor of a new emphasis on nutrition management. The promise of successful intervention lies not so much in planning nutrition programs as in managing the new strategies that exist and in making them work in live situations. Good management includes both the planning for and implementation of action. It is the operational link between the desirable and the feasible, and between the economically rational and the politically possible.

Management is not a panacea; good management is no substitute for bad policy. Nor is it likely to be adequate compensation for an adverse political economy. Rather, it must be nurtured, encouraged, and given rein to develop. Nevertheless, the role of management in bringing nutrition goals to fruition is compelling. Management is the administrative crystallization of purpose, custodian of policy, and orchestration of action. Few nutrition programs can succeed without it.

Finally, although managers are not politicians in the formal sense, they must function politically nonetheless. How well they do so is likely to influence nutritional outcomes, especially in low-income countries where there are so many obstacles to overcome, where a plan by itself is "an object with no velocity" (Warwick 1979), and where even "the best structure is only inert opportunity" (Johnston and Clark 1982).

---

34. A study of nutrition programs supported by the World Bank indicates that they are better learning experiences, precisely because responsible officials are prominently involved in the experimentation (Berg 1984).

12 Integrating Political and Economic Factors within Nutrition-Related Policy Research: An Economic Perspective

URBAN JONSSON

Nutrition-Related Policy Research

It is important to distinguish between policies and strategies. Policies are set by the highest political authority of a country—the parliament, the president, or the party in a one-party state—and reflect its ideology. They are usually long term and of a normative character. Policy goals subsume a set of impact objectives for economic growth, internal and external economic balances, income distribution, levels of literacy, mortality rates, etc.

Strategies outline the ways to achieve policy goals. A food policy may define national food self-sufficiency as its main goal, with specific conditions on land ownership, income distribution, etc. A food strategy may consist of specific recommendations about crop mixtures, use of fertilizers, irrigation, prices, etc. An infant mortality rate of 50 per 1,000 live births is a policy goal; the training and deployment of village health workers is part of a strategy.

Strategies are most often worked out by government ministries or parastatal bodies. In most countries, they change more often than policies. In Tanzania, the policy of "socialism and self-reliance" has not changed since it was declared in 1967, but the strategies to achieve its goals have changed several times since then.

Programs, finally, describe how to achieve a set of outcome objectives through a specified set of inputs and outputs. At best, a strategy is translated into a limited number of programs so that the specified impact objective subsumes all program objectives—that is, if all the outcome objectives are achieved, then the impact objective will also be achieved.

Policy research is defined as a systematic process (1) to assess and analyze the relevance, effectiveness and efficiency of existing strategies to achieve the goals of a given policy; (2) to define criteria and recommendations for the development and design of alternative strategies to achieve the goals of a policy; and (3) to assess and analyze the effect of all policies on the achievement of nutrition policy goals.

Nutrition-oriented policy research requires a detailed understanding of the causes of malnutrition in society, but it is too often based on reductionistic models that reflect the bias of the researcher. Agricultural economists, for example, often tend to equate malnutrition with inadequate aggregate food production, and many national food strategies are also based on the same assumption (Tanzanian Ministry of Agriculture 1984). Except for drought-stricken crisis areas, the correlation between malnutrition and food production or even food availability is very low or nonexisting. Much of this policy research is, therefore, not valid and often misleading, giving a false impression that national food and agriculture strategies are nutrition-oriented.

Such research also illustrates the lack of communication and dialogue between economists and nutritionists. The two groups seldom work together at national and subnational levels to develop strategies to improve nutrition. Often people may agree on the existence of a problem—for example, high infant mortality rate or malnutrition—but they may disagree on its cause. This has serious implications. If there is disagreement on what causes the problem, there is probably also disagreement on which strategy should be adopted to alleviate it. In order to assess and analyze a problem so that the maximum number of people understand it, it is important to make the underlying values and assumptions as explicit as possible, by the formulation of a conceptual framework.

Understanding the Causes of Malnutrition

The Need for a Conceptual Framework

In trying to analyze the causes of malnutrition, it is easy to arrive at the conclusion that everything depends on everything. Most analyses are sectoral-biased, and only occasionally have multisectoral nutrition-oriented programs been implemented. It is also a well-known fact that nutritional status is often more influenced by policies and strategies that are not commonly identified as nutrition-oriented than by those that are. Nutrition-related policy research has a big challenge to address all policies, whether they are labelled nutrition-oriented or not.

For a long time, nutrition-oriented research has been polarized. Natural scientists have been preoccupied with increasingly complex analyses of human nutrient requirements and the development of diets to fulfill these, while social scientists have seen malnutrition as a poverty phenomenon that could not be eradicated until development policies were enacted. Both perspectives are necessary and complementary.

To facilitate a multidisciplinary dialogue, there is a need for a unified conceptual framework. Such a framework should accommodate all important aspects of the nutrition problem and provide guidance for its assessment and analysis, as well as the design of actions to alleviate it.

The following criteria have been considered in the development of such a conceptual framework:[1]

1. It should reflect both the biological and humanistic (social, cultural, etc.) aspects of the nutrition problem (nontraditional paradigm).
2. It should facilitate the identification and analysis of the causes of malnutrition and include a set of hypotheses concerning the most important ones.
3. It should accommodate the potentially multisectoral nature of the situation—that is, it should be comprehensive enough to accommodate all possible main determinants and flexible enough to deduce the most important determinants in a given context (integrative and contextual paradigm).
4. It should facilitate a dialogue among people of different disciplines, especially between natural and social scientists.
5. It should facilitate the consideration of the time dimension.
6. It should accommodate the analyses of processes occurring at different levels of society.
7. It should be easy to popularize and so facilitate communication, training, and mobilization (service-oriented paradigm).

Proposed Conceptual Framework

The conceptual framework presented in this chapter has been developed for a better understanding of the causes of death in children between 6 months and 5 years of age. Malnutrition is recognized as both an important cause of child deaths and the result of several causative processes in society. The framework has three important dimensions or aspects: level of analysis, level of society, and time.

Level of Analysis

In many countries, a specified reduction in infant or child mortality rates is stated as a policy goal. Deaths of children are the final result of a long sequence of interlinked causes, the understanding of which comprises the first level of the analysis. The immediate causes of deaths of young children are primarily malnutrition and disease. Malnutrition is almost always a combined result of various diseases and dietary inadequacies interacting in a mutually reinforcing manner. In a given context, it is possible to identify the immediate causes of death of an individual child or of a higher child death rate in a community. An example might be diarrheal diseases in combination with low energy intake. With this information, actions could be taken to reduce the child death rate by promoting oral rehydration therapy and food supplementation.

Nutrition and health policies and strategies are often geared toward the achievement of impact objectives at this level. However, they often have only a

---

[1] For further discussion and definitions, see Tornebohm (1976).

short-term effect. If long-term improvements are to be secured, it will be necessary to address the causes of, for example, low energy intake and diarrheal diseases.

Dietary inadequacies might be caused by a low supply of food or by inadequate time to prepare food or feed children. Similarly, deaths from diseases may result from one or a combination of causes, such as lack of health services, poor water supplies and sanitary environment, poor food hygiene, or inadequate child care. Causes of malnutrition at this level are underlying causes. They are numerous, usually interrelated, and can be considered as failures to satisfy the basic needs of children and women. They may be grouped in three clusters: mother and child health services, household food security, and child care.

In order to assess the relation between morbidity and mother and child health services, attention should be given to health service coverage and actual utilization, especially of preventive and promotive services. Such an assessment will automatically guide the analysis into questions of affordability, community participation, and health worker's performance.

Several studies have shown that adequate food availability at the household level is a necessary but insufficient condition for the adequate dietary intake of young children. This can be understood if food intake is divided into the following components: number of meals per day; amount of food per meal; energy and nutrient density of the food consumed; and utilization of energy and nutrients. The number of meals per day is influenced by the availability of food in the household, fuel, time for preparing the meal and feeding the young child, etc. The amount of food per meal is influenced by food availability, method of preparation, and the age of the child. Energy concentration is determined by the bulk of the food, how it is prepared, and how the diet is composed. Utilization, finally, is affected by type of food, method of preparation, and the presence of illness.

The type and quality of child care influences the prevalence of both disease and malnutrition among children. The most important health-related factors are (1) utilization of health services, (2) provision of proper home care, and (3) provision of a safe environment for the children.

Nutrition-related factors include (1) breast-feeding frequency, (2) capability to prepare meals and feed children many times per day, and (3) capability to select the most appropriate foods available to meet the nutritional needs of children. By disaggregating the underlying causes in this way, the analysis becomes more operational.

Most of the underlying causes of death in young children reflect an unequal distribution of income, availability of services, and educational and production opportunities. In a specific context, it may be possible to identify which causes and relationships are the most important ones and which can be addressed with the available resources.

The production, distribution, and consumption of commodities and services depend on the socioeconomic structure of society. There is no society in which production is fully determined by basic human needs. In some, the maldistribution is extreme, with excessive poverty and great material wealth existing side by side. The determinants of the reasons for maldistribution of commodities and services in the community and within the household must be analyzed and understood. They comprise the basic causes of hunger and malnutrition. Most attempts to conceptualize them—for example, Joy, Cravioto, Call, and Levinson (Berg, Scrimshaw, and Call 1971)—have not done so adequately.

The basic causes are related to the production process and can be divided into groups that reflect the various conditions of production. Ecological constraints, especially the unreliability of rainfall, and factors such as the availability of tools, natural resources, technology, knowledge, and skills form a system that defines potential production at a given point in time.

Existing property relations are the most important determinants of the social conditions of production. Ownership or access to the means of production, the division of labor, and the power structure of society determine the economic structure of society. They form structural constraints of the economy and must be understood in any policy analysis. However, production, distribution, and consumption are also influenced by political and ideological factors.

Political factors primarily reflect the structure and the function of the state. They include such important issues as national policies for agriculture, health, education, income and prices, and the existing legal systems. In most developing countries, the ideology of the state coexists with traditional ideologies, such as religion, culture, and beliefs. Both political and ideological structures are reflected in formal and nonformal institutions that provide basic services or promote proper practices regarding, for example, food production and child care. With respect to basic services, nonformal structures—for example, extended families, traditional birth attendants, and age-group formations—play a very important role.

It is necessary to consider the above in analyses of the situation of children and women, because although an analysis of specific problems and their causes might indicate what should be done (factual analysis), it does not indicate how or by whom (operational analysis). These structures are at the interface between the underlying and basic causes within the conceptual framework because they reflect the socioeconomic superstructure and the economic systems operating at the level of basic causes. It is not until the basic causes of deaths of young children are attacked that a permanent improvement of the condition of children and women can be achieved. Even so, much can be done on a short- or medium-term basis to deal with the immediate and underlying causes (see figure 12.1 for a suggested conceptual framework).

FIGURE 12.1 Causes of deaths of young children

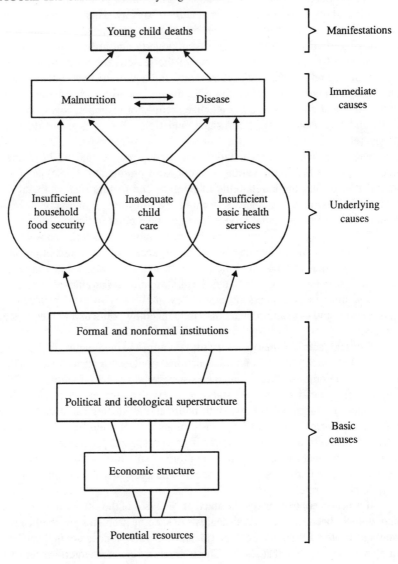

Level of Society

The second dimension of the conceptual framework is the level of society at which the causes are operating. The causes of maldistribution of food, for example, may vary. At the national level, ecological causes may dominate, while at the village level, socioeconomic causes may be most important.

Before ameliorative actions can be designed, the level of society at which the most important causes occur must be identified, and an assessment of the resources commanded at this level, and by whom, must be made. Most policies are formulated at the national level, while the implementation of these policies often requires reallocation of human and other resources at subnational levels.

Time

Time is the third and last dimension of the proposed conceptual framework. Any society at a specific point in time is, to a large extent, a result of what it was before; it is part of a historical process. Many determinants of young child deaths and malnutrition show a seasonal variation. Food availability, water supply, and diseases, such as malaria, vary with time. The seasonal variation of women's work-load also affects child survival. The time dimension at the individual level is also important to consider. The etiology of hunger, malnutrition, and disease often shows that these problems can be traced to time before conception.[2]

The Impact of Policies and Strategies on the Nutritional Status of Young Children

Most national policies and strategies affect the economy, and economic policies are generally adopted in order to achieve certain goals of economic growth and equity. Strategies that are adopted to increase production and maintain external economic balance also affect income distribution, trade, and agricultural development. In addition, the desire to provide adequate social services makes it difficult to achieve internal economic balance, resulting in large budget deficits, increased bank borrowing, and inflation.

Policies and strategies may affect different levels of society to a larger or lesser extent and may be divided into two broad groups. The first directly affects distribution and consumption of commodities, the most important of which are income and consumer price policies (e.g., minimum income, the tax system, subsidies, etc.) Most of these policies are difficult to administer and are often not targeted for specific groups. In analyzing their impact on nutrition, it is sometimes more important to identify who controls production at the household level than to assess the household income as such. Studies in Tanzania have shown that when a village grows economically, malnutrition sometimes increases. This can be understood if the causes of malnutrition at different societal levels are identified (Ljungqvist 1981). Food subsidies are expensive and primarily benefit the urban population. They are difficult to target and must be combined with some rationing system if the food supply is low, which is most often the case in Africa, for example.

2. A more detailed description of this conceptual framework is given in UNICEF (1990).

The second broad group of policies affects the economic base and is therefore more important in the long term. They influence one or more of the following: (1) ecology and technology, (2) social conditions, and (3) ideologies.

Policies targeted toward ecological and technological change affect nutrition in several ways. In many countries, the agricultural production base is threatened by deforestation and land erosion. Policies and strategies on land use are therefore of great importance. The survival of many agropastoral societies requires a proper and viable balance between people, cattle, land, and water resources. Too often governments have not been aware of this delicate balance and have adopted policies that have resulted in the gradual breakdown of the ecological system.

Resettlement of groups of people has often been an important strategy for facilitating the universal provision of health and education services, although in some areas this is not possible, given the available technology (Andersson and Andersson 1984). The social conditions of production and the prevailing ideologies of the communities also affect resettlement. People may be moved overnight, but their social system, customs, and beliefs may remain for another generation.

The introduction of new technologies may alter the ecological balance in many ways. New seeds may require more reliable water sources, plowing by tractor may reduce the quality of topsoil, and chain saws may accelerate deforestation.

All these policies and strategies affect the production base, often resulting in lower carrying capacity. This leads to decreased food production and is a threat to household food security, an important determinant of dietary intake and nutrition.

Policies that affect the social conditions of production also affect nutrition. The ownership and control of the means of production and appropriation patterns vary considerably among societies. The different modes of production—peasant, private farm, state, commercial, or cooperative—not only influence what is being produced but also, to some extent, for whom. Surplus production generates money. The extent to which this extra money is used to improve the condition of children and women is determined by whoever controls the income. In the African context, the prevailing sexual division of labor is important, as most food production is controlled by women, while cash production is dominated by men. A shift toward production for sale, therefore, very often decreases women's command of resources and tends to affect child care and nutrition negatively (Mascarenhas 1984).

The effect of technological change is especially important in this context. New technologies most often affect both the sexual division of labor and the control of resources and income. Strategies on the expanded use of oxen, water supply, milling technologies, etc. should be assessed from both these aspects.

From the nutritional point of view, priority should be given to technologies that both reduce the work load of women and increase their control of household resources. Such technologies will increase their time for child care and provide them with better opportunities to obtain commodities and utilize services.

Policies can also affect nutrition through changes in ideology. Most new states have adopted a national ideology that is partly enforced through legislation and partly communicated through the educational system. In most countries, the state tries to influence people to adopt an ideology that legitimizes state intervention.

A recent analysis of the causes of young child malnutrition in Tanzania found the persistent subordination of women to be most important (Tanzanian Government/UNICEF 1985). The subordination of women is in many societies legitimized by existing traditional ideologies. Even if the legal system gives equal rights to women and men, interpretations of the law still reflect male dominance. The fundamental inequality between the sexes, which is typical in most African societies, is probably best reflected in the institution of polygamy (Meillassoux 1972). The neglect of women in the research and design of strategies and programs for improved nutrition policies has contributed to low impact during implementation. It is not enough to hire a token female consultant—these issues must be emphasized and understood by all policy-oriented researchers.

Priorities of Research on the Political Economy of Nutrition Improvement

From the beginning of this century, new discoveries in biochemistry provided new knowledge about the dietary needs of human beings that was soon systematized in a new scientific discipline—human nutrition (Atwater and Benedict 1899). For a number of decades, nutrition scientists were preoccupied with investigating the human requirements for all possible nutrients and their combinations, the precise nutrient composition of foods, and all possible relationships between malnutrition and disease. Sophisticated instruments were developed to increase accuracy and to study new biological and biochemical processes. There is no doubt that the scientific paradigm for human nutrition is a valid and powerful approach to the problems defined by most nutrition scientists.

During the 1960s, the enormous problem of hunger and malnutrition in the Third World was discovered. Some nutritionists broadened their scope of interest from problems in the human nutrition science to the problem of malnutrition in society. New departments of nutrition in developing countries or international nutrition were established at universities; conferences were arranged; books and reports were published—all concentrating on the problem of hunger and malnutrition in the developing world. The problem of malnutrition was reduced to a problem of the inadequate consumption of protein (Science Advisory Committee 1967; United Nations 1986). This theory fit well into the conventional wisdom of development theory and legitimized the donor agency philosophy: "they" lack something "we" have—let us give it to them. The problem of malnutrition in the world had been reduced to an uncontroversial technical problem.

Increasingly, however, this approach was challenged. The first attack came from some nutrition scientists. The intensive debate that was triggered by McLaren (1974) in the *Lancet* accused the "protein-school" of trying to avoid a discussion on the maldistribution of food. Harper, Payne, and Waterlow (1973) made it even more clear:

> The most likely effect of such statements (for example, the cause is the lack of protein) is simply to distract attention from a broad-based attack on the social and economic deprivation of which ill-health and malnutrition are both symptoms.

The United Nations World Food Conference was held in 1974, a year when world hunger had reached an unacceptable level. In the main document adopted by the conference, the views on the causes of hunger now reflected a more politically conscious perspective (FAO 1974):

> The situation of the people afflicted by hunger and malnutrition arises from their historical circumstances, including social inequalities, including in many cases alien and colonial domination, foreign occupation, racial discrimination, apartheid and neocolonialism in all its forms, which continue to be among the greatest obstacles to the full emancipation and progress of the developing countries and all the people involved.

This new awareness triggered an increasing interest among social scientists to study the problem of hunger and malnutrition in society. Scientists within such different fields as public health, agriculture, education, demography, economy, anthropology, and political science extended their research interests into the field of nutrition. Soon a number of subdisciplines were established—for example, nutrition education and nutrition authropology. (Most of these subdisciplines are reductionistic in the sense that they primarily form a part of the dominant paradigm of the "mother science.")

The first priority for research on the political economy of nutrition is therefore to develop conceptual models (or paradigms) that are nontraditional, integrative, contextual, and service-oriented. Some criteria for such a conceptual framework were given in the beginning of this chapter.

Most nutrition and other policy research in Africa is done by foreign institutions. Models, research methodologies, and protocols are often developed outside the country of study, with little or no attention given to the specific context of the country. For example, most economic policy analyses still assume that all peasants try to maximize their cash income. This is simply not true. If the researchers had direct African experience, they would know that cash income is just one of several determinants of individual satisfaction and that income satisfaction as an individual goal is very common. Therefore, the big challenge for research on the political economy in general and on nutrition in particular is to break out of the "normal science" as defined in the Western countries. We can no longer assume that peasants in a small African village behave the same way as people in industrialized countries.

The invisibility of women is perhaps the most significant characteristic of present policy research on agriculture, food, and nutrition. In the context of Sub-Saharan Africa—where the majority of people live in subsistence or semi-subsistence agriculture—an improved understanding of the subordination of women in society should have a very high priority in research on the political economy of nutrition. Research is needed to analyze the impact of present policies on women as well as to design strategies that empower women—that is, increase women's control of household resources. Protein-energy malnutrition is often a result of inadequate child care, especially low feeding frequency (including breast-feeding), which to a large extent is a result of the overburdening of women. Agriculture and food strategies should, therefore, be carefully analyzed as to their effect on the sexual division of labor. In most policy research, household food security is only studied from the technical input/output aspect, but it is a process that affects women's time pattern to a large extent. In Eastern Africa, weeding, for example, is always regarded as the woman's responsibility, regardless of whether the field has been prepared by hoe or by tractor (Kjaerby 1983).

The invisibility of women in policy research on food and nutrition is not so much a reflection of male dominance as a logical result of the unwillingness and incapability of researchers to address the basic causes of hunger and malnutrition in society.

Several developing countries are at present in a process of economic structural adjustment. So far, research has been focused on macroeconomic analysis, employment effects, inflation, etc. Very few studies have tried to assess the impact of this process on nutrition. Policy research is urgently needed to understand the impact of structural adjustment on the social conditions of women and children. But again, such research requires rethinking traditional approaches and developing a more adequate conceptualization of the problem.

In many developing countries, especially in Africa, universal primary education (UPE) and literacy programs have a very high priority and absorb a substantial amount of total government budgets. Far too little policy research has been made on the positive and negative effects of UPE on nutrition. Not only do most UPE systems produce jobless graduates with a negative attitude toward agriculture, but UPE has also meant that young children, especially girls, are no longer at home to assist in important child-care tasks. Research on the political economy of nutrition should recognize that UPE is one of the most dramatic processes in the transformation of rural areas in Africa.

Most policies and strategies aimed specifically toward nutritional improvements are still biased toward provision of physical inputs in order to improve the nutritional situation. More emphasis should be given to initiating and supporting endogenous development. Such research, however, requires a thorough knowledge of the communities to be assisted. In Tanzania, for example, most policy-oriented research is still undertaken by foreigners who do not speak the national language. African peasants are repeatedly confronted with researchers and other experts who cannot talk to them, which is why so much policy research becomes superficial, macrolevel-oriented, and relatively unsophisticated.

Integrating Economics, Political Science, Nutrition, and Other Disciplines

Research is a process that involves the selection of a research topic, methodology, field work, analysis, and communication of results. The malnourished are seldom, if ever, involved in any of these steps; they are merely passive study subjects. This lack of direct participation is the most glaring weakness in present policy research on nutrition. Researchers often explain that their subjects would not understand economic theory, social analysis, etc. But many researchers do not understand their subjects, treating them as merely "consumer units" with certain behavioral characteristics.

Another problem is the compartmentalization and specialization of most sciences. Many of the classic economists during the nineteenth century based their work on a deep concern for the existing problems of poverty, exploitation, and hunger. Ricardo, Malthus, Marx, etc., all addressed their research in a holistic way. This approach almost completely disappeared with the explosive development of science in the twentieth century.

The two problems mentioned above are interconnected. Involvement and understanding of people require a holistic approach, and the development and refinement of a holistic approach requires full participation of the people affected by the problem. The first step toward increased integration of the disciplines studying malnutrition in society is the development of more integrative paradigms. As long as research is focusing on immediate and underlying causes, the integration is not felt necessary. It is not until the basic causes are addressed, which requires community-based studies, that the integration of disciplines becomes necessary.

For many years, several multidisciplinary teams of researchers have tried to work together on the problem of malnutrition in society. The result has not been encouraging. Real integration seldom takes place, and the final report is as compartmentalized as the university departments the researchers come from.

In the majority of cases, malnutrition is *created;* it is a result of social processes that are conditioned by power structures that reflect the economic and political contradictions in the community and are legitimized by prevailing ideologies. Therefore, the initiative for integration must come from the field of political economy in its broadest definition. If policy research focused more on how policies and strategies affect people in communities, a more integrated, contextual, and service-oriented paradigm would emerge. Such a paradigm would generate more valid and useful methodologies for economic policy research in the field of nutritional improvement.

13 Nutrition-Related Policy Research: A Political Science Perspective on the Role of Economic and Political Factors

RAYMOND F. HOPKINS

Introduction

Political scientists are classically interested in who gets what, when, and how (Lasswell 1936). Nutrition-related policies viewed in this light constitute the outcome of contending interests. Typically, research on nutrition seeks efficient ways to improve people's nutrition. Seldom are political factors integrated into such nutrition research. To add a political economy perspective requires treating nutrition policies and their effects as outcomes of competition among various interests. Both the outcomes and the interests tend to be denominated in economic, not caloric, terms.

The political economy approach has many derivations. In all of them, it is explicitly assumed that interests and not ideals drive social processes and shape policy.[1] Research on the process that determines nutrition-related outcomes, therefore, should be sensitive to antagonisms in each context.[2] Contending interests affect nutrition both directly and indirectly. Both deserve attention since policies to achieve nutrition goals, as well as broad socioeconomic conditions, are necessarily shaped by their political and economic environment.

In general, four political economy questions deserve inclusion in research on nutrition-related policy. First, what political and economic factors induce a state to make direct nutrition interventions? This question relates broadly to the literature on agenda setting and decision-versus-nondecision analyses. It asks: How does nutrition become a focus of public attention and an object of state intervention? (Cobb, Ross, and Ross 1976; Bachrach and Baratz 1970). Empirical research would focus on the events that moved nutrition issues into the political arena.

Second, what are the goals that shape government nutrition-related pol-

1. This point is frequently made, especially in studies of transitional policies (see Brewer 1975; Hyden 1983).
2. Staniland (1985) identifies several streams, both Marxist and non-Marxist, of political economy approaches.

icy? This question is important because formally declared policy goals seldom conform exactly to "operational goals," that is, what is actually sought by those in power. This discrepancy is different from the conventional distinction between intent and results. The gap between the intended and actual effects of policy is, of course, of major significance. However, even before this prospective gap arises, it is important to distinguish between formal and effective policy intent. For example, the formal intent of the Sri Lankan food stamp program was to better target a nutritional intervention, but the effective intent may also have included greater state control over welfare allocations and a savings for the state and for those bearing the costs of the previous ration program. Similarly, the shifts in United States food stamp policy in 1981 and 1982 may have had better targeting only as a subsidiary goal, while their primary goal was to increase pressure on poor groups to seek employment. Certainly, in conflict situations, starvation as a goal may not be proclaimed, but it is nevertheless real. Consider the case of Poles in Nazi concentration camps (1939–45), Kampucheans in Khmer Rouge areas of Kampuchea (1978–80), or rebels in areas of Afghanistan not under Russian control (1980–85). Thus, a government's intent in amplifying or contracting the food available to particular groups may be to help or punish specific groups, either directly or indirectly. Food aid programs, for example, are notorious for seeking multiple goals simultaneously—such as welfare, surplus disposal, and diplomatic amity.

Third, how do political and economic factors impact differently at different stages in the policy process? This question looks at the various stages in the policy process to see how political and economic forces, generally the ones exogenous to the formation of policy itself, affect the outcome. We generally recognize that the interests of food producers in expanding demand have been a factor in promoting nutrition programs. The goal of increased farm income, however, is basically endogenous to the policy itself; it normally would be identified in answering the first and second questions about policy formulation. Political and economic factors, analogous to the role of producer interests in food aid programs, impact policy at the implementation and evaluation stages (Pressman and Wildavsky 1984). Consider that producers want surpluses targeted to noncommercial markets to expand demand. Thus the coverage of surplus disposal programs tends to exclude powerful groups from direct benefits and to include weaker and perhaps rival ones. One result can be the mobilizing of sentiments against this targeting, as powerful groups seek to secure the benefits for themselves. Often such outcomes result in diversions variously described as "leakage," corruption, patronage, or welfare rip-offs.[3]

Fourth, what are the economic and political determinants of nutritional status? This question moves beyond the focus on specific nutrition policy

3. An example of distortion of nutrition aims to political purposes is clearly documented by Wallerstein (1980) in his review of U.S. food aid.

processes. It asks about the broad effects of economic and political factors on the nutritional well-being of individuals or groups. The notion that poverty explains hunger and that political weakness and poverty are intertwined is well established.[4] Research that established the independent effects of different factors would enhance the likelihood that nutrition objectives can be pursued more effectively and that nutrition policy can be designed without myopia regarding its political dimension.

Making Nutrition a Public Policy Objective

For most people, nutrition is a personal or family responsibility. This has been true throughout history and remains so today. From subsistence households to families who patronize urban fast-food shops, the role of the state in nutrition remains largely indirect. This is important—after all, states set the broad rules for economic activity, provide order, and enforce rules by which food is exchanged. In most cases, however, the state does not directly provide the ration nor does it prescribe what is to be consumed. Exchange-rate policy, for example, may affect nutrition, but exchange rates are almost never determined by nutritional considerations. The role of the state in nutrition-related outcomes becomes more direct when it makes sectoral interventions in the food system—for example, to expand production, improve marketing, subsidize consumer prices or guarantee the quality of commodities. The effects of these actions can dramatically improve nutrition even if their primary aim is to satisfy broad economic or safety objectives. Food grading, for example, can have positive external effects on nutrition by providing incentives to producers and distributors to maintain quality and avoid food contamination. The ending of food grading by African governments has been related to a deterioration in the nutritional quality of food (Bates 1981).

In the twentieth century, states have increasingly undertaken direct nutrition policies by prescribing diets, especially in state-run feeding programs, setting minimum food standards, or providing supplementary feeding to targeted groups. These direct interventions may have less net impact on the food status of a populace than other nutrition-related policies whose primary goal is not the provision of nutritional benefits.[5] Weak administrative and fiscal resources that most less developed countries have at their disposal make state action—whether direct or indirect—even less important in shaping nutritional status. Weather, international prices, and cultural barriers to production and trade expansion may all exceed the impact of the state per se. Nevertheless, to

---

4. The evidence for these connections is widely scattered. One useful review is Berg (1984).

5. The distinction between nutrition policies and policies related to food, public health, or income is ambiguous. Timmer et al. (1983), for example, label targeted ration systems as food policies and call nutrition policies only very specific interventions, such as education or fortification of foods.

the extent that social control over human consumption is possible, state action remains central.

The political economist is interested in all three policy domains described above—macroeconomic policies, food-sector policies, and direct nutrition policies—when state action represents a response to nutrition concerns. Nutrition has been politicized in varying situations. Three basic conditions, however, seem to frequently be the immediate reason for nutrition goals to gain priority—the occurrence of acute food shortages; the establishment of new scientific understanding regarding the relation of food to health and economic productivity; and an increase in the power of undernourished groups. Nutrition research need not focus only on the second condition. Political economy analyses appropriately touch on all three, most certainly where priority for nutrition programs increases as a function of power changes.

In all three cases, a shift in the relative perceived value of nutrition occurs. In the first instance, famine threatens to bring with it great social costs that private-sector nutrition practices cannot avoid. In the second situation, research findings prompt a recalculation of nutritional costs and benefits compared to other valued items. In the third case, the perceived value of nutrition policy rises thanks to greater weight being accorded to an ascendent political group. After Castro came to power in Cuba, for instance, the poor population experienced substantial nutritional gains.

Research that examines cases of heightened government attention to nutrition is needed. One class of changes to investigate is where nutritional considerations affect macropolicy. I hypothesize that changes in such policies, however relevant to nutrition, are seldom a product of conscious nutritional cost/benefit calculations. Furthermore, interest groups focused on nutritional status—even if amorphous and volatile in character, such as the urban poor—are also unlikely to affect macropolicy. The growing reference to "food security" in many countries, however, may indicate that a change is occurring that may end the general absence of nutrition goals from macropolicy. Food security represents a symbol formulated to consolidate and articulate the importance of nutritional considerations. Because it focuses on diffuse, structural conditions, it is particularly salient. When policies are justified in the name of food security (or some other broad referent, such as basic needs), this could be taken as evidence of increased attention to nutrition. Direct nutrition interventions, such as emergency feeding programs or special programs for the poor, continue to be the major policy actions taken in response to food security concerns, but food sector and macroissues are increasingly considered, at least by analysts examining policy solutions to this nutritional objective (Valdes 1981; World Bank 1985). Many nutrition effects arise from indirect subsidies, such as price-depressing policies for food. To shift to overt direct subsidies requires greater support, but it may also be more politically controversial. Research on the comparative advantages of direct and indirect subsidies is in order, as well as research on the extent to which changes in the salience of nutrition goals can affect policy changes. This is especially important in that most rhetoric on food security has been nonoperational because of lack of agreement on how to effectively use macropolicy for nutrition gains.

Another area for investigation is the use in judicatory and administrative law of nutritional criteria or status in defining the rights and relevant facts about claimants. If there is a changing view about the importance of nutrition for health, emotional stability, or the right of people to a minimum diet, it should be reflected in the application of law within the state. Such changes might arise in administrative law outside the legislative arena. Likewise, we should investigate possible growth in funding of nutrition programs and research. The way key groups, notably the medical establishment, perceive nutrition improvements to be in their interest is likely to measurably affect their support for research and for direct nutrition interventions.[6] Changes would be reflected in the medical profession's position on budget and administrative law issues. Nutrition research may also expose consequences of malnutrition that expand state responsibility for oversight of the food system and for setting standards. The latter is especially likely in the state's custodial and licensing functions. Thus, new research findings may affect nutritional requirements in state-supported or mandated institutions, such as the military, prisons, hospitals, and schools, and in state-licensed facilities, such as nurseries.

Public sector responsibility for nutrition may also expand when groups advocating redistribution of income gain power or when research exposes opportunities for gain. Due to the large proportion of income expended by the poor on food, a practical effect of food and nutrition programs, even untargeted ones, is that they provide a greater relative benefit to low-income groups. Thus, those seeking progressive distributional effects normally favor nutritional policies. Private corporations may also increase spending on nutrition policies, usually when research indicates that a better diet is cost-effective in reducing losses in the work force due to illness.

It is no accident that socialist states frequently set up strong food-price controls and create implicit subsidies as a major policy objective. The impetus for this seems to be a distributional goal. Seldom are nutritional criteria used, however, in selecting foods targeted for expanded production or subsidies. Doctors and scientists, as significant interest groups, may become more interested in nutrition thanks to research discoveries. Their interest in promoting state action to improve nutrition usually rests on an appeal to others to recalculate their interests rather than to reorganize power relations; alternatively, when poorer classes acquire greater power, they are also likely to promote policies designed to enhance general nutrition but, as a result of changed power, not

6. One nutrition expert proposed studying the possible effects of nutrition on the crime rate, arguing that if good evidence were uncovered that inadequate nutrition promoted crime, it would generate political support for nutrition intervention.

interests.[7] Comparative cases of power shifts as causes of state expansion of nutritional interventions are instructive. Peron's Argentina, for example, attempted to promote cheap food for the urban poor when urban labor came to power. The result left Argentina economically disadvantaged by putting the burden of the redistributional program on agriculture and rural producers, who had represented a major export and growth sector. Egypt's extensive food subsidies are clearly related to the power of the urban poor. They constitute a broad social contract between the Egyptian elite and the populace, but one that is borne largely by foreign aid and general revenue rather than by producers.

The costs of food subsidies, school feeding programs, and the like may be justified by either efficiency or equity—that is, by societal savings from reduced unemployment or health burdens or by principles of social justice imposed through the rise to power of middle and working classes. Whatever the case, however, the manner in which direct costs of such public interventions are distributed will be important for maintaining support of these policies. As such, the growth of public sector involvement in nutrition can be best explained by political and economic factors. In addition to research on the changing role of nutrition in the political agenda, details of nutrition policies that are adopted should be included. The policies themselves may be treated as intervening variables between interests and outcomes. As such, they are capable of affecting the subsequent support for nutrition policy through their impact on political and economic factors, including the creation or maintenance of an "interested" constituency and the effectiveness that people perceive the programs as having.

Goals of Nutrition Policy

The classic practice in nutrition policy is to specify goals in fairly narrow terms of benefits to targeted recipients. This is often a misspecification of the process by which a policy was adopted and of the interests it was intended to serve. The most obvious instance is programs that arise from a need to dispose of surplus food. In nutrition programs that transfer food, and perhaps in all welfare and charitable undertakings, some self-interest of sponsors or supporters is to be expected. It is curious, however, that research evaluating the goals used in cost/benefit analyses often overlooks benefits to groups other than the targeted recipients or (occasionally) society in general. In order to understand the working of nutrition policy in realistic terms—that is, in terms of the effective interests shaping policy—the features of the policy that led various interests to support it in the first place need to be identified.

Among the goals of nutrition programs might be an integrated welfare

---

7. A classic argument in political science exists between those who see change as necessarily reflecting a shift in power, e.g., Marxists and realists, and those who explain change as a function of learning and culture, e.g., liberals and political sociologists, such as Weber, Durkheim, and Lasswell.

structure in which nutrition programs are a cost-efficient means to improve health or ameliorate unacceptable conditions resulting from market failures. The Colombia food stamp program, the United States WIC program, and the Chinese system of basic food subsidies are examples of programs with both welfare and health goals. In these cases, the poorer the country, the less appropriate or necessary it was to target the delivery of nutrition. All three programs, interestingly, have been the subject of curtailment; in Colombia the program was terminated. What was the problem? Was it the inability of nutrition benefits to satisfy health and welfare goals? Or was it that the interests served were politically too weak to sustain the program? Did strong political opposition arise because the perceived program costs exceeded benefits or the effects of the program on recipients posed threats to other interests, such as social control by an elite? Research on these questions, which integrate political economy factors, is called for. It should involve both measuring the effects of a program, as in evaluation studies of WIC, and analyzing support for the program among various bureaucracies, legislative organs, and interest formations.[8]

At the international level, the delivery of food aid poses another interesting research issue. For many donors, even those that are net food importers, surplus disposal and market development goals are seldom absent from the program. Thus Sweden pushes wheat; Norway, fish products; and Saudi Arabia, dates. The United States, as a major food exporter, certainly has many rules and practices for providing food aid that conform to these goals and hence embody the interests of producers. Nevertheless, though these commodity goals are not nutritionally derived, if they are satisfied, the result may be a greater reliability of such programs. If surplus disposal and market development goals can be pursued in ways that do not seriously distort or harm recipient country interests, then it is reasonable to accept such practical aspects of policy goals and look for opportunities to serve these nonnutritional objectives while at the same time looking for nutrition-based criteria for the allocation of food aid.[9]

It is also useful to ascertain whether income transfer effects are the major or at least an important objective of nutrition policies. Political economists regularly explain that food subsidy programs whose benefits go heavily to urban groups are caused by an "urban bias."[10] In Bangladesh, for instance, there is a clear entitlement for city and government workers in the ration shop system. Analyses of subsidy programs frequently assume that nutrition—not income goals—is at stake. They analyze the income effects of such programs but do so

---

8. See the United States Department of Agriculture's effort to rewrite the external evaluation of WIC to a less favorable one, apparently as a way to make requests for cuts in the program consistent with the evaluation (*New York Times*, February 1, 1985, p. 7).

9. The extent to which nutrition is an objective in the allocation of food aid is a major concern in reviews of food aid policy (see Huddleston 1984; Hopkins 1984a).

10. A classic statement of this is found in Lipton (1976).

with a view to assessing the efficiency or fairness of such programs compared to nutritional goals. However, it is desirable to question whether such programs do not have important nonnutritional intents, such as providing income or extra security to economically or politically important groups. If the intent of such programs is to offer visible, regular, and valued transfers from the state to particular groups, then the goals of the policy may be realized even if nutritional objectives are not optimally or efficiently served.

Research to identify and weigh effective goals of policies related to nutrition would appropriately incorporate several methodologies. At least three kinds of data can be sought—historical, social-accounting, and interview. Historical evidence would be found in parliamentary debates and records of committee and politburo meetings. Diaries, speeches, and other interpretations by those making decisions would also be helpful. Where the legislative process is fairly open, as in democratic societies, the role and published views of pressure groups would be germane. Such historical data from the records of individuals and organizations would help establish the legislative and executive intent of a policy. A second technique would look at social accounting data— that is, information based on state-mandated tallies, such as measures of hospital intakes, government expenditures, and food prices. Statistical analyses can then be used to account for variations in policy. For example, if a country's food stamp or ration system's food outlays varied with changes in unemployment, then it would be acting as if one of its purposes was income stabilization; while if it varied more closely with the costs of agricultural production support programs, the inference would be that its likely intent and certain effect was surplus disposal. Similarly, if Thai rice export levies varied with national revenue needs or with ministry of agriculture projects rather than domestic feeding considerations, the intent of the program would not appear to be primarily nutritional. Most studies estimate the nutritional effects of subsidies, such as the indirect one in Thailand, but do not attempt to use statistical data to explain them.

Finally, interview data can be used to develop more interpretative explanations. Interviews and survey research can provide spot checks on explanations or can explore new areas, such as how nutritional programs are perceived by recipients.

Historical, social-accounting, and interview data would also be useful in establishing the effective intent of policies as well as in probing questions about earlier and later stages in the policy process. Different evidence should be combined when possible, because the intent of policy is an illusive element to determine. A study by Lipsky and Thibodeau (1985) combines such data to criticize implementation failures in the temporary emergency assistance programs of the United States.

Distortions of Nutrition Policy

The third stage at which political and economic factors affect nutrition policies is during their implementation phase. The fungibility of resources often allows powerful actors to undercut a policy's intent or to diminish its effect. Targeted feeding programs, for example, are frequently vitiated by the benefits being indirectly appropriated to others. Food provided to women and children may end up benefiting male heads of households. This happens when food from household sources normally available to women and children is reduced once they become beneficiaries. Thus food is transferred, at least in part, away from the targeted beneficiary so that actual additional food ends up elsewhere in the household.

Local governments and national bureaucracies may do the same with nutrition programs they administer. Such bodies can effectively transfer benefits intended as additional help for undernourished people to other programs, such as transport or housing subsidies. By changing existing procedures, additional contributions to nutrition programs can end up adding monies to other budget expenditures and leaving the nutrition program benefits close to where they were. It is also possible for nutrition benefits to simply disappear through illegal appropriation. For example, in Bangladesh, 15 to 35 percent of the grain earmarked for food-for-work projects disappeared between arrival and disbursement to project workers.[11] This diversion is often in the form of small appropriations in kind by low-paid handlers rather than organized high-level corruption. Nevertheless, it changes the outcome of the policy. Food aid may also be distorted by outright theft, as occurred in Ghana and Nigeria in the 1970s.

Bureaucratic regulations governing the administration of national nutrition programs may also distort policy intent. A classic problem is the oversupply of regulations and personnel. Its usual effect on program implementation is to expand middle-class employment of a nonproductive kind in industrialized countries and less-skilled employment in many less-developed ones. Even though this was not the intent of the nutrition policy, it may be one of its major consequences.

There have been serious problems of distortions from intent in the United States food stamp program. The rules for the program created anomalies so that some of the poorest and most malnourished people were excluded, while middle-class college students met eligibility tests and administrative hurdles. In spite of this, food stamps account for about 5 percent of the value of food purchased for home consumption and have proved more effective and less distortive than direct distribution programs (Food Research Action Center 1981; Berry 1984).

Other distortions of intent arise when budgetary pressures or the absence

11. Based on discussions with Bangladesh officials at the World Food Program meetings of the CFA, Rome, June 3–8, 1984.

of resources lead to the suspension of nutrition programs. A most poignant example of this occurred in Africa in 1984–85, when food rotted in ports while relief camps up-country were filled with starving people. In Nigeria, the universities could not open in 1984–85 until the large food subsidy was deleted from the educational budget and students were required to pay the full costs of their food needs.[12] There are other implementation problems, for instance, when rules for safety in food products do not cover the results of promotional efforts that inappropriately expand their use. From simple overindulgence to the bitter controversy over Nestle's promotion of infant formula in Africa, nutritional and commercial interest groups have debated regulation propriety. In the Nestle case, its product for many African families came to displace more nutritious and inexpensive breast-feeding. Substantial rectification of this issue required the formation of an international lobby to pressure for corporate restraint and an international code of conduct.

To review, three major stages in the policy process can be distinguished. At each point, competing economic and political factors shape the outcomes. These stages are: (1) the formation of interests, during which the priority given to nutrition in public policy is settled; (2) interest incorporation, in which effective goals of particular policies are settled; and (3) policy implementation, during which distortions in priority and intent take place. Different issues move along such paths from policy inception through implementation (see table 13.1). Research on policies directly related to nutrition should appropriately look at the entire process by which nutrition outcomes are shaped.

In table 13.1, several political and economic factors have been chosen to illustrate the previous argument. The schema assumes that interest in nutrition policy arises in competition with other political and economic interests. A rise in priority for nutrition, in turn, gives rise to new policies or to the reshaping of existing ones at a second stage. At a third stage, policy implementation, the interests of those affected by the policy, including those charged with implementing it—for example, researchers, welfare workers, or teachers—will lead to a more or less faithful realization of the policy's intent.

Consider what happens in the first example. A significant change in food production and, as a result, availability occurs. Various groups seek to protect themselves from the adverse effects of this change and look to state action. If the change is a shortfall and prices are rising, this tends to give rise to calls for aiding those most hurt. The Ethiopian famine of 1983–85 is a concrete case that led to special emergency relief legislation in the United States Congress and to emergency food supplements approved by the ECC at stage two. Thus, the priority accorded to relieving famine conditions led to specific policies. Additional food was to be shipped, and new arrangements for its distribution were

12. Based on a conversation with Vremudia P. Diejomaoh, director of the Nigerian Institute of Social and Economic Research, Ibadan University, at Swarthmore College, November 1, 1984.

TABLE 13.1 Political economy episodes in nutrition policy

(a)	Stages in Policy	Policy priority setting	Policy declaration	Policy implementation
(b)	Role of Interests	Formation or discovery	Incorporation	Realization or distortion
(c)	Selected Factors That Give Rise to Change		Examples of Policy Activity	
	Physical (food storage)	Emergency relief	Rules for delivery	Allocation to favored groups
	Political strife	Rationing	Government control of stocks	Black market sales
	Economic cycles	Entitlement programs	Macrostabiliza-tion: state/ voluntary association coordination	Uneven food-stamp coverage
	Research results	Importance of special nutrients	Mandated fortifi-cation, e.g., iodine in salt	Substitute food components
	Political support search	School milk	State program for school feeding	Erratic delivery
	Surplus food	Nonmarket disposal	"New" feeding programs	Processor profits

negotiated. In the Ethiopian case, implementation was controversial. It is claimed that the distribution of food excluded famine victims opposing the government and favored military and forced-resettlement efforts.

Fluctuations in family income, food prices, or the economy in general can also lead (at stage one) to heightened interest in nutrition policy. In order to reduce the hardships such cycles impose, consumer food subsidy and food stamp programs have been developed in many countries. War or internal politi-cal crises can foster rationing systems. These and other interests become em-bodied in concrete programs at stage two. Equitable distribution of a vital resource—welfare-burden sharing between local and national governments—and forced savings may simultaneously be elements of policies. As a result, such policies often incorporate disparate, sometimes nonnutrition, interests in the same undertaking. On occasion, a search for enhanced political popularity may be an important factor in giving a nutrition policy its initial impetus. In Kenya, President Moi announced in 1979 that the government would provide milk to school children. His vision was ahead of bureaucratic planning and the crystallized ideas of regular interest promoters, but it was nevertheless implemented on a modest basis, due less to educational and dairy interests than to a need to maintain presidential authority and credibility. In the Philippines in June 1974, shortly after President Marcos declared martial law, his government had a strong interest in promoting symbolically benevolent undertakings, and the Philippine Food and Nutrition Program was inaugurated. Thus nutrition became a priority by presidential decree, and evidence of its importance was subsequently clarified in the first national nutrition survey in 1978. These are two instances in which nutrition priority grew as a result of a search for politically popular measures.

Food surpluses, especially when acquired by a government, can also create interests in nutrition programs. The United States Temporary Emergency Food Program, which aimed to give away surplus dairy stocks in the early 1980s, is a good example of a new program incorporating more than the interests of targeted recipients. It is also one in which distribution was hampered by bureaucratic interests, but its very presence on the national scene drew attention to the more general nutritional and economic plight of many poor American families (Lipsky and Thibodeau 1985).

Little political economy research on the above stages of explicit nutrition programming exists. Especially absent are studies on the changing levels of understanding and priority accorded nutrition concerns in various countries. Indeed, more conventional national surveys on the material components of nutrition, such as food and micronutrient consumption and their potential effects on body weight and height, are sorely needed (Huddleston 1985). As such surveys are undertaken, however, information from survey respondents should also include political economy data on sociopolitical characteristics of respondents, their attitudes, and their economic situation.

Economic and Political Determinants of Hunger

We now turn from a focus on the political economy of the nutrition policy process to the broader issue of the causes and consequences of hunger. State authority and market exchange are the two major mechanisms for allocating values in society (Lindblom 1977). Today, hunger or inadequate nutrition occurs in a world with ample production. Nutritional deprivation, therefore, is fundamentally a consequence of economic and political factors. This truism does not lead us very far, however.[13] To promote improvements in existing

---

13. There is a myriad of works on hunger, its causes, and its solutions. A bibliography of over three thousand articles and books was compiled by Ball (1981). After reading a sampling of books, studies by government commissions, and the like, nearly all observers agree on the fundamental role of poverty and on the complex character of forces that create and sustain it. See Sen (1981) for an excellent analysis.

FIGURE 13.1 Determinants and effects of inadequate nutrition, a syndrome of features

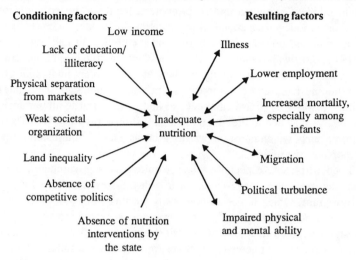

nutrition availabilities, specific economic and political constraints need to be identified, and political and economic gains from improved nutrition need to be demonstrated. This identification is inherently contextual, looking at individual countries over many years.

There exist many causes and consequences of inadequate nutritional status (see figure 13.1), including health factors that cumulatively affect economic and political factors (Berg 1973, 1987a; Winikoff 1978; Johnston and Clark 1982). A syndrome of causes and consequences operates in ways that are generally undesirable and may be self-perpetuating. Reciprocal causation also exists, a feature easy to understand but difficult to assess empirically.[14] Some links are well documented (as between low education, inadequate nutrition, and impaired health), but others, for example, between political repression and inadequate nutrition, though often asserted, are unexamined.

Additional macrostudies, especially on the effect of the role of the state and class structure on nutrition outcomes, are in order. For instance, one study worth undertaking would investigate whether centrally planned societies are more likely to pursue nutritional interventions, with positive effects on health, urban drift, or political quiescence. Studies in the pluralist tradition have influenced works such as that of Johnston and Clark (1982) to propose incrementalist reform and the encouragement of political participation and organization. This might be less useful advice if central planning achieved better nutrition outcomes. What does cross-national evidence show about the positive impact

14. A similar scheme with multiple, nonrecursive causal factors surrounding nutritional deficits was drawn up by Field (1978).

of such factors on nutrition? For the most part, we do not know to what extent participation can be a determining factor. Since little work on this topic has been undertaken, the World Bank and other research groups could well undertake such studies.[15]

A classical problem in achieving broad social objectives, such as adequate nutrition for all, has been the "collective goods" quality of such goals. The range of nutrition interventions by the state to offset market deficiencies, especially in poor countries where poverty and illiteracy make the nutrition problem acute, is limited by two factors—a weak capacity that limits the range of effective action a state can take, and the lack of motivation of beneficiaries of collective goods to recognize and pursue their interests. The second and classic collective-goods problem arises regularly when smaller, more intense interests working to secure goods from which others may be excluded dominate policymaking, overriding more general interests of a population in relatively nonexcludable goods. Nutrition-intervention attempts aimed at a collective good that threaten specific or selected interests can thus be thwarted. This failure is a widely observed problem of political economy, found in varying situations.[16] In Tanzania, the effort to develop basic village units to improve life generally met with a number of problems, but the one not usually mentioned in this context was the unwillingness of the national party to tolerate decisions and cooperative efforts outside of party control. In 1969, for example, the country's most successful development experiment, the Ruvuma Development Association, was disbanded because it threatened the specific political interests of party leaders. Although it was successful in improving the lives of association members and creating local self-reliance, it was not under party control.[17]

In industrialized countries, the interplay of strong organized interests versus more diffused ones is also clear. In the United Kingdom, a government guide to healthy eating, which recommended reduced meat, butter, and milk consumption, was edited to remove strong statements as a result of pressure from food industry groups lobbying through the ministry of agriculture.[18]

Finally, it may turn out from macrostudies that the institutionalization of policy is very important. In Chile, the swing in government from the middle-class cabinets of the 1960s to the Allende socialist government of the 1971–73 period to the repressive Pinochet military regime of 1974 was accompanied by major shifts in attention to poverty and redistribution issues. The nutritional

15. This approach is found in the World Bank statistics, e.g., *World Development Report, 1982,* which deals briefly with these issues, and in Winikoff (1978), whose book asks the right questions but contains only individual case studies.

16. See Olsen (1965) for a seminal statement of the concept, and Russel and Nicholson (1981) for a series of illustrative analyses.

17. A good account of this is in Coulson (1982).

18. See *Manchester Guardian,* "Nutritionist's Threat to Quit over Censorship," May 8, 1985.

programs, however, continued and enjoyed modest expansion in coverage and increased efficiency in targeting throughout the period, affected by only a short interruption after the 1973 coup. This case suggests that at some level of social complexity, nutrition policy can be functionally isolated from macropolitical economic forces, sustained and protected by its own integrity and importance. Broad macrofactors of differentiated political interests may account for Chile's deviation from an expectation that more adequate nutrition would be associated with increased political participation and opportunities. That nutrition programs did not suffer under Pinochet does not mean nutrition improved, of course. Nevertheless, the maintenance of targeted nutrition in Chile may be analogous to cases of welfare lobbies in industrial states that can sustain nutrition programs in the face of changing and exogenous political and economic impacts.

There is also a need for research in microstudies. Leonard's (1972) work on Kenya's agricultural extension bureaucracy would be quite valuable to duplicate in several countries and focus on the administration of nutrition programs. Particularly important to document would be the impact of nutrition policies and targeted feeding programs on local politics and on diffused political attitudes. Scott (1986) makes a convincing case that important responses to government policy occur in the form of foot-dragging and other everyday types of resistance. Such small-scale, unarticulated, individualized reactions to state intervention are more common in peasant societies in which policies providing nutritional benefits to certain classes or locales are to be principally paid for by petty producers.

To date, most studies on the political consequences of nutritional deficiencies have focused on disturbances, such as riots or government overthrows, that followed changes in price subsidies or the mishandling of famine conditions, such as the food riots in Egypt, Morocco, and elsewhere, and the coups in Ethiopia, Niger, and Bangladesh (Bienen and Gersovitz 1984; Shepherd 1975; Alamgir 1980).

The complex causal chain linking inadequate nutrition to political and economic factors has, therefore, required both macro and micro research. At the macrolevel, it will be useful to understand the constraints on policy-making so that feasible efforts to lift barriers to nutrition can be chosen. Promoting nutrition priority with a policy recommending an attack on entrenched elite interests is a fruitless strategy.[19] Even modest efforts to change nutritional recommendations can encounter strong resistance if a few intense interests are aroused in opposition. The United States National Academy of Science proposal in October 1985 to lower minimum vitamin requirements met with strong resistance from consumer lobbies that argued that this would allow a reduction

19. It may be especially irrelevant in Latin America (see Tullis 1985).

in dietary guidelines for feeding programs for the poor. In this case, the lobby for the undernourished seems to have prevailed.

At the microlevel, nutrition surveys on household behavior and case studies of the bureaucratic and local-level operation of nutrition-related policies are especially needed.[20] The state's institutional role and the class, ethnic, and other political factors that bear upon nutrition outcomes are most concretely revealed by microlevel studies that look for these determinants.

Conclusion

Casting the study of nutrition-related policy in the framework of political economy invites faddishness and superficiality. However, there is virtue to the political economy framework. It establishes a broad, open-ended context for research on nutrition, and it encourages investigators to see connections that link macropolitical and economic features to particular nutritional outcomes. It also recognizes the increasingly dense policy environment of twentieth-century society and the value of making recommendations for improved policy in the setting of concrete political and economic circumstances in which the policies are to operate.

This chapter has reviewed the policy process and pointed to the roles of political and economic factors in nutrition-related policy. It has argued that research is needed on market failures and the political basis of policy. Insufficient political support for public goods, negative externalities of state regulation (or its absence), and monopolistic inefficiencies in land use and marketing all contribute to nutrition failures, most poignantly in Africa (Hopkins 1984b).

The general argument has been that research is needed to recognize interests that are served in existing situations. In addition, the prospects for changing interests through research should be pursued, recognizing that evidence supporting the value of improved nutrition may encourage individual self-interested responses and also improve the prospect of attaining collective goods. The macropolitical and economic effects of the alleviation of malnourishment may be inadequate to move policy decisions in the absence of ways to mobilize such interests. Military commanders give high priority to an army's food supply; the provision of nutrition-oriented food policies by states deserves the same priority. A better understanding of the political and economic constraints that limit achievement of malnourishment alleviation, and of its benefits to society as well as to such targeted populations as children and mothers is an important step toward improving nutrition policy. Where political

---

20. Eicher (1985) points out the relative paucity of good data of this kind from Africa. Indeed, there are few food balance sheets for African countries, and consumption data reports are particularly weak.

support for such a collective good is insufficient and where those without adequate nutrition lack political power, the political economy approach can at least suggest what individualized benefits to established, nontargeted groups may be most cost-efficient and thereby induce the changes desired by political leaders or international agencies seeking broader goals of equity and social justice.

PART V

Conclusions and Policy Implications

14 Integrating Political and Economic Considerations in Programs and Policies to Improve Nutrition: Lessons Learned

PER PINSTRUP-ANDERSEN

The purpose of this chapter is to identify and synthesize the main lessons learned from the work reported in previous chapters and from other relevant evidence. The principal types of policies and programs with nutrition implications will be discussed first. The key actors in the policy process will be identified and their goals, rationales, relative power, behavior, and interaction as revealed in past action analyzed. Then follows a discussion of the various coalitions and support groups that may be considered in efforts to improve nutrition. The macroeconomic constraints within a political economy framework are discussed, and the chapter concludes with a brief summary of the overall implications of the findings in this book for action, research, and information generation.

Policy and Program Types

It seems clear from the evidence presented in this book and elsewhere that food and nutrition-related policies and programs are at least as susceptible to political economy considerations and manipulations as other government policies and programs. Since nutrition-related policies and programs are needed to correct for undesired effects of a skewed asset distribution and insufficient endowment among certain population groups, they usually involve direct government transfers or market distortions. Opportunities for capturing the resulting benefits and rents are present, and the competition from groups that are not at risk of malnutrition is strong.

Nutrition does not have a natural home in government, in contrast to, say, agriculture or health. Therefore, in the traditional structure and organization of the government, it is unlikely that any government agency places first priority on nutrition improvements. Past multisectoral nutrition planning efforts were made to remedy this situation by creating new institutional arrangements, including nutrition units in various ministries or the president's office and in semiautonomous nutrition institutes. However, even in cases where special responsibilities and powers were given to these new units to override priorities of existing sectoral ministries and related agencies, the results were disappointing. The existing power structure and vested interests within it made it virtually impossible for the nutrition units to achieve the prescribed goals. In spite of a great deal of rhetoric, integrated multidisciplinary nutrition strategies or policies generally exist only on paper. Although an integrated multidisciplinary approach makes eminent sense from a nutrition perspective, such an approach cannot be effective within most countries' political economy framework.

This does not mean, however, that efforts to improve nutrition should be relegated to the ministry of health and limited to small, direct intervention programs as practiced in the past. Most government policies and programs have implications for the nutritional status of the poor, irrespective of their intent. Therefore, rather than dealing with nutrition problems only in programs designed specifically for that purpose, it is important to consider explicitly the nutritional effects in deliberations, design, and implementation of all policies and programs expected to have significant nutrition implications.

Policies and programs that can be expected to influence incomes of the poor, the prices of food and other basic necessities, access to primary health care, sanitary conditions, and access to clean water offer great promise for improving nutrition. Unfortunately, these same types of policies and programs may also be harmful for nutrition. If the nutrition effects are explicitly considered at the time of policy choice, design, and implementation, desirable effects may be enhanced and undesirable ones avoided.

In addition to food price, wage, and employment policies, transfer and social programs of various kinds, and health programs, close attention should be paid to macroeconomic and sectoral adjustment as well as to agricultural policies and programs affecting productivity, cost of production and marketing, access to input and output markets by small-scale farmers, and land tenure. Finally, the magnitudes and nature of changes in rural infrastructure may have important implications for the rural poor's nutrition within as well as outside agriculture, because their income-generating capabilities as well as their access to food and nonfood commodities and the prices they have to pay for them may change.

Decisions regarding the above policy and program types are made in different government agencies and influenced by different interest groups with different priorities, which in most cases probably do not include nutrition improvement. Therefore, it is important to generate information not only about the potential effects on the nutritionally at-risk groups but also the effects on the groups who make or influence the policy decisions and the extent to which they are likely to achieve their goals under policy scenarios that are beneficial to nutrition. It is important to explicitly consider the trade-offs, if any, between the achievement of the policy goals and the desired nutrition effects. However, one should not assume that such trade-offs always exist. Better information may identify policy modifications that will result in better nutrition without sacrificing the achievement of the policy goals.

A policy or program may be justified in part by malnutrition, even though the principal policy goal is different. For example, cheap-food policies for the urban populations are frequently justified by the poor's need for sufficient food to meet nutritional requirements, even though no attempts are made to limit access to cheap food to the poor. While nutrition is a convenient justification, other interests are being served. Knowing what those interests are and whom they serve may be an important tool for the enhancement of the nutrition effect. Could the most powerful interests be served by some alternative policy that would increase the nutrition effect without compromising the political sustainability of the policy? A two-pronged targeting of the nutritionally vulnerable and a large enough subset of the politically powerful to assure sustainability, leaving the rest of the urban population to pay market prices for food, would be one option.

The Key Actors

Many groups and institutions may influence food and nutrition policy. Some are more influential in policy choice and design, others in the implementation phase. The key actors within a given country are (1) households, through their response to policies and programs and their market response, or household groups, such as consumer associations, labor unions, or community groups; (2) public-sector agencies including parliament, the president's or prime minister's office, sectoral ministries, nutrition institutes, planning units, and various commissions, and elected, appointed, or self-appointed politicians and bureaucrats in these agencies; and (3) private sector agents, such as producers, processors, distributors, and exporters and importers of pharmaceutical, food, and other commodities.

Each of these three groups of actors may be disaggregated into separate subgroups, each with its own agenda, goals, behavior, and related power over specific components of the policy process. Several actors outside the country may also exercise considerable influence over nutrition-related government policies, including the international financing institutions and bilateral assistance agencies.

Following the reasoning of the neoclassical political economy theory, those among the above actors who perceive that they can influence policy decisions to enhance their gains or reduce their losses will do so unless the expected costs of such action exceed expected gains. Both intended and unintended beneficiaries will seek such net gains, and opportunities for coalitions between the two groups may be of mutual interest.

Goals, Rationales, Behavior, and Relative Power

As illustrated in previous chapters, various interest groups attempt to capture benefits or "rents" from public-sector action. Politicians, whether elected or otherwise in power, are likely to have a number of goals and objectives. Some of them are compatible with improved food security and nutrition, and some are not. Conflicting self-interests and trade-offs among them play an important role in the formulation of nutrition-related policies and programs, and the resulting policies are frequently inconsistent and reflect these conflicting self-interests. They need not represent the goals of a monolithic government entity (Allison 1971). Similarly, bureaucrats tend to pursue their own objectives whether or not they are compatible with either stated overall government goals or efforts to improve nutrition. According to this bureaucratic politics model, "decision-makers are viewed as actors or players in a game of politics, promoting bureaucratic interests in competition for various stakes and prizes. Bureaucratic positions on policy issues are determined by bureaucratic interests. Policy outcomes, more often than not, reflect a synthesis or compromise among different positions" (Kozak and Keagle 1988). This is in sharp contrast to the explicit or implicit assumption of many food and nutrition policy analyses: the state bureaucracy is a neutral implementing agent.

According to Keagle (1988), bureaucrats tend to make changes at the margins of existing policies rather than propose large changes including new policies. Such behavior contributes to stability and continuity in government action as opposed to large changes frequently favored by politicians entering office.

Many private-sector interest groups also seek rents or directly unproductive profit (DUP) from government action related to nutrition. Market distortions resulting from food-price subsidies, government interventions, and food and agricultural marketing and foreign trade regulations, as well as direct transfer schemes, such as food stamp programs and social programs of various types, are examples of nutritional-related government action that generates opportunities for DUP. Exclusive licensing of import or wholesale and milling of wheat for subsidy programs is a case in point. The DUP created by licensing may be captured solely by the entity obtaining the license, or it may be divided among the license holder and the politicians or bureaucrats who have the power to issue exclusive licenses. If licensing is needed, DUP might be reduced by creating a competitive license market using, for example, periodic public auctions. However, this would reduce or eliminate the ability of the corresponding public-sector agencies or individuals to extract from rents or confer them on others.

Similar opportunities for capturing DUP exist in many other cases of government intervention in the markets for food, pharmaceutical, and other nutrition-related commodities through price policies, marketing, and foreign trade regulations. Whether the DUP is an economic or a fiscal cost, it has implications for the cost-effectiveness of efforts to reduce malnutrition and should be considered explicitly in policy and program analysis and design. Explicit consideration will also identify and expose the extent of DUP generated and by whom it is captured.

Private and public-sector agents and groups not targeted for transfers will attempt to capture benefits from transfer programs either directly, by diverting transfers to themselves, or indirectly. Indirect benefits can take many forms. For example, indirect economic benefits may be obtained by means of exclusive rights to the production and distribution of transfer goods, such as food and drugs. Indirect political benefits in the form of support of the government as a political entity, specific government agencies, and politicians who the transfer recipients associate with the transfers may also be significant. The need for such political support may be strong and may be a major reason for the program. When this is so, governments are likely to avoid narrow targeting on the poorest household groups and, instead, direct transfers to the less poor and nonpoor, where the cost-effectiveness with respect to political support is more favorable. Narrow targeting on the poor and powerless generally does not generate much political support, and some past programs, such as the Colombian food stamp program, targeted themselves out of existence.

In countries with a relatively small population that is considered poor, government support for narrowly-targeted transfer programs may come from the nonpoor on the basis of altruism and the desire to keep transfer costs low. Such support will favor transfers that appear to be directly focused on alleviating human misery. Food stamps limited to basic staple foods are likely to receive more support than cash transfers, food supplementation schemes directed at preschool children in poor families will receive more support than food stamps for the same families, and efforts to promote child survival will receive more support than general primary health care.

The net results on the recipient households and their members are likely to be the same or similar whether transfers are received in stamps, cash, or food supplementation for preschool children, because households make corresponding adjustments in overall food acquisition and allocation. Therefore, the program preferences expressed by the nonpoor may be based on an illusion. As long as the perceptions exist, however, they are important considerations in policy and program design because they increase political sustainability.

The nonpoor's greater willingness to support transfer programs they perceive to be directly linked to the alleviation of human misery is closely related to their greater willingness to transfer income than to transfer income-earning assets. Asset redistribution is more likely to result in the redistribution of relative power and self-sustained nutrition improvements, and less likely to have the support of those in power. Most income-transfer schemes influence nutrition only for their duration. A recent proposal by the Sri Lankan government (Gunatilleke 1990) offers a refreshing new approach. The existing food stamp program would be replaced by a two-pronged program that transfers funds for current household food consumption and a lump sum to be used only for investment in income earning activities.

As Latham and Strauss show in chapters 9 and 10, improved nutrition may increase labor productivity, reduce health costs, enhance school performance, and thus contribute to economic growth. Opportunities for capturing some of the economic surplus resulting from improved nutrition may provide an incentive to support policies and programs favorable for nutrition. While this is true in principle, Field (chapter 11) argues that, generally, such opportunities are not sufficient to convince the nonpoor to provide strong support for nutrition programs, although Hopkins claims that they may trigger new programs (chapter 13).

There are several reasons why the promise of enhanced economic growth is insufficient to support modifications in policies and programs to better serve nutritional needs. First, the lag between investment in improved nutrition of preschool children—the most vulnerable group—and the resulting economic gains is long and probably exceeds the time horizon of most public and private-sector interest groups. Second, the payoff is uncertain partly because of the long time lag and partly because it depends on other factors, for example, employment or income earning opportunities, which must be present to permit potential productivity gains from better nutrition to materialize. Third, when the investment in improved nutrition is made, it is unclear which groups will benefit. To enlightened dictatorships with a long-time horizon, it would not matter so much who would gain as long as society as a whole did. However, with the exception of Cuba, which made heavy investments in education, health, and nutrition, such dictatorships are hard to find.

Potential income gains play a more important role in supporting nutritional improvements in cases where the gains occur with a much shorter time lag and when beneficiaries of these gains can be identified with greater certainty. Primary health care and subsidized feeding for workers may have short-run positive effects on labor productivity that exceed their cost. Therefore, unless the higher productivity results in wage increases, such programs may be in the economic interest of employers. Similarly, primary health care and subsidized feeding of children of workers may reduce child morbidity and worker absenteeism and thus be in the interest of both private and public-sector employers.

Although the individual household has little or no influence on policy and program formulation, it has the ultimate power to participate in or reject the programs that are available. As discussed in chapter 8, policies and programs that disregard household behavior will be successful only by chance. Fortunately, a relatively rich theory of the behavior of households as producers, consumers, and suppliers of labor is available for predicting their response to specific programs and policies.

Ideally, target households would communicate their perceptions, constraints, and preferences to those responsible for program design and implementation. In some countries, such as Nicaragua (chapter 6), this is done through consumer associations and labor unions. However, in most developing countries, consumer associations possess little political power, and labor unions, where they are powerful, frequently do not effectively represent the poor and malnourished.

Direct participation in problem diagnosis and program design and implementation by target households at the community level appears to offer promising prospects. Such an approach has been successful in a number of cases, such as the Iringa project in Tanzania (Yambi, Jonsson, and Ljungqvist 1990) and many smaller village-level projects around the world. However, unless the target group possesses all the resources necessary to support the project, a very rare situation, the success of this approach depends on support and protection from nontarget groups that could attempt to divert such support for their own benefit. Therefore, the critical political economy question becomes one of identifying a source of sustainable and reliable support, that is, a group or agency that will meet its own goals by providing such support and protection. As illustrated in chapters 6 and 7, identifying such a source is no easy task. The existing power structure will make every effort to avoid a significant shift in the relative balance of power while attempting to siphon off some or all program benefits. Thus, benefits from programs and policies targeted on the poor are frequently captured by others.

Coalitions

Two options may be open for the poor to assure that government policies and programs reflect their interests. They may threaten the power and legitimacy of the government through social unrest or by way of the voting booth, or they may enter into coalitions with the nonpoor.

Street violence and related action have been effective in avoiding adverse changes in food and economic policies in many countries, including Egypt, Morocco, and Tunisia. However, although the evidence is not clear, it appears that where such action has been successful, it has not been limited to the poor. Since the poor consist of a large number of heterogenous groups that are widely diffused geographically, organization for action is extremely difficult. Furthermore, due to the many potential beneficiaries of such action, each with very little power, attempts to organize will suffer from the free-rider problem. The risk of losing well-established patronage relationships with the nonpoor will also discourage many low-income people from participation in demonstrations and violence.

In a well-functioning democracy, the voting booth offers an opportunity for the poor to influence at least the broad types of policies and programs to be pursued. However, even in such countries—whose number is unhappily small—the poor have relatively little influence on the design and implementation of specific policies and programs.

Therefore, the most promising avenue for the poor is coalition with the nonpoor. Such coalitions may be broadly aimed at power and influence beyond nutrition, or they may be narrowly focused. The poor have two things to offer their partners. First, because their poor and malnourished status is generally perceived to be undesirable, they provide legitimacy for transfers and market interventions that generate benefits, which, in turn, can be shared with the nonpoor. Second, the economic surplus generated as a result of improved nutrition may be shared with nonpoor coalition partners.

The expected benefits to potential partners must exceed expected costs of participating in the coalition. If the desired policies and programs move the economy away from the Pareto optimum, that is, they cause overall national income to fall, the incidence of costs should be separated from the incidence of benefits. For example, programs can be designed to assure benefits to nonpoor coalition partners, while costs are diffused among other groups of society. If the economy is moved closer to the Pareto optimum, as might be the case if the benefits from increased labor productivity exceed the cost of the nutrition intervention, and if the potential coalition partners derive a net benefit, it is not essential that the incidence of costs and benefits be separated. For example, provision of primary health care and improved sanitary conditions to workers may result in net benefits to the employer because the gains in labor productivity exceed the cost of the services.

The cost-effectiveness of government policies and programs from a nutrition point of view is a function of the degree to which the benefits are targeted to the malnourished. Effective targeting will reduce leakage to nontarget groups and increase the cost-effectiveness. However, as mentioned above, sharing the benefits with nontarget groups may be essential to assure political sustainability. This latter point is frequently overlooked in economic analyses of food and nutrition policies. In order to make relevant recommendations to policymakers, the trade-offs between cost-effectiveness and political sustainability must be explicitly considered. Taking political sustainability into account in efforts to increase the cost-effectiveness of nutrition-related policies and programs may result in either a two-pronged targeting approach aimed at the malnourished and the group providing the necessary support or a less exact targeting that would include a relatively large number of households that are not expected to have malnourished members. The latter will reduce the targeting cost and the error of exclusion, that is, the error of excluding target households from participating, while reducing the program's cost-effectiveness.

Targeting is essential to keep costs of some programs and policies, such as food price subsidies, reasonable without diluting the benefits received by the malnourished. For other programs, such as primary health care and the provision of clean water and improved sanitation, universal coverage may be appropriate. The cost of such programs may be reduced by charging user fees graduated according to ability to pay.

Most of the more likely coalition partners have been identified in this section. Some who have not but were discussed earlier in the chapter include importers, wholesalers, retailers, and processors whose incomes depend on a particular policy or program, and politicians and bureaucrats who are able to derive direct or indirect economic benefits from nutrition-related policies or who may derive power from the patronage the policy makes available to them. Agricultural producer associations may support food-related transfer programs that are expected to increase effective food demand and prices. Finally, program implementors and others whose employment depends on the policy will be logical coalition partners.

Macroeconomic Constraints

As de Janvry and Subramanian illustrate in chapter 1, system imperatives or macroeconomic constraints limit the political economy choices. When macroeconomic constraints are ignored over time, policies and programs may become unsustainable, as Utting illustrates in chapter 6 on Nicaragua. Current economic crises in many developing countries are partly an outcome of a failure to limit policies to a sustainable level within the macroeconomic constraints.

However, in most cases, it would be incorrect to blame current domestic crises solely on erroneous domestic policies. Changes in the international economic environment play a major role. Thus, the national governments and their agents are constrained in the long run by national macroeconomic conditions, which, in turn, are constrained by the international economic environment. Failure to conform to the macroeconomic constraints in the short run will result in the need for macroeconomic and sectoral reforms in the longer run, reforms that may be painful for the poor and cause deteriorations in their nutritional situation (Pinstrup-Andersen 1988b).

If national governments behave according to what Allison (1971) calls the "rational actor model," they would consider the macroeconomic constraints in the short run within the constraints of information availability. If, on the other hand, government behavior is better characterized by the "governmental (bureaucratic) politics model" (Allison 1971) and if the economy as a whole behaves according to the neoclassical political economy theory as argued by most authors in this book, it is no surprise that macroeconomic constraints are not adhered to in the short run. There is no reason for each actor to believe that the long-term costs they will incur by ignoring long-run macroeconomic constraints will exceed the short-term benefits.

Conclusions and Implications for Analysis and Action

In order to understand the complex process leading to specific nutrition-related action and to predict how this process will respond to alternative stimuli, it is essential not only to identify the key actors but also their goals and rationales, to assess their relative power within the process, and to attempt to model their behavior. It is also essential to better understand these actors' interactions, their dependencies and competitive relationships, their vested interests, and opportunities they may have to coalesce into mutually beneficial groups to the exclusion of others.

For policy analysts and advisors, such understanding is critically important to prioritize their work and to appropriately design analyses, policy papers, and other means of generating and transferring information.

Policy analysis based on a solid understanding of the political economy issues mentioned above is likely to result in information that is more relevant to the policy decisions at hand, more realistic within the existing power structure, and therefore more useful for the decision maker.

Unfortunately, a large part of past economic analysis applied to food and nutrition policy has ignored most of the important political economy issues and has consequently been of less use to the policymaker. This is not to argue that information from such analyses is useless; solid economic estimates of the consequences of alternative policy action is essential to good policy analysis. It is necessary but not sufficient to guide policy decisions.

One of the principal difficulties of integrating political and economic analyses into policy research is that neither the neoclassical political economy theory nor existing models of public-sector behavior in general and public and private sector rent-seeking behavior in particular are yet developed enough to be quantified and effectively integrated with quantitative economic models. Recent attempts by de Janvry, Roe, and others to endogenize certain political economy factors in economic models have promise, although unacceptably strong assumptions are often needed to avoid excessive model complexity. This book was conceived on the notion that an enhanced qualitative understanding of the political economy issues and relationships would assist in further improving the political economy approach to policy analysis, advice, design, and implementation.

The political economy analyses presented in this book illustrate clearly the vulnerability of the poor and malnourished who must depend on government for their survival. In most cases, government cannot be relied upon for continued support, unless the poor enter into coalitions with more powerful groups. A number of such coalition possibilities exist. Better still are efforts to reduce dependency on government by building elements of self-sustainability into policies and programs and to eliminate the causes of malnutrition, not just the symptoms, which would make government transfers unnecessary. To the extent that such efforts imply redistribution of relative power between the poor and other groups in the public and private sector, they will face opposition. They will also be opposed by groups of nonpoor who capture benefits from transfers and market distortions justified by the existence of poverty and malnutrition.

Efforts to alleviate malnutrition may be divided into programs focused directly on nutrition and the monitoring and modifications of broader policies, and programs with nutrition implications. The former should emphasize community participation, particularly the participation of the intended beneficiaries, in program design, implementation, and financing. The capacity to solve nutrition problems at the household and community levels should be strengthened to enhance the sustainability of the efforts and reduce the dependency on the national government. Local institutions should be strengthened, viable local coalitions identified, and efforts to generate information relevant to household and community decision-making, including community-based growth monitoring, promoted.

In order to ensure that nutrition is explicitly considered in the choice, design, and implementation of broader policies and programs and to support community level efforts, institutional strengthening at the national level is needed. Lessons from multisectoral nutrition planning and subsequent experience with alternative institutional models should be taken into account. As Jonsson and Hopkins delineate in chapters 12 and 13, more and better information about a variety of issues is needed to guide government action related to nutrition. In particular, more information about the costs and benefits of alternative policies and programs is needed, not just with respect to the malnourished but also to other groups that may support or oppose specific policies. Merely estimating costs to the government and benefits to the malnourished is clearly insufficient for policy guidance. Ignoring conflicts and potential compatibility among interest groups or other related political economy aspects of nutrition-related policies and programs in policy analysis and advice may result in erroneous recommendations and policies to the detriment of the malnourished who provided the rationale for this book.

References and Bibliography

Adams, Richard. 1985. "Development and Structural Change in Rural Egypt, 1952 to 1982." *World Development* 13(6):705–23.

———. 1986. *Development and Social Change in Rural Egypt*. Syracuse: Syracuse University Press.

———. 1991. The Effects of International Remittances on Poverty, Inequality, and Development in Rural Egypt. Research Report No. 86. Washington, D.C.: International Food Policy Research Institute.

Adelman, I.; Adelman, M.; and Taft, C. 1973. *Economic Growth and Social Equality in Developing Countries*. Stanford: Stanford University Press.

Administrative Committee on Coordination/Sub-Committee on Nutrition. 1985. "Report on the Eleventh Session of the ACC Sub-Committee on Nutrition and its Advisory Group on Nutrition." Nairobi: ACC/SCN.

Ahmed, B. 1972. *Leadership in Village Cooperatives*. Comilla: Bangladesh Academy of Rural Development.

Ahmed, R. 1981. "Foodgrain Distribution Policies within Dual Pricing Mechanisms: The Case of Bangladesh." In *Development Issues in an Agrarian Economy*, edited by W. Mahmud. Dacca: Center for Administrative Studies.

Akin, J.; Guilkey, D.; and Popkin, B. 1983. "The School Lunch Program and Nutrient Intake: A Switching Regression Analysis." *American Journal of Agricultural Economics* 65:477–85.

Alamgir, Mohiuddin. 1978. *Bangladesh: A Case of below Poverty Level Equilibrium Trap*. Dacca: Bangladesh Institute of Development Studies.

———. 1980. *Famine in South Asia*. Cambridge, Mass.: Oelgeschlager, Gunn and Hain.

———. 1981. "Towards Land Reform in Bangladesh." In *Land Reform in Bangladesh*, edited by M. K. Alamgir. Dacca: Bangladesh Centre for Social Studies.

Alderman, Harold, and Braun, Joachim von. 1984. *The Effects of the Egyptian Food Ration and Subsidy Scheme on Income Distribution and Consumption*. Research Report No. 45. Washington, D.C.: International Food Policy Research Institute.

Allen, S. R., and Koval, A. J. 1982. "Food Aid for Supplementary Feeding: A Case Study from Egypt." In *Nutrition Policy Implementation: Issues and Experience*, edited by N. S. Scrimshaw and M. B. Wallerstein, 115–30. New York: Plenum Press.

237

Allison, G. T. 1971. *Essence of Decision*. Boston: Little, Brown and Co.

Anderson, K., and Hayami, Y., with associates. 1986. *The Political Economy of Agricultural Protection: East Asia in International Perspective*. London: Allen and Unwin.

Andersson, I., and Andersson, C. 1984. *Development of Water Supplies in Singida Region, Tanzania*. Research Report 62. Dar es Salaam: Institute of Resource Development Assessment, University of Dar es Salaam.

Arens, J., and van Beurden, J. 1977. *Jhagrapur: Poor Peasants and Women in a Village in Bangladesh*. Amsterdam: Third World Publications.

Aschcraft, N. 1972. "Economic Opportunities and Patterns of Work: The Case of British Honduras." *Human Organization* 31:425–33.

Asociación Nacional De Industriales (ANDI). 1976. "An Analysis of the National Development to Close the Gap." *Revista* 29. Bogotá, Colombia: ANDI.

———. 1981. Various titles. *Revista* 53. Bogotá, Colombia: ANDI.

Atwater, W. O., and Benedict, F. G. 1899. "Experiments on the Metabolism of Matter and Energy in the Human Body." Bulletin No. 69, p. 76. Washington, D.C.: United States Department of Agriculture.

Austin, J. E., and Quelch, J. A. 1979. "U.S. National Dietary Goals: Food Industry Threat or Opportunity." *Food Policy* 4(2):115–28.

Bachrach, Peter, and Baratz, Morton. 1970. *Power and Poverty, Theory and Practice*. New York: Oxford University Press.

Baldwin, R., and Weisbrod, B. 1974. "Disease and Labor Productivity." *Economic Development and Cultural Change* 22:414–35.

Ball, Nicole, 1981. *World Hunger: A Guide to the Economic and Political Dimensions*. Santa Barbara, Calif.: ABC-Clio Press.

Banerji, D. 1973. "Health Behaviour of Rural Populations." *Economic and Political Weekly* 7:2261–68.

Banfield, E. C. 1958. *The Moral Basis of a Backward Society*. New York: Free Press.

Bangladesh Rural Advancement Committee. 1979. *Who Gets What and Why: Resource Allocation in a Bangladesh Village*. Dacca: Bangladesh Rural Advancement Committee.

Bardach, E. 1977. *The Implementation Game: What Happens after a Bill Becomes a Law?* Cambridge, Mass.: MIT Press.

Bardhan, Pranab. 1984a. *Land, Labor, and Rural Poverty: Essays in Development Economics*. New York: Columbia University Press.

———. 1984b. *The Political Economy of Development in India*. Cambridge: Basil Blackwell.

Barker, J. 1985. "Gaps in the Debates about Agriculture in Senegal, Tanzania, and Mozambique." *World Development* 13(1):67.

Barraclough, S. 1982. *A Preliminary Analysis of the Nicaraguan Food System*. Geneva: UNRISD.

Barrera, A. 1988. "The Role of Maternal Schooling and Its Interaction with Public Health Programs in Child Health Production." Economic Growth Center Discussion Paper No. 551, Yale University.

Basiotis, P.; Brown, M.; Johnson, S. R.; and Morgan, K. 1982. "Nutrient Availability, Food Costs, and Food Stamp Program Participation for Low-Income Households,

1979–80." Report prepared under USDA Grant No. 53–3244–9–88. Department of Agricultural Economics, University of Missouri.

————. 1983. "Nutrient Availability, Food Costs, and Food Stamps." *American Journal of Agricultural Economics* 65(4):685–93.

Basta, S. S.; Soekirman; Karyadi, D.; and Scrimshaw, N. S. 1979. "Iron Deficiency Anemia and Productivity of Adult Males in Indonesia." *American Journal of Clinical Nutrition* 32:916–25.

Bates, Robert. 1981. *Markets and States in Tropical Africa.* Berkeley: University of California Press.

Baumeister, E., and Neira, O. 1984. "Economia y Politica en las Relaciones Entre el Estado y el Sector Privado en el Procesos Nicaraguense." Paper presented at the seminar Los Problemas de la Transicion en Pequenas Economias Perifiericas, Managua, Nicaragua.

Beaton, G. 1983. "Energy in Human Nutrition: Perspectives and Problems." W. O. Atwater Memorial Lecture, Miami Beach, Florida.

Beaton, G. H., and Ghassemi, H. 1979. "Supplementary Feeding Programs for Young Children in Developing Countries." *American Journal of Clinical Nutrition* 35:864–916.

Beck, G., and Van den Berg, B. 1975. "The Relationship of the Rate of Intrauterine Growth of Low Birthweight Infants to Later Growth." *Journal of Pediatrics* 86:504–11.

Beghin, I. 1979a. "The Holistic Approach in the Causation of Hunger and Malnutrition, and the Identification of General Goals for Their Prevention." Paper presented at Workshop on Goals, Processes and Indicators for Food and Nutrition Policy and Planning, Massachusetts Institute of Technology.

————. 1979b. "Nutrition and National Development Planning." *Bibliotheca Nutritio et Dieta* 28:137–47.

Behrman, J., and Wolfe, B. 1984. "More Evidence on Nutrition Demand: Income Seems Overrated and Women's Schooling Underemphasized." *Journal of Development Economics* 14:105–28.

————. 1987. "How Does Mother's Schooling Affect Family, Health, Nutrition, Medical Care Usage and Household Sanitation?" *Journal of Econometrics* 36:185–204.

Behrman, J.; Wolfe, B.; and Blau, D. 1985. "Human Capital and Earnings Distribution in a Developing Country: The Case of Prerevolutionary Nicaragua." *Economic Development and Cultural Change* 34:1–30.

Belden, J. 1978. "Food Strategy for Canada." *Food Policy* 3(2):82–83.

Belize, Government of. 1964. *Seven-Year Development Plan, 1964–1970.* Belmopan, Belize: Office of the Prime Minister.

————. 1974. *Agricultural Census, 1973–1974.* Belmopan, Belize: Ministry of Natural Resources.

————. 1980. *The Belize Home Production and Consumption Survey, 1980.* Belmopan, Belize: Planning Unit.

————. 1982. *The Belize Home Production and Consumption Survey, 1982.* Belmopan, Belize: Planning Unit.

Belli, P. 1971. "The Economic Implications of Malnutrition: The Dismal Science Revisited." *Economic Development and Cultural Change* 20:1–23.

Bensel, Richard F. 1984. *Sectionalism and American Political Development.* Madison: University of Wisconsin Press.

Berg, Alan. 1973. *The Nutrition Factor.* Washington, D.C.: The Brookings Institution.

———. 1984. *Nutrition Review.* Washington, D.C.: World Bank Population, Health and Nutrition Department.

———. 1987a. *Malnutrition: What Can Be Done?* Washington, D.C.: World Bank.

———. 1987b. "Rejoinder: Nutrition Planning is Alive and Well, Thank You." *Food Policy* 4(12):365–75.

Berg, A.; Scrimshaw, N. S.; and Call, D. L. 1971. *Nutrition, Nutritional Development and Planning.* Cambridge, Mass.: MIT Press.

Berry, Jeffrey, 1978. "Food Stamps: The Recurring Issues." In *The New Politics of Food,* edited by D. Hadwiger and W. Browne. Lexington, Mass.: Lexington Books.

———. 1982. "Consumers and the Hunger Lobby." In *Food Policy and Farm Programs,* edited by D. Hadwiger and R. Talbot. Montpelier, Vt.: Capital City Press.

———. 1984. *Feeding Hungry People: Rule Making in the Food Stamp Program.* New Brunswick: Rutgers University Press.

Bertocci, Peter J. 1972. "Community Structure and Social Rank in Two Indian Villages in Bangladesh." *Contributions to Indian Sociology* 6:28–52.

Beutler, E. 1980. "Iron." In *Modern Nutrition in Health and Disease,* 6th ed., edited by J. G. Wohl and R. S. Goodhant, 324–54. Philadelphia: Lea and Febiger.

Bhaduri, A. 1973. "A Study of Agricultural Backwardness under Semi-Feudalism." *Economic Journal* 73:120–37.

Bhalla, Surjit. 1985. "Living Standards in Sri Lanka in the Seventies: Mirage and Reality." Washington, D.C.: World Bank. Mimeo.

———. 1986. "Is Sri Lanka an Exception? A Comparative Study of Living Standards." In *Rural Poverty in South Asia,* edited by T. N. Srinivasan and P. Bardhan. New York: Columbia University Press.

Bienen, Henry S., and Gersovitz, Mark. 1984. "Consumer Subsidy Cuts, Violence and Political Stability." Princeton University. Typescript.

Binder, Leonard. 1978. *In a Moment of Enthusiasm: Political Power and the Second Stratum in Egypt.* Chicago: University of Chicago Press.

Blair, Harry. 1978. "Rural Development, Class Structure and Bureaucracy in Bangladesh." *World Development* 6(1):65–82.

Blau, D. 1984. "A Model of Child Nutrition, Fertility and Women's Time Allocation: The Case of Nicaragua." In *Research in Population Economics 5,* edited by T. P. Schultz and K. Wolpin. Greenwich, Conn. JAI Press.

Blythe, C. 1978. "Norwegian Nutrition and Food Policy: Consumer Information and Price Policy Aspects." *Food Policy* 3(3):163–79.

Bodemann, Y. M. 1981. "Class Rule as Patronage-Kinship, Local Ruling Cliques and the State in Rural Sardinia." *Journal of Peasant Studies* 9.

Bonnen, J. 1984. "U.S. Agriculture, Instability, and National Political Institutions: The Shift from Representative to Participatory Democracy." In *United States Agricultural Policy: 1984 and Beyond,* edited by J. Hillman, 58. A series of monographs prepared by the Department of Agricultural Economics, University of Arizona, and Resources for the Future.

Boyd-Orr, J. 1937. "The Science of Nutrition and Agriculture Policy." In *N.F.U. Yearbook 1937*, 312–31. London: National Farmers' Union.

Bratton, Michael. 1980. *The Local Politics of Rural Development: Peasant and Party-State in Zambia*. Hanover, N.H.: University Press of New England.

Braun, Joachim von, and de Haen, Hartwig. 1983. *The Effects of Food Price and Subsidy Policies on Egyptian Agriculture*. Research Report 42. Washington, D.C.: International Food Policy Research Institute.

Brewer, Garry, ed. 1975. *A Policy Approach to the Study of Political Development and Change*. New York: Free Press.

Brewster, J. 1970. "The Cultural Crisis of Our Time." In *A Philosopher among Economists*. Philadelphia: J. T. Murphy Co.

Brock, W. A., and Magee, S. P. 1978. *The Economics of Pork-Barrel Politics*. Working Paper 78–78. University of Texas at Austin: Bureau of Business Research.

Brockman, Tom C. 1977. "The Farmers and Agriculture of Orange Walk Town." *Journal of Belizean Affairs*. Special Issue.

Brooks, R. M.; Latham, M. C.; and Crompton, D. W. T. 1979. "The Relationship of Nutrition and Health to Worker Productivity in Kenya." *East African Medical Journal* 56:413–21.

Browne, A., and Wildavsky, A. 1984. "Implementation as Mutual Adaptation." In *Implementation*, edited by J. L. Pressman and A. Wildavsky, 206–31. Berkeley: University of California Press.

———. 1984. "Implementation as Exploration." In *Implementation*, edited by J. L. Pressman and A. Wildavsky, 232–56. Berkeley: University of California Press.

Burkhalter, B. R. 1974. *A Critical Review of Nutrition Planning Models and Experience*. Ann Arbor, Mich.: Community Systems Foundation.

Caiden, N., and Wildavsky, A. 1974. *Planning and Budgeting in Poor Countries*. New York: Wiley.

Caribbean Agricultural Extension Project (CAEP). 1983. *Institutional Analysis of Agricultural Extension in Belize*. Trinidad: University of the West Indies.

Caribbean Food and Nutrition Institute (CFNI). 1976. *An Assessment of the Food and Nutrition Situation in Belize*. Kingston, Jamaica: CFNI.

———. 1977. *Identification of the Food and Nutrition Problem in Belize*. Kingston, Jamaica: CFNI.

———. 1978. *A Food and Nutrition Policy for Belize*. Kingston, Jamaica: CFNI.

Center for National Policy. 1985. "Food and Agriculture Policies: Proposals for Change." Washington, D.C.: CNP. Mimeo.

Center on Budget and Policy Priorities. 1984. "End Results: The Impact of Federal Policies since 1980 on Low-Income Americans." Washington, D.C.: Interfaith Action for Economic Justice.

Central Bank of Ceylon. 1984. *Annual Reports*. Colombo, Sri Lanka.

———. 1973, 1978–79, 1981–82. *Central Bank's Finances and Socio-Economic Survey*. Colombo, Sri Lanka.

———. 1980–81. *Report on Consumer Finances and Socio-Economic Survey*. Colombo, Sri Lanka.

Centre for Agricultural Strategy. 1979. *National Food Policy in the U.K.* CAS Report No. 5. University of Reading.

Chambers, Robert. 1966. "Harnessing Social Science." *East Africa Journal* 3(8):30–38.

———. 1974. *Managing Rural Development: Ideas and Experience from East Africa.* Uppsala, Sweden: Scandinavian Institute of African Studies.

———. 1977. "Poverty and Future Rural Development in Africa: Perceptions, Pitfalls, and Proposals." Paper prepared for the Ninth International Conference of the Institute for International Cooperation, University of Ottawa.

Chandra, R. K. 1982. "Malnutrition and Infection." In *Nutrition Policy Implementation: Issues and Experience,* edited by N. S. Scrimshaw and M. B. Wallerstein. New York: Plenum Press.

Chen, J. S., and Johnson, S. R. 1983. "Food Stamp Program Participation and Food Cost: A Simultaneous Equations Analysis with Qualitative and Continuous Dependent Variables." Report prepared under USDA Grant No. 53–3244–9–1988. University of Missouri, Department of Agricultural Economics.

Chen, L.; Chowdhury, A. K. M. A.; and Huffman, S. 1980. "Anthropometric Assessment of Energy—Protein Malnutrition and Subsequent Risk of Mortality among Preschool Aged Children." *American Journal of Clinical Nutrition* 33:1836–45.

Chernichovsky, D. 1979. "The Economic Theory of the Household and the Impact Measurement of Nutrition and Related Programs." In *Evaluating the Impact of Nutrition and Health Programs,* edited by R. Klein, M. Read, H. Riecken, J. Brown, A. Pradilla, and C. Daza. New York: Plenum Press.

Chernichovsky, D., et al. 1983. "Correlates of Preschool Child Growth in Rural Punjab." In *Child and Maternal Health Services in Rural India: The Narangwal Experiment,* edited by A. Kielmann. Baltimore: Johns Hopkins University Press.

CIERA (Centro de Investigaciones y Estudios de la Reforma Agraria. 1984. *Directorio de Politicas Alimentaires.* Managua, Nicaragua: CIERA.

———. 1985. "El ABC del Abastecimiento." Internal Document. Managua, Nicaragua: CIERA.

Claffey, B., and Stucker, T. 1982. "The Food Stamp Program." In *Food Policy and Farm Programs,* edited by D. Hadwiger and R. Talbot. Montpelier, Vt.: Capital City Press.

Cleaves, P. S. 1980. "Implementation amidst Scarcity and Apathy: Political Power and Policy Design." In *Politics and Policy Implementation in the Third World,* edited by M. S. Grindle, 281–303. Princeton: Princeton University Press.

Cobb, Roger; Ross, Jennie-Kieth; and Ross, Marc. 1976. "Agenda Building as a Comparative Political Process." *American Political Science Review* 70(1):126–38.

Cochrane, S.; Leslie, J.; and O'Hara, D. 1982. "Parental Education and Child Health: Intracountry Evidence. *Health Policy and Education* 2:213–50. Congressional Budget Office. 1977. "The Food Stamp Program: Income or Food Supplementation?" Washington, D.C.

Congressional Research Service. 1984. *Final Report of the President's Task Force on Food Assistance.* Washington, D.C.

Consolazio, C. F.; Johnson, R. E.; and Pecora, L. J. 1963. *Physiological Measurements of Metabolic Functions in Man.* New York: McGraw-Hill.

Coulson, Andrew. 1982. *Tanzania: A Political Economy.* New York: Oxford University Press.

Cravioto, J., and DeLicardie, E. 1973. "Nutrition and Behavior and Learning." *World Review of Nutrition* 16:80–96.

Cuddihy, William. 1980. *Agricultural Price Management in Egypt*. Staff Working Paper 388. Washington, D.C.: World Bank.

Dahl, R. A. 1961. *Who Governs? Democracy and Power in an American City*. New Haven, Conn.: Yale University Press.

Danziger, S., and Gottschalk, P. 1985. "The Poverty of Losing Ground." *Challenge* (May–June):32–39.

Davies, C. 1973. "Relationship of Maximum Aerobic Power Output to Productivity and Absenteeism of East African Sugarcane Workers." *British Journal of Industrial Medicine* 30:146–54.

———. 1982. "Linkages between Socioeconomic Characteristics, Food Expenditure Patterns, and Nutritional Status of Low-Income Households: A Critical Review." *American Journal of Agricultural Economics* 64(5):1016–25.

Davis, C. G.; Sanderson, J. H.; Bailey, L. B.; Wagner, P. A.; Dinning, J.; and Christakis, G. J. 1985. "Factors Affecting Food Consumption and Nutrient Achievement of Elderly Minority Households: Metropolitan Dade County, Florida." University of Florida Experiment Station Bulletin.

De Bello, J. 1980. "The Food Stamp Plan of 1939–1943." Honors Thesis, Harvard University.

de Janvry, Alain. 1981. *The Agrarian Question and Reformism in Latin America*. Baltimore: Johns Hopkins University Press.

de Janvry, Alain, and Subbarao, K. 1984. *Agricultural Price Policy and Income Distribution in India*. Giannini Foundation of Agricultural Economics Working Paper 274. Berkeley: University of California.

de Melo, Martha. 1981. "Modeling the Effects of Alternative Approaches to Basic Human Needs: Case Study of Sri Lanka." In *Basic Needs and Development*, edited by D. Leipziger and P. Streeten. Cambridge, Mass.: Oelgeschlager, Gunn, and Hain.

Deolalikar, A. 1984. "Are There Pecuniary Returns to Health in Agricultural Work? An Econometric Analysis of Agricultural Wages and Farm Productivity in Rural South India." Economic Program Progress Report 38. Hyderabad, India: ICRISAT.

———. 1988. "Nutrition and Labor Productivity in Agriculture: Estimates for Rural South India." *Review of Economics and Statistics* 70:406–13.

Departamento Nacional de Planeación (DNP). 1975. *To Close the Gap/Social, Economic and Regional Development Plan 1974–78*. Bogotá, Colombia.

———. 1980. *National Integration Plan 1979–82*. Bogotá, Colombia.

Departamento Nacional de Planeación–National Food and Nutrition Program DNP-PAN. 1977–1982. *Evaluation and Implementation Reports*. Bogotá, Colombia.

Dethier, Jean-Jacques. 1985. "The Political Economy of Food Prices in Egypt." Ph.D. diss., University of California, Berkeley.

DeVault, M., and Pitts, J. 1984. "Surplus and Scarcity: Hunger and the Origins of the Food Stamp Program." *Social Problems* 31(5):545–57.

Dewey, Katherine G. 1981. "Nutritional Consequences of the Transformation from Subsistence to Commercial Agriculture in Tabasco, Mexico." *Human Ecology* 9:151–87.

Downs, A. 1967. *Economic Theory of Democracy.* New York: Harper and Row.

Dumont, R. 1963. "A Development Plan for British Honduras: Part Two." In *The Modernization of Agriculture.* Government of Belize and the United Nations.

Economic Commission for Africa. 1982. "Situation of Food and Agriculture in Africa: A Synopsis." New York: United Nations.

Economic Commission for Latin America (ECLA). 1984. "Balance Preliminar de la Economia Latinoamericano Durante 1984." Santiago: ECLA.

Edgerton, V. R.; Gardner, G. W.; Okira, Y.; Gunawardens, K. A.; and Senewiratne, B. 1979. "Iron Deficiency Anemia and Its Effect on Worker Productivity and Activity Patterns." *British Medical Journal* 2:1546–49.

Edirisinghe, Neville. 1984. "The Implications of the Change from Ration Shops to Food Stamps in Sri Lanka for Fiscal Costs, Income Distribution, and Nutrition." Washington, D.C.: International Food Policy Research Institute.

———. 1985. "Preliminary Report on the Food Stamp Scheme in Sri Lanka: Distribution of Benefits and Impact on Nutrition." Washington, D.C.: International Food Policy Research Institute. Mimeo.

Edirisinghe, Neville, and Poleman, Thomas T. 1976. "Implications of Government Intervention in the Rice Economy of Sri Lanka." International Monograph 48. Ithaca, N.Y.: Cornell University.

Eicher, Carl K. 1985. "Agricultural Research for African Development: Problems and Priorities for 1985–2000." Paper prepared for a World Bank Conference on Research Priorities for Sub-Saharan Africa, Bellagio, Italy.

Engelmann, E.; Wittung, W.; and Mohr, U. 1983. *Mischmehl für die menschliche Ernährung.* GTZ-Project No. 77.2285.03.01.100. Final Report. Lima: GTZ.

Esman, Milton. 1978. "Landlessness and Near-Landlessness in Developing Countries." Paper prepared for United States Agency for International Development. Washington, D.C.: USAID.

Esman, M., and Montgomery, J. D. 1980. "The Administration of Human Development." In *Implementing Programs of Human Development,* edited by P. Knight, 183–234. Washington, D.C.: World Bank.

Fadil, Mahmoud Abdel. 1975. *Development, Income Distribution and Social Change in Rural Egypt, 1952–1970.* Cambridge: Cambridge University Press.

Fairclough, E. H. 1981. *The Belize Household Expenditure Survey, 1980.* Belize: Government of Belize, Central Planning Unit.

Fallows, S. J., and Wheelock, J. V. 1982. "Strategies for Reducing Fat in the U.K. Diet." *Food Policy* 7(3):222–28.

Ferejohn, J. 1983. "Congress and Redistribution." In *Making Economic Policy in Congress,* edited by A. Schick, 139–46. Washington, D.C.: American Enterprise Institute.

Field, John Osgood. 1977. "The Soft Underbelly of Applied Knowledge: Conceptual and Operational Problems in Nutrition Planning." *Food Policy* 2:228–39.

———. 1978. "Nutrition, Malnutrition, and Disease: A Social Science Perspective." Paper prepared for workshop on Nutritional Intake and Disease Response, Hyannis, Massachusetts.

———. 1983a. "Development at the Grassroots: The Organizational Imperative." In *Nutrition in the Community,* 2d ed., edited by D. S. McLaren, 357–71. Chichester, England: Wiley.

———. 1983b. "The Importance of Context: Nutrition Planning and Development Reconsidered." In *Nutrition in the Community,* 2d ed., edited by D. S. McLaren, 61–78. Chichester, England: Wiley.

———. 1985. "Implementing Nutrition Programs: Lessons from an Unheeded Literature." *Annual Review of Nutrition* 5:143–72.

———. 1987. "Multisectoral Nutrition Planning: A Post-Mortem." *Food Policy* 1(12):15–28.

Field, J. O.; Burkhardt, R.; and Ropes, G. 1981. "Supplementary Feeding in Rural Egypt: The Health System in Action." *Food Policy* 6:163–72.

Field, J. O., and Levinson, F. J. 1975. "Nutrition and Development: Dynamics of Political Commitment." *Food Policy* 1:53–61.

Fishbein, B. K. 1977. "The Food Stamp Program: A Legislative History with an Analysis of the Program in Westchester County." *Journal of the Institute for Socioeconomic Studies,* Special Supplement.

Fitzgerald, E. V. K. 1984. "Diez Problemas para el Analisis de la Pequena Economia Periferica en Transicion." Paper presented at seminar on Los Problemas de la Transicion en Pequenas Economias Perifericas, Managua, Nicaragua.

———. 1985. "La Economia Nacional en 1985: La Transicion como Coyuntara." Paper presented at the 1985 Annual Congress of Nicaraguan Social Scientists, Managua, Nicaragua.

Fleuret, P., and Fleuret, A. 1980. "Nutrition, Consumption, and Agricultural Change." *Human Organization* 39:250–60.

Flynn, Peter. 1974. "Class, Clientelism and Coercion: Some Mechanisms of Internal Dependency and Control." *Journal of Commonwealth and Comparative Politics* 12(2).

Food and Agriculture Organization of the United Nations (FAO). 1981. "Introducing Nutrition into Agricultural and Rural Development." Paper prepared for the 6th session of the Committee on Agriculture, COAG 81/6.

———. 1982. *Integrating Nutrition into Agricultural and Rural Development Projects: A Manual.* Rome: FAO Food Policy and Nutrition Division.

———. 1984. "Declaration on the Eradication of Hunger and Malnutrition." World Food Conference.

Food Research and Action Center (FRAC). 1981. *Food and Nutrition Issues in the Food Stamp Program.* Washington, D.C.: FRAC.

———. 1983. "Still Hungry: A Survey of People's Need of Emergency Food." Washington, D.C.

Foster, George. 1960. "Interpersonal Relations in Peasant Society." *Human Organization* 19(4):174–80.

———. 1961. "The Dyadic Contract: A Model for Social Structure of a Mexican Peasant Village." *American Anthropologist* 63:1173–92.

———. 1965. "Peasant Society and the Image of the Limited Good." *American Anthropologist* 65(4):296.

Gann, Thomas W. F. 1919. *The Maya Indians of Southern Yucatan and Northern British Honduras.* Bulletin 64. Washington: Smithsonian Institution, Bureau of American Ethnology.

García, Jorge G. 1979. "¿Hay Inseguridad Alimentaría en Colombia?" *Planning and Development Journal* 21(3).

Garcia, Marito, and Pinstrup-Andersen, Per. 1987. *The Pilot Food Price Subsidy Scheme in the Philippines: Its Impact on Income, Food Consumption, and Nutritional Status.* Research Report 61. Washington, D.C.: International Food Policy Research Institute.

Gardner, G. W.; Edgerton, R. V.; Senewiratne, B.; Barnard, R. J.; and Okira, Y. 1977. "Physical Work Capacity and Metabolic Stress in Subjects with Iron Deficiency Anemia." *American Journal of Clinical Nutrition* 30:910–17.

Gavan, James D., and Chandrasekera, Indrani Sri. 1979. *The Impact of Public Food-grain Distribution on Food Consumption and Welfare in Sri Lanka.* Research Report 13. Washington, D.C.: International Food Policy Research Institute.

George, P. S. 1979. *Public Distribution of Foodgrains in Kerala—Income Distribution Implications and Effectiveness.* Research Report 7. Washington, D.C.: International Food Policy Research Institute.

Gesellschaft für Technische Zusammenarbeit (GTZ). 1982. *Introduction Nutrition Consideration into the Bo-Pujehun Rural Development Project, Sierra Leone.* Eschborn Germany: GTZ.

———. 1985. *Fachseminar: Ernährungsaspekte in der Ländlichen Entwicklung.* Feldafing Germany: DSE.

Gilman, R. H., and Skillicorn, P. 1984. "Boiling of Drinking Water: Can a Fuel Scarce Community Afford It?" Johns Hopkins School of Medicine and Bangladesh International Center for Diarrheal Disease Research. Typescript.

Gopalan, C. 1983. "Small Is Healthy?" Bulletin 8:33–37. Nutrition Foundation of India.

Gopaldas, T. 1975. *Project Poshak,* vols. 1 and 2. New Delhi: CARE.

Gorostiaga, X. 1982. *Dilemas de la Revolucion Popular Sandinista a Tṛes Anos del Triunfo.* Managua, Nicaragua: INIES/CRIES.

Grant, J. P. 1982. "The State of the World's Children, 1982–83." New York: UNICEF.

———. 1985. *The State of the World's Children, 1985.* Oxford: Oxford University Press.

Greenstein, R. 1985. Testimony in Hearings before the House Agriculture Subcommittee on Domestic Marketing, Consumer Affairs, and Nutrition. 99th Cong., 1st sess.

Greger, J. 1985. "A Review of the Thrifty Food Plan and its Use in the Food Stamp Program." Committee on Agriculture, U.S. House of Representatives.

Griffin, Keith. 1974. *The Political Economy of Agrarian Change.* Cambridge: Harvard University Press.

Gunatilleke, G. 1990. "Government Policies and Nutrition In Sri Lanka: Changes during the Last Ten Years and Lessons Learned." Pew/Cornell Lecture Series on Food and Nutrition Policy. Ithaca, N.Y.: Cornell Food and Nutrition Policy Program.

Gwatkin, D. R. 1979a. "Food Policy, Nutrition Planning, and Survival—The Cases, Kerala and Sri Lanka." *Food Policy* 4:4.

———. 1979b. "Political Will and Family Planning: The Implications of India's Emergency Experience." *Population and Development Review* 5:29–59.

Gwatkin, D. R.; Wilcox, J. R.; and Wray, J. D. 1980. *Can Health and Nutrition Interventions Make a Difference?* Washington, D.C.: Overseas Development Council.

Habicht, J. P., and Butz, W. P. 1979. "Measurement of Health and Nutrition Effects of Large Scale Intervention Projects." In *Evaluating the Impact of Nutrition and Health Programs,* edited by R. Klein, M. Read, H. Riecken, J. Brown, A. Pradilla, and C. Daza, 133–69. New York: Plenum Press.

Hagedorn, K. 1983. "The Methodology of Agricultural Policy Research." *European Review of Agricultural Economics* 10(4):303–23.

Hager, C. 1980. "Policy Implications of USDA Food Plans." NED-ESCS-USDA. ESS Staff Report No. AGESS 801212. Washington, D.C.: U.S. Department of Agriculture.

Hakim, Peter, and Solimano, Giorgio. 1976. "Nutrition and National Development: Establishing the Connection." *Food Policy* 1:249–59.

———. 1978. *Development, Reform and Malnutrition in Chile.* Cambridge: MIT Press.

Hambraeus, L. 1979. "The Nutritionist's Role in Food and Nutrition Policymaking in Affluent Societies." In *Nutrition in Europe,* edited by L. Hambraeus. Stockholm: Almqvist and Wiksell International.

Hamermesh, D., and Johannes, J. 1985. "Food Stamps as Money: The Macroeconomics of a Transfer Program." *Journal of Political Economy* 93(1):205–13.

Hannah, L. M. 1976. "Hand Pump Irrigation in Bangladesh." *Bangladesh Development Studies* 4.

Harberger, Arnold C. 1979. *Basic Needs Versus Distributional Weights in Social Cost-Benefit Analysis.* Background notes for a seminar, World Bank. Typescript.

Harbert, Lloyd, and Scandizzo, Pasquale. 1982. *Food Distribution and Nutritional Intervention—The Case of Chile.* Staff Working Paper 512. Washington, D.C.: World Bank.

Harik, Iliya. 1979. *Distribution of Land, Employment and Income in Rural Egypt.* Special Series on Landlessness and Near-Landlessness, Rural Development Committee. Ithaca, N.Y.: Cornell University Press.

Harper, A. E.; Payne, P. R.; and Waterlow, J. C. 1973. "Human Protein Needs." *The Lancet* (June).

Havnevik, K., and Skarstein, R. 1983. "Some Notes on Agricultural Backwardness in Tanzania." In *Poverty and Aid,* edited by J. R. Parkinson, 152–59. Oxford: Basil Blackwell.

Hayami, Yujiro; Subbarao, K.; and Otsuka, K. 1982. "Efficiency and Equity in Producer Levy of India." *American Journal of Agricultural Economics* 64:654–63.

Health Education Council. 1983. "A Discussion Paper on Proposals for Nutritional Guidelines for Health Education in Britain." Prepared for the National Advisory Committee on Nutrition Education by an ad hoc working group.

Heginbotham, S. J. 1975. *Cultures in Conflict: The Four Faces of Indian Bureaucracy.* New York: Columbia University Press.

Heller, P. S., and Drake, W. D. 1979. "Malnutrition, Child Morbidity and the Family Decision Process." *Journal of Development Economics* 6:203–35.

Hernandez, M.; Perez Hidalgo, C.; Ramirez Hernandez, J.; Madrigal, H.; and Chavez,

A. 1974. "Effect of Economic Growth on Nutrition in a Tropical Community." *Ecology of Food and Nutrition* 3:283–91.

Herring, Ronald. 1981. "The Janus-Faced State in a Dependent Society: Sri Lanka's Shifts in Development Strategy." Northwestern University, Evanston, Ill. Mimeo.

————. 1985. "Food, Policy and Welfare in Sri Lanka: Before and after the Liberal Regime." Paper presented at the Conference on Food Security and the International Political Economy, Logan, Utah.

Heywood, P. F. 1974. "Malnutrition and Productivity in Jamaican Sugarcane Cutters." Ph.D. diss., Cornell University, Ithaca, N.Y.

Heywood, P. F.; Latham, M. C.; and Cook, R. 1974. "Nutritional Status and Productivity of Jamaican Sugar Cane Cutters." *Federation Proceedings* 33:2646.

Hirschman, A. O. 1967. *Development Projects Observed*. Washington, D.C.: The Brookings Institution.

Hoagland, W. 1984. "Perception and Reality in Nutrition Programs." In *Maintaining the Safety Net*, edited by J. Weicher, 43–55. Washington, D.C.: American Enterprise Institute.

Hopkins, Raymond F. 1984a. "The Evolution of Food Aid." *Food Policy* (November):345–62.

————. 1984b. "Food, Agriculture, and Famine." In *Africa in the Post Decolonization Era*, edited by Richard Bissele and Michael Radu, 59–82. New Brunswick: Transaction Books.

————. 1986. "Food Security, Policy Options and the Evolution of State Responsibility." In *Food, the State, and International Political Economy*, edited by F. Lamond Tullis and W. Ladd Hollis. Lincoln: University of Nebraska Press.

————. 1988. "Political Calculations in Subsidizing Food." In *Food Subsidies in Developing Countries*, edited by Per Pinstrup-Andersen, 107–26. Baltimore: Johns Hopkins University Press.

Horton, S. 1986. "Child Nutrition and Family Size in the Philippines." *Journal of Development Economics* 23:161–76.

————. 1988. "Birth Order and Nutritional Status: Evidence from the Philippines." *Economic Development and Cultural Change* 36:341–54.

Huddleston, Barbara. 1984. *Closing the Cereal Gap with Trade and Food Aid*. Research Report 43. Washington, D.C.: International Food Policy Research Institute.

————. 1985. "Quantifying the Evolving Food Problem." Paper prepared for IDS Seminar, Sussex, Brighton, England.

Hunter, Guy. 1969. *Modernizing Peasant Societies*. London: Oxford University Press.

Huntington, S. P. 1968. *Political Order in Changing Societies*. New Haven: Yale University Press.

Hyden, Goran. 1975. "Ujamaa Villagization and Rural Development in Tanzania." *ODI Review* 1:66.

————. 1980. *Beyond Ujamaa in Tanzania: Underdevelopment and an Uncaptured Peasantry*. Berkeley: University of California Press.

————. 1983. *No Shortcuts to Progress: African Development Management in Perspective*. Berkeley: University of California Press.

Ilchman, W. F., and Uphoff, N. T. 1971. *The Political Economy of Change*. Berkeley: University of California Press.

Immink, M., and Viteri, F. 1981a. "Energy Intake and Productivity of Guatemalan Sugarcane Cutters: An Empirical Test of the Efficiency Wage Hypothesis, Part I." *Journal of Development Economics* 9:251–72.

———. 1981b. "Energy Intake and Productivity of Guatemalan Sugarcane Cutters: An Empirical Test of the Efficiency Wage Hypothesis, Part II." *Journal of Development Economics* 9:273–87.

Immink, M.; Viteri, F.; and Helms, R. 1982. "Energy Intake over the Life Cycle and Human Capital Formation in Guatemalan Sugarcane Cutters." *Economic Development and Cultural Change* 30:351–72.

Institute of Nutrition and Food Science. 1977. *Nutrition Survey of Rural Bangladesh, 1975–76.* Dacca: University of Dacca.

Isenman, Paul. 1980. "Basic Needs: The Case of Sri Lanka." *World Development* 8:237–58.

Jabbar, M. S.; Mandal, M. A. S.; and Elahi, K. K. 1980. "Usufructuary Land Mortgage: A Process Contributing to Growing Landlessness in Bangladesh." *Bangladesh Journal of Agricultural Economics.*

Jahangir, B. K. 1979. *Differentiation, Polarization, and Confrontation in Rural Bangladesh.* Dacca: Center for Social Studies.

Jamison, D. 1983. "Child Malnutrition and School Performance in China." Washington, D.C.: World Bank, Population, Health, Nutrition Department. Typescript.

Jamison, D., and Lau, L. 1982. *Farmer Education and Farm Efficiency.* Baltimore: Johns Hopkins University Press.

Jannuzi, F. T., and Peach, J. T. 1980. *The Agrarian Structure of Bangladesh: An Impediment to Development.* Boulder, Colorado: Westview Press.

Jenkins, C. L. 1980. "Patterns of Protein-Energy Malnutrition among Preschoolers in Belize." Ph.D. diss., University of Tennessee.

Johnston, B. F., and Clark, W. C. 1982. *Redesigning Rural Development: A Strategic Perspective.* Baltimore: Johns Hopkins University Press.

Jonsson, U. 1983. "A Conceptual Approach to the Understanding and Explanation of Hunger and Malnutrition in Society." Paper presented at TFNC-UNICEF Workshop on Hunger and Society, 5–9 December, Suleiwayo, Tanzania.

———. 1988. "A Conceptual Approach to the Understanding and Explanation of Hunger and Malnutrition in Society." In *Hunger and Society,* edited by M. Latham et al. Monograph No. 17. Ithaca, New York: Cornell University International Monograph Series.

Joy, L. 1983. "Food and Nutrition Planning." *Journal of Agricultural Economics* 24:165–92.

Joy, L., ed. 1978. *Nutrition Planning: The State of the Art.* Guildford, England: IPC.

Joy, L. and Payne, P. R. 1975. *Food and Nutrition Planning.* Nutrition Consultants Reports Series 35. Rome: FAO.

Keagle, J. M. 1988. "Introduction and Framework." In *Bureaucratic Politics and National Security,* edited by D. C. Kozak and J. M. Keagle. Boulder, Colo., and London: Lynne Rienner Publishers.

Kees van Donge, J. 1982. "Politicians, Bureaucrats, and Farmers: A Zambian Case Study." *Journal of Development Studies* 19(1):102.

Keller, W. D., and Kraut, H. A. 1959. "Work and Nutrition." *World Review of Nutrition and Dietetics* 3:69–81.

Kenski, H. C. 1978. "U.S. Food Stamp Policy: Political Considerations." *Food Policy* 3(2):95–103.

Keys, A.; Brozek, J.; Henschel, A.; Mickelson, O.; and Taylor, H. L. 1950. *The Biology of Human Starvation*. Minneapolis: University of Minnesota Press.

Kielmann, A., and Associates. 1983. *Child and Maternal Health Services in Rural India: The Narangwal Experiment*. Integrated Nutrition and Health Care, vol. 1. Baltimore: Johns Hopkins University Press.

Kishimba, A. H. 1985. "Depleted Soils Enhance Famine." Paper presented at the Food Security Workshop in Mikumi, Tanzania.

Kjaerby, F. 1983. *Problems and Contradictions in the Development of Ox-Cultivation in Tanzania*. Uppsala, Sweden: Scandinavian Institute of African Studies.

Kocher, J. E. 1973. *Rural Development, Income Distribution, and Fertility Decline*. New York: The Population Council.

Korte, F. 1977. "Nutrition in Developing Countries; A Seminar for Technical Assistance Personnel." Recommendation working group on Nutrition and Development Planning, Schriftenreihe No. 71. Eschborn, Germany: GTZ.

Korte, R. 1969. "The Nutritional and Health Status of the People Living on the Mwea Tebere Irrigation Settlement." In *Investigations into Health and Nutrition in East Africa*, Africa Studien Nr. 42, edited by H. Kraut and H. D. Cremer, 267–334. München: Weltforum Verlag.

Korten, D. 1980. "Community Organization and Rural Development: A Learning Process Approach." *Public Administration Review* 40:480–511.

Korten, D. C., and Alfonso, F. B., eds. 1981. *Bureaucracy and the Poor: Closing the Gap*. Singapore: McGraw-Hill.

Kotz, N. 1969. *Let Them Eat Promises: The Politics of Hunger in America*. New York: Doubleday Anchor.

Kozak, D. C., and J. M. Keagle, eds. 1988. *Bureaucratic Politics and National Security*. Boulder, Colo., and London: Lynne Rienner Publishers.

Kracht, U. 1980. *Action to Stimulate International Cooperation in Food and Nutrition Proceedings 11*. International Congress of Nutrition, World Food Council. New York: Plenning Press.

———. 1983. Entwicklungspolitische Maßnahmen zur Verbesserung der Ernährungslage. In *Nahrung und Ernährung,* edited by H. D. Cremer. Stuttgart: Ulmer Verlag.

Kraut, H. A., and Muller, E. A. 1946. "Calorie Intake and Industrial Output." *Science* 104:495–97.

Krueger, A. O. 1974. "The Political Economy of the Rent-Seeking Society." *American Economic Review* 64:291–303.

———. 1980. *Foreign Exchange Regimes and Economic Development: Liberalization Attempts and Consequences*. Cambridge, Mass.: Ballinger.

Kuznets, S. 1972. *Economic Growth of Nations*. Cambridge, Mass.: Harvard University Press.

Laing, W. A. 1981. "Cost of Diet-Related Disease." In *Preventive Nutrition and Society,* edited by M. R. Turner. New York and London: Academic Press.

Lancet. 1984. "A Measure of Agreement on Growth Standards." *Lancet* 1:142–43.

Lane, S. 1978. "Food Distribution and Food Stamp Programme Effects on Food Consumption and Nutritional Achievement of Low Income Persons in Kern County, California." *American Journal of Agricultural Economics* 60(1):108–16.

Langsford, W. A. 1979. "A Food and Nutrition Policy." *Food and Nutrition Notes and Reviews* 36(3):100–103.

Lappe, F. M., and Collins, J. 1977. *Food First: Beyond the Myth of Scarcity.* Boston: Houghton Mifflin.

Lasswell, Harold D. 1936. *Politics: Who Gets What, When, and How.* New York: McGraw-Hill.

Latham, M. C. 1971. "The Edibility Gap: Differences between Promise and Delivery in the Family Food Commodity Program." Testimony in Hearings before the U.S. Senate Select Committee on Nutrition and Human Needs, 92d Cong., 1st sess.

———. 1974. "Protein-Calorie Malnutrition in Children and Its Relation to Psychological Development and Behavior." *Physiological Reviews* 54:541–65.

———. 1975. "Nutrition and Infection in National Development." *Science* 188:561–66.

———. 1983. "Dietary and Health Interventions to Improve Worker Productivity in Kenya." *Tropical Doctor* 13:34–38.

———. 1984a. "Smallness—A Symptom of Deprivation." *Nutrition Foundation of India Bulletin* 5(6):3–4.

———. 1984b. "Strategies for the Control of Malnutrition and the Influence of the Nutritional Sciences." *Food and Nutrition* 10:5–32.

Latham, M. C., and Stephenson, L. S. 1981. "Kenya: Health, Nutrition and Worker Productivity Studies." Final Report. Washington, D.C.: World Bank.

Latham, M. C.; Stephenson, L. S.; Hall, A.; Wolgemuth, J. C.; Elliott, T. C.; and Crompton, D. W. T. 1983. "Parasitic Infections, Anaemia and Nutritional Status: A Study of Their Interrelationships and the Effect of Prophylaxis and Treatment on Workers in Kwale District, Kenya." *Transactions Royal Society of Tropical Medicine and Hygiene* 77:41–48.

Latham, M. C.; Stephenson, L. S.; Wolgemuth, J. C.; Elliott, T. C.; Hall, A.; and Crompton, D. W. T. 1983. "Nutritional Status, Parasitic Infections and Health in Roadworkers in Kenya. Part 1. Kwale District—Coastal Lowlands." *East African Medical Journal* 60:2–10.

Lattimore, R., and Schuh, G. E. 1976. "A Policy Model of the Brazilian Beef Cattle Economy." *Chilean Journal of Economics* 39:51–75.

League of Nations. 1937. *The Relation of Nutrition to Health, Agriculture and Economic Policy.* Geneva: League of Nations.

Lele, Uma. 1975. *The Design of Rural Development: Lessons from Africa.* Baltimore: Johns Hopkins University Press.

Leman, C. 1980. *The Collapse of Welfare Reform: Political Institutions, Policy, and the Poor in Canada and the United States.* Cambridge, Mass.: MIT Press.

Leonard, David. 1972. "Organizational Structures for Productivity in Kenyan Agricultural Extension." Institute for Development Studies Paper 20. Kenya: University of Nairobi.

———. 1977. *Reaching the Peasant Farmer: Organization Theory and Practice in Kenya.* Chicago: University of Chicago Press.

Levinson, F. J. 1974. *Morida: An Economic Analysis of Malnutrition among Young Children in Rural India.* Cornell/MIT International Nutrition Policy Series No. 1. Ithaca, N.Y.: Cornell University.

———. Forthcoming. "Multisectoral Nutrition Planning: A Synthesis of Experience." In *Beyond Child Survival: Enhancing Child Growth and Nutrition in Developing Countries,* edited by Per Pinstrup-Andersen, David Pelletier, and Harold Alderman.

Levitan, S., and Belous, R. 1981. *What's Happening to the American Family.* Baltimore: Johns Hopkins University Press.

Lindblom, Charles E. 1959. "The Science of Muddling Through." *Public Administration Review* 19:79–88.

———. 1977. *Politics and Markets.* New York: Basic Books.

Lipsky, M. 1980. *Street-Level Bureaucracy: Dilemmas of the Individual in Public Services.* New York: Russell Sage.

Lipsky, Michael, and Thibodeau, Marc. 1985. *Food in the Warehouses, Hunger in the Streets.* Cambridge, Mass.: MIT Political Science Department. Typescript.

Lipton, Michael. 1974. "Towards a Theory of Land Reform." In *Peasants, Landlords, and Governments: Agrarian Reform in the Third World,* edited by D. Lehmann, 307. New York: Holmes and Meier.

———. 1976. *Why Poor People Stay Poor.* Cambridge, Mass.: Harvard University Press.

———. 1985. "Coase's Theorem versus Prisoner's Dilemma: A Case for Democracy in Less Developed Countries." In *Economics and Democracy,* edited by R. C. O. Matthews, 76. London: Macmillan.

Ljungqvist, B. 1981. "Iringa Nutrition Survey, Main Report." Report No. 692. Dar es Salaam: Tanzania Food and Nutrition Centre.

Longhurst, R. 1984. *The Energy Trap: Work, Nutrition and Child Malnutrition in Northern Nigeria.* Cornell International Nutrition Monograph Series 13. Ithaca, N.Y.: Cornell University.

Lukes, Steven. 1974. *Power: A Radical View.* Studies in Sociology, British Sociological Association. London: Macmillan.

Lynch, L. E. 1978. "Nutrition Planning Methodologies: A Comparative Review of Typology and Applications." Report to the ACC Subcommittee on Nutrition, United Nations.

Machado, Absalon. 1981. "The National Food and Nutrition Plan and the Food Industry." *Revista de la ANDI* 53.

———. 1977. "Nutrition Planning: The Poverty of Holism." *Nature* 267:742.

———, ed. 1983. *Nutrition in the Community: A Critical Look at Nutrition Policy, Planning and Programmes.* Chichester, England: John Wiley.

McLaren, D. S. 1974. "The Great Protein Fiasco." *The Lancet* (July):93.

———. 1977. "Nutrition Planning: The Poverty of Holism." *Nature* 267:742.

Madden, P., and Yoder, M. 1972. "Program Evaluation: Food Stamps and Commodity Distribution in Rural Areas of Central Pennsylvania." Pennsylvania State University Agricultural Experiment Station Bulletin No. 780.

Majone, G., and Wildavsky, A. 1979. "Implementation as Evolution." In *Implementation,* edited by J. L. Pressman, 177–94. Berkeley: University of California Press.

Malentlema, T. N. 1985. "Food and Nutrition as a Tool in Programs for Food Security in Tanzania." Paper presented at the Food Security Workshop in Mikumi, Tanzania.

Malony, C. 1974. *Peoples of South Asia.* New York: Holt Rinehart and Winston.

March, M. 1981. "An Analysis of the Development and Rationales of the United States Income Security System, 1776–1980." U.S. Congress, House Select Committee on Aging. Publication No. 97–303, 97th Cong., 1st sess.

Martorell, R., and Arroyave, G. 1984. "Malnutrition, Work Output and Energy Needs." Paper presented at the International Union of Biological Sciences Symposium on Variations in Working Capacity in Tropical Populations.

Martorell, R.; Delgado, H.; Valverde, V.; and Klein, R. E. 1981. "Maternal Stature, Fertility and Infant Mortality." *Human Biology* 53:303–12.

Martorell, R.; Habicht, J. P.; and Klein, R. 1982. "Anthropometric Indicators of Changes in Nutritional Status in Malnourished Populations." In *Methodologies for Human Population Studies in Nutrition Related to Health,* NIH Publication No. 82–2462, edited by B. A. Underwood. Washington, D.C.: U.S. Government Printing Office.

Martorell, R., and Ho, T. J. 1984. "Malnutrition, Morbidity and Mortality." *Population and Development Review* (supplement to volume 10):49–68.

Martorell, R.; Leslie, J.; and Moock, P. 1984. "Characteristics and Determinants of Child Nutritional Status in Nepal." *American Journal of Clinical Nutrition* 39:74–86.

Maru, R. 1981. "Organizing for Rural Health." In *Bureaucracy and the Poor: Closing the Gap,* edited by D. C. Korten and F. B. Alfonso, 35–43. Singapore: McGraw-Hill.

Mascarenhas, A. 1985. "Contribution towards a National Food Strategy." Institute of Resource Assessment. Mimeo.

Mascarenhas. O. 1984. *Women's Control of Resources and Its Implications for the Food and Nutritional Status of Their Families.* Report, University of Dar es Salaam.

Mathematica Policy Research. 1985. "Puerto Rico Nutrition Evaluation: Interim Report." Report prepared under contract for USDA-FNS.

Meillassoux, C. 1972. "From Reproduction to Production." *Economy and Society* 1:93–105.

Merton, R. K. 1949. "Bureaucratic Structure and Personality." In *Social Theory and Social Structure,* edited by R. K. Merton. Glencoe, Ill.: Free Press.

Meuer, Gerd. 1984. "Food and Politics in Africa: How to Hit the Hunger List." Development and Cooperation: Contributions to Development Policy by DSE, No. 5, 4–9, Bonn.

Migdal, J. S. 1977. "Policy and Power: A Framework for the Study of Comparative Policy Contexts in Third World Countries." *Public Policy* 25:243–60.

Migot Adhola, S. E. 1979. "Rural Development Policy and Equality." In *Politics and Public Policy,* edited by Barkan and Okumu. Kenya and Tanzania: Praeger.

Mitra, Ashok. 1977. *Terms of trade and class relations: An essay in political economy.* London: F. Cass.

Moock, P., and Leslie, J. 1986. "Childhood Malnutrition and Schooling in the Terai Region of Nepal." *Journal of Development Economics* 20:33–52.

Moore, Clement Henry. 1977. "Clientalist Ideology and Political Change: Fictitious

Networks in Egypt and Tunisia." In *Patrons and Clients,* edited by E. Gellner and J. Waterbury, 258. London: Duckworth and Company.

Moore, Mick. 1985. "On the Political Economy of Stabilization." *World Development* 13(9):1087–91.

Mora, Jose Obdulio. 1982a. "Nutritional Situation of the Colombian Population, 1977–80." Vol. 1. Minsalud/INS/ASCOFAME. Bogotá, Colombia.

———. 1982b. "Nutritional Situation of the Colombian Population, 1977–80." In *Encuesfor Nacional de Salud 1977–80,* vol. 1. Ministry of Health, National Health Institute and Colombian Association of Health Faculties. ASCOFAME. Bogotá, Colombia.

Mora, J. S.; de Paredes, B.; Wagner, M.; de Navarro, L.; Suescun, J.; Christiansen, N.; and Herrera, M. G. 1979. "Nutritional Supplementation and the Outcome of Pregnancy." *American Journal of Clinical Nutrition* 32:455–62.

Morawetz, D. 1987. *Twenty-Five Years of Economic Development, 1950–1975.* Baltimore: Johns Hopkins University Press.

Moris, Jon. 1972. "Administrative Authority and the Problems of Effective Agricultural Administration in East Africa." *The African Review* 1(1):105–46.

———. 1981. *Managing Induced Rural Development.* International Development Institute. Bloomington: Indiana University.

Morris, Morris D. 1979. *Measuring the Condition of the World's Poor.* Pergamon Policy Studies No. 42. Published for the Overseas Development Council. New York: Pergamon Press.

Mueller, Suzanne. 1980. "Retarded Capitalism in Tanzania." *Socialist Register* 208.

Mukherjee, R. 1971. *Six Villages of Bengal.* Bombay: Popular Prakashan.

Muller, D. C. 1979. *Public Choice.* Cambridge: Cambridge University Press.

Muratorio, B. 1980. "Protestantism and Capitalism Revisited in the Rural Highlands of Ecuador." *Journal of Peasant Studies* 8:37–60.

Murray, C. *Losing Ground.* 1984. New York: Basic Books.

Myrdal, Gunnar. 1968. *Asian Drama: An Enquiry into the Poverty of Nations.* New York: Pantheon.

Nathan, R. P. 1980. "Public Assistance Programs and Food Purchasing." *Agricultural Food Policy Review,* ESCS-AFPR-2, 25–29. Washington, D.C.: U.S. Department of Agriculture.

National Agricultural Policy and Presidential Commission on the Reestablishment of Cooperatives. 1981. Report. Dar es Salaam.

Nelson, Joan. 1985. "Sri Lanka: 1977–1982." Washington, D.C.: Overseas Development Council. Mimeo.

Nelson, Joan, et al., eds. 1989. *Fragile Coalitions: The Politics of Economic Adjustment.* New Brunswick, N.J.: Transaction Books.

Obeyesekere, A. 1984. "The Origins and Institutionalization of Political Violence." In *Sri Lanka in Change and Crises,* edited by James Manor. London: Groom Helon.

Ochoa, Mario. 1984. "The Colombian Food System: Design, Results, Nutritional Impact, and Political Constraints." Draft study prepared for the International Food Policy Research Institute. Bogotá, Colombia.

Olson, Mancur. 1965. *The Logic of Collective Action.* Cambridge, Mass.: Harvard University Press.

Omawale. 1980. "Nutrition Problem Identification and Development Policy Implications." *Ecology of Food and Nutrition* 9:113–22.

――――. 1982. "The Evaluation of the Belize Food and Nutrition Policy." Report to the Ministry of Health, Belize.

Osborn, Ann. 1982. "Socio-Anthropological Aspects of Development in Southern Belize, Toledo Rural Development Project." End of Tour Report. Belize: Ministry of Natural Resources.

Paarlberg, D. 1981. "Power and the U.S. Food Policy Agenda." *Food Policy* 6(3):158–62.

Packard, R. M. 1984. "Maize, Cattle, and Mosquitoes: The Political Economy of Malaria Epidemics in Colonial Swaziland." *Journal of African History* 25:189–212.

Palmer, J., and Sawhill, I. 1984. *The Reagan Record: An Assessment of America's Changing Domestic Priorities*. Cambridge, Mass.: Ballinger Publishing.

Paul, S. 1982. *Managing Development Programs: The Lessons of Success*. Boulder, Colo.: Westview.

Pearce, D. 1984. "Farewell to Alms: Women's Fare Under Welfare." In *Women: A Feminist Perspective*, edited by J. Freeman, 510. Palo Alto, Calif.: Mayfield Publishing.

Peltzman, S. 1976. "Toward a More General Theory of Regulation." *The Journal of Law and Economics* 19:211–40.

Penn, J. B. 1980. "The Federal Policy Process in Developing the Food and Agriculture Act of 1977." *Agricultural Food Policy Review*, ESCS-AFPR-3, 9–35. Washington, D.C.: U.S. Department of Agriculture.

Peterkin, B.; Kerr, R. L.; and Hama, M. 1982. "Nutritional Adequacy of Diets of Low-Income Households." *Journal of Nutritional Education* 14(3):102–4.

Petit, Michel. 1985a. *Determinants of Agricultural Policies in the United States and the European Community*. Research Report 51. Washington, D.C.: International Food Policy Research Institute.

――――. 1985b. "For an Analytical Political Economy, Relevance to the Study of Domestic and International Trade Agricultural Policies." In *Agriculture and International Relations*, edited by H. de Haen et al., 31–44. London: Macmillan.

Petit, M.; de Benedictis, M.; Britton, D.; de Groot, M.; Henrichsmeyer, W.; and Lechi, F. 1987. *Agricultural Policy Formation in the European Community: The Birth of Milk Quotas and CAP Reform*. Amsterdam: Elsevier.

Petras, J. F., and Zemelman Merino, H. 1972. *Peasants in Revolt*. Austin: University of Texas Press.

Physician Task Force on Hunger in America. 1985. *Hunger in America: The Growing Epidemic*. Cambridge, Mass.: Harvard University.

Pines, J. M. 1982. "National Nutrition Planning: The Lessons of Experience." *Food Policy* 7:275–301.

Pinstrup-Andersen, Per. 1985. "Food Prices and the Poor in Developing Countries." *European Review of Agricultural Economics* 12:69–85.

――――. ed. 1988a. *Consumer-Oriented Food Subsidies: Costs, Benefits, and Policy Options for Developing Countries*. Baltimore: Johns Hopkins University Press.

――――. 1988b. "Macroeconomic Adjustment and Human Nutrition." *Food Policy* 13(1):37–46.

Pinstrup-Andersen, Per, and Caicedo, E. 1978. "The Potential Impact of Changes in Income Distribution on Food Demand and Human Nutrition." *American Journal of Agricultural Economics* 60:402–15.

Pitt, M., and Rosenzweig. 1985. "Agricultural Prices, Food Consumption, and the Health and Productivity of Farmers." *Review of Economics and Statistics* 67:212–23.

———. 1985. "Health and Nutrient Consumption across and within Farm Households." *Review of Economics and Statistics* 67:212–23.

Piven, F. F., and Cloward, R. 1971. *Regulating the Poor: The Functions of Public Welfare.* New York: Vintage.

———. 1977. *Poor People's Movements.* New York: Vintage.

Polsby, N. W. 1963. *Community Power and Political Theory.* New Haven, Conn., and London: Yale University Press.

Popkin, B. 1978. "Nutrition and Labor Productivity." *Social Science and Medicine* 12:117–25.

Popkin, B., and Lim-Ybanez, M. 1982. "Nutrition and School Achievement." *Social Science and Medicine* 16:53–61.

Poppendieck, J. 1985. "Policy, Advocacy, and Justice: The Case of Food Assistance Reform." In *Toward Social and Economic Justice,* edited by D. Gil and E. Gil. Cambridge, Mass.: Schonkman.

———. 1986. *Breadlines Knee Deep in Wheat: Food Assistance in the Great Depression.* New Brunswick, N.J.: Rutgers University Press.

Prescott, N. M. 1974. "Schistosomiasis and Development." *World Development* 7:1–14.

Pressman, Jeffrey L., and Wildavsky, Aaron. 1973. *Implementation: How Great Expectations in Washington are Dashed in Oakland; or Why It's Amazing that Federal Programs Work at All. This Being a Saga of the Economic Development Administration as Told by Two Sympathetic Observers Who Seek to Build Morals on a Foundation of Ruined Hopes.* Berkeley: University of California Press.

———. 1984. *Implementation.* 3d ed. Berkeley: University of California Press.

Price, D. W.; West, D. A.; Scheier, G. E.; and Price, D. Z. 1978. "Food Delivery Programs and Other Factors Affecting Nutrient Intake of Children." *American Journal of Agricultural Economics* 60:609–18.

Pyle, D. F. 1980. "From Pilot Project to Operational Program in India: The Problems of Transition." In *Politics and Policy Implementation in the Third World,* edited by M. S. Grindle, 123–44. Princeton: Princeton University Press.

———. 1985. "Life after Project: A Multi-Dimensional Analysis of Implementing Social Development Programs at the Community Level." Typescript derived from Ph.D. diss., Department of Political Science, MIT.

Raikes, P. 1985. "National Food Balance or Food Security as a Basic Need. Is There a Policy Option for Tanzania?" Paper presented at the Food Security Workshop in Mikumi, Tanzania.

Rao, N. P. 1980. "Determinants of Nutritional Status in India." In *Rural Household Studies in Asia,* edited by H. P. Binswanger, R. E. Evenson, C. Florencio, and B. White. Singapore: Singapore University Press.

Rashid, H. E. 1977. *Geography of Bangladesh.* Bangladesh: Bangladesh University Press.

Ratcliffe, J. W. 1977. "Poverty, Politics, and Fertility: The Anomaly of Kerala." *Hastings Center Report* (February):34–42.

Rausser, G. 1982. "Political Economic Markets: PERTS and PESTS in Food and Agriculture." *American Journal of Agricultural Economics* 61:821–33.

Rausser, Gordon C.; Lichtenberg, Erik; and Lattimore, R. 1983. "New Developments in Theory and Empirical Applications of Endogenous Governmental Behavior." In *New Directions in Econometric Modeling and Forecasting in U.S. Agriculture,* edited by Gordon C. Rausser. New York: Elsevier North-Holland.

Redclift, M. 1983. "Production Programs for Small Farmers: Plan Puebla as Myth and Reality." *Economic Development and Social Change* 31:551–86.

Reynolds, T. 1980. "The Food Stamp Explosion." Master's thesis, University of Texas, Austin.

Rich, W. C. 1973. *Smaller Families through Social and Economic Progress.* Washington, D.C.: Overseas Development Council.

Richards, Alan. 1984. "Ten Years of Infitah: Class, Rent and Policy Status in Egypt." *Journal of Development Studies* 20(4):323–38.

Richards, Peter, and Gooneratne, Wilbert. 1980. *Basic Needs, Poverty, and Government Policies in Sri Lanka.* Geneva: International Labor Organization.

Ringen, K. 1983. "Norway's Nutrition and Food Policy: Overview, Results and Future Directions." In *Nutrition in the Community,* 2d ed., edited by D. S. McLaren. Chichester, England: Wiley.

Ripley, R. B. 1969. "Legislative Bargaining and the Food Stamp Act, 1964." In *Congress and Urban Problems,* edited by F. Cleaveland. Washington, D.C.: Brookings Institution.

Rondinelli, D. A. 1983. *Development Projects as Policy Experiments: An Adaptive Approach to Development Administration.* New York: Methuen.

Rosenzweig, M. 1980. "Neo-Classical Theory and the Optimizing Peasant: An Econometric Analysis of Market Labor Supply in a Developing Country." *Quarterly Journal of Economics* 94:31–55.

Rosenzweig, M., and Schultz, T. P. 1983. "Estimating a Household Production Function: Heterogeneity, the Demand for Health Inputs, and Their Effects on Birthweight." *Journal of Political Economy* 91:723–46.

Rosenzweig, M., and Wolpin, K. 1984. "Migration Selectivity and the Effects of Public Programs." Economic Growth Center Discussion Paper 464, Yale University.

Russell, C. S., and Nicholson, N. K., eds. 1981. *Public Choice and Rural Development.* Beverly Hills: Sage.

Ryan, J., Bidinger, P., Rao, N., and Pushpamma, P. 1984. "The Determinants of Individual Diets and Nutritional Status in Six Villages of South India." International Crops Research for the Semiarid Tropics, Research Bulletin No. 7, Hyderabad, India.

Sahn, David E. 1986. "Changes in the Living Standards of the Poor in Sri Lanka during a Period of Macroeconomic Restructuring." World Development 15(6).

———. 1988. "The Effect of Price and Income Changes in Food-Energy Intake Sri Lanka." *Economic Development and Cultural Change* 36(1).

Sahn, D., and Alderman, H. 1988. "The Effects of Human Capital on Wages, and the Determinants of Labor Supply in a Developing Country." *Journal of Development Economics* 29:157–84.

Satyanarayana, K.; Naidu, A. N.; Chatterjee, B.; and Rao, B. S. N. 1977. "Body Size and Work Output." *American Journal of Clinical Nutrition* 30:322–25.

Save the Children. 1980. *CBIRD Methodology: Introduction to CBIRD.* Westport, Conn.

Scandizzo, Pasquale L., and Knudsen, Odin K. 1980. "The Evaluation of the Benefits of Basic Need Policies." *American Journal of Agricultural Economics* 62(1):46–57.

Scandizzo, P. L., and Swamy, G. 1982. *Benefits and Costs of Food Distribution Policies.* Staff Working Paper 509. Washington, D.C.: World Bank.

Schattschneider, E. E. 1960. *The Semi-Sovereign People: A Realist's View of Democracy in America.* New York: Holt, Rinehart and Winston.

Scheback, Emmerich. 1982. "Targeted Food Subsidies vs. Targeted Food Marketing Interventions: Myth and Reality." Washington, D.C.: World Bank. Mimeo.

Schelp, F. P.; Sornmani, S.; Gormaiphol, S. Emil; Pongaew, P.; Keller, W.; Harinasuta, C.; Migasena, P. 1982. "Physical Growth of Pre-School Children in Relation to a Water Resource Development Scheme in Thailand." *Journal of Tropical Pediatrics* 28(August):187.

Schneider, C. 1985. "1984 Developments in the Federal Food Programs: Calm Before the Storm." *Clearinghouse Review* 19(1):988–95.

Schultz, T. P. 1984. "Studying the Impact of Household Economic and Community Variables on Child Mortality." *Population and Development Review* (supplement to volume 10):215–35.

Science Advisory Committee. 1967. *The World Food Problem.* A Report of the Panel on the World Food Situation.

Scobie, Grant. 1981. *Government Policy and Food Imports: The Case of Wheat in Egypt.* Research Report 29. Washington, D.C.: International Food Policy Research Institute.

————. 1983. *Food Subsidies in Egypt: Their Impact on Foreign Exchange and Trade.* Research Report 40. Washington, D.C.: International Food Policy Research Institute.

Scott, James, 1969. "Corruption, Machine Politics, and Political Change." *American Political Science Review* 63:1142–58.

————. 1972. "Patron-Client Politics and Political Change in Southeast Asia." *American Political Science Review* 66:91–113.

————. 1986. *Everyday Forms of Peasant Resistance.* New Haven: Yale University Press.

Scrimshaw, N. S.; Behar, M.; Guzman, M. A.; and Gordon, J. E. 1967. "Nutrition and Infection Field Study in Guatemalan Villages, 1959–1964; I: Study Plan and Experimental Designs." *Archives of Environmental Health* 14:657–62.

Scrimshaw, N. S.; Taylor, C. E.; and Gordon, J. E. 1968. "Interactions of Nutrition and Infection." Geneva: WHO.

Scrimshaw, N. S., and Wallerstein, M. B., eds. 1982. *Nutrition Policy Implementation: Issues and Experience.* New York: Plenum.

Seckler, D. 1982. "Small but Healthy." In *Newer Concepts in Nutrition and Their Implications for Policy,* edited by P. V. Sukhatme, 127. India: Maharashtra Association for the Cultivation of Science.

Selowsky, Marcelo. 1979. *Balancing Trickle Down and Basic Needs Strategies: Income*

Distribution Issues in Large Middle-Income Countries with Special Reference to Latin America. Staff Working Paper 335. Washington, D.C.: World Bank.

————. 1980. "Nutrition, Health and Education: The Economic Significance of Complementarities at Early Ages." Paper presented at the Sixth World Congress of the International Economic Association, Mexico City.

Selowsky, Marcelo, and Taylor, Lance. 1973. "The Economics of Malnourished Children: An Example of Disinvestment in Human Capital." *Economic Development and Cultural Change* 22(1):17–30.

Sen, Amartya. 1980. *Levels of Poverty: Policy and Change.* Staff Working Paper 401. Washington, D.C.: The World Bank.

————. 1981. *Poverty and Famines.* London: Oxford University Press.

————. 1986. "Sri Lanka's Achievements: How and When." In *Rural Poverty in South Asia,* edited by T. N. Srinivasan and P. Bardhan. New York: Columbia University Press.

Senauer, Benjamin. 1982. "The Current Status of Food and Nutrition Policy and the Food Programs." *American Journal of Agricultural Economics* 64(5):1009–16.

Shepard, R. J. 1978. *Human Physiological Work Capacity.* Cambridge: Cambridge University Press.

Shepherd, Jack. 1975. *The Politics of Starvation.* New York: Carnegie Endowment.

Shils, E. A. 1975. *Center and Periphery: Essays in Macrosociology.* Chicago: University of Chicago Press.

Shortridge, K. 1984. "Poverty is a Woman's Problem." In *Women: A Feminist Perspective,* edited by J. Freeman, 492–97. Palo Alto, Calif.: Mayfield Publishing.

Silva, C. R. 1984. "Plebiscitary Democracy or Creeping Authoritarianism? The Presidential Election and Referendum of 1982." In *Sri Lanka: In Change and Crises,* edited by James Manor. New York: St. Martin's Press.

Singh, I. J.; Squire, L.; and Strauss, J., eds. 1986. *Agricultural Household Models: Extensions, Applications and Policy.* Baltimore: Johns Hopkins University Press.

Soiffer, S. M., and Howe, G. N. 1981. "Patrons, Clients, and the Articulation of Modes of Production and Capitalism into Peripheral Agriculture in Northeastern Brazil." *Journal of Peasant Studies* 9.

Soshan, Boas. 1980. "Grain Riots and the 'Moral Economy': Cairo, 1350–1517." *Journal of Interdisciplinary History* 10(3):1350–1517.

Spurr, G. B. 1983. "Nutritional Status and Physical Work Capacity." *Yearbook of Physical Anthropology* 26:5–35.

Spurr, G. B.; Barac-Nieto, M.; and Maksud, M. G. 1977. "Productivity and Maximal Oxygen Consumption in Sugar Cane Cutters." *American Journal of Clinical Nutrition* 30:316–21.

Spurr, G. B.; Maksud, M. G.; and Barac-Nieto, M. 1977. "Energy Expenditure, Productivity and Physical Work Capacity of Sugar Cane Loaders." *American Journal of Clinical Nutrition* 30:1740–46.

Sri Lanka Department of Government Printing. 1985. "Parliament of the Democratic Republic of Sri Lanka: Poor Relief Act No. 32 of 1985." Colombo.

Staniland, Martin. 1985. *What is Political Economy?* New Haven: Yale University Press.

Stavrakis, O. 1979. "The Effect of Agricultural Change upon Social Relations and Diet in a Village in Northern Belize, Central America." Ph.D. diss., University of Minnesota.

———. 1981. "Cane Farming in Belize: A Sociological Viewpoint." In *Proceedings of First Sugarcane Extension Workshop,* edited by Awe, Cawich, and Zetina. Belize: Belize Sugar Industries.

Stavrakis, O., and Omawale. 1985. "Why Nutrition-Related Projects Fail to Impact the Poor." In *Cultural Aspects of Economic Development.* Michigan State University.

Stavrakis, O., and Teck, A. 1983. "Survey of Sugarcane Benefits Distribution in Northern Belize." Report for Development Services, Minneapolis.

Steiner, G. 1971. *The State of Welfare.* Washington, D.C.: Brookings Institution.

———. 1981. *The Futility of Family Policy.* Washington, D.C.: Brookings Institution.

Steinmo, S. 1982. "Linking the Village to Modern Health Systems." In *Institutions of Rural Development for the Poor: Decentralization and Organizational Linkages,* edited by D. K. Leonard and D. R. Marshall, 151–92. Berkeley: University of California Press.

Stepanek, J. F. 1979. *Bangladesh—Equitable Growth?* New York: Pergamon Press.

Stephenson, L. S.; Latham, M. C.; and Jansen, A. 1983. *A Comparison of Growth Standards: Similarities between NCHS, Harvard, Denver and Privileged African Children and Differences with Kenyan Rural Children.* Cornell International Nutrition Monograph Series 12. Ithaca, N.Y.: Cornell University.

Stephenson, L. S.; Latham, M. C.; Kurz, K. M.; Miller, D.; Kinoti, S. N.; and Oduori, M. L. 1985. "Urinary Iron Loss and Physical Fitness of Kenyan Children with Urinary Schistosomiasis." *American Journal of Tropical Medicine and Hygiene* 34(2):322–30.

Stevens, R. D. 1976. "Comilla Rural Development Programs to 1971." In *Rural Development in Bangladesh and Pakistan,* edited by Stevens, Alavi, and Bertocci. Honolulu: University of Hawaii Press.

Stigler, G. 1970. "Director's Law of Public Income Redistribution." *The Journal of Law and Economics* 13:1–10.

Stiglitz, J. 1984. "Alternative Theories of Wage Determination and Unemployment: The Efficiency Wage Model." In *The Theory and Experience of Economic Development: Essays in Honor of Sir W. Arthur Lewis,* edited by M. Gersovitz, C. Diaz-Alejandro, G. Ranis, and M. Rosenzweig. London: Allen and Unwin.

Strauss, J. 1986. "Does Better Nutrition Raise Farm Productivity?" *Journal of Political Economy* 94:297–320.

———. Forthcoming. "Households, Communities and Preschool Children's Nutrition Outcomes: Evidence from Rural Côte d'Ivoire." *Economic Development and Cultural Change.*

Sukhatme, P. V., and Morgen, S. 1982. "Autoregulatory Homeostatic Nature of Energy Balance." *American Journal of Clinical Nutrition* 35:355–65.

Sultan, K. M. Tipu. 1974. *Problems Associated with Democratization of Cooperatives in Bangladesh.* Comilla: Bangladesh Academy of Rural Development.

Sussman, G. E. 1980. "The Pilot Project and the Choice of an Implementing Strategy: Community Development in India." In *Politics and Policy Implementation in the Third World,* edited by M. S. Grindle, 103–22. Princeton: Princeton University Press.

Tanzania Food and Nutrition Centre. *Ten Years of Nutrition Work in Tanzania.* Dar es Salaam.

Tanzanian Ministry of Agriculture. 1982. Marketing Development Board. Dar es Salaam: Government of Tanzania, Ministry of Agriculture.

――――. 1982. "The National Agricultural Policy, Final Report." Dar es Salaam: Government of Tanzania, Ministry of Agriculture.

――――. 1984. *Tanzania: National Food Strategy.* Vols. 1–2. Dar es Salaam: Government of Tanzania, Ministry of Agriculture.

Tanzanian Government/UNICEF. 1985. *Analysis of the Situation of Children and Women.* Vols. 1–2. Dar es Salaam: Government of Tanzania, Ministry of Agriculture and UNICEF.

Taylor, Lance; Horton, Susan; and Ruff, Daniel. 1983. "Food Subsidy Programs—Practice and Policy Lessons." Massachusetts Institute of Technology. Mimeo.

Thoden van Velzen, H. U. E. 1976. "Staff, Kulaks and Peasants: A Study of a Political Field." In *Government and Rural Development in East Africa,* edited by L. Cliffe, J. Coleman, and M. Doornbas. The Hague: Martinus Nijhoff.

Thomas, D.; Strauss, J.; and Henriques, M.-H. 1987. "Child Survival, Nutritional Status and Household Characteristics: Evidence from Brazil." Economic Growth Center Discussion Paper No. 542, Yale University.

Thorbecke, Erik, and Svejnar, Jan. 1987. *Effects of Macroeconomic Policies on Agricultural Performance in Sri Lanka, 1960–82.* Paris: OECD.

Thurow, L. 1974. "Cash vs. In-Kind Transfers." *American Economic Review* 64(1): 190–95.

Timmer, C. Peter; Falcon, W. P.; and Pearson, S. R. 1983. *Food Policy Analysis.* Baltimore: Johns Hopkins University Press.

Tornebohm, H. 1976. "A Systematization of Paradigms." Report No. 85. University of Gothenburg, Department of Theory of Science.

Trairatvorakul, Prasarn. 1984. *The Effects on Income Distribution and Nutrition of Alternative Rice Price Policies in Thailand.* Research Report 46. Washington, D.C.: International Food Policy Research Institute.

Tullis, Lamond. 1985. "The Current View on Rural Development: Fad or Breakthrough in Latin America?" In *An International Political Economy,* edited by W. Ladd Hollist and Lamond Tullis, 223–54. Boulder, Colo.: Westview.

Tullock, G. 1965. *The Politics of Bureaucracy.* Washington, D.C.: Public Affairs Press.

Underwood, B. A. 1978. "Success or Failure of Supplementary Feeding Programs as a Nutritional Intervention." Paper presented at the International Symposium on Nutrition Interventions, Santiago, Chile.

UNICEF (United Nations Children's Fund). 1990. *Strategy for Improved Nutrition of Children and Women in Developing Countries.* UNICEF Policy Review No. 1. New York.

United Nations. 1945. *Five Technical Reports on Food and Agriculture.* UN Interim Commission on Food and Agriculture. Washington, D.C.: United Nations.

――――. 1986. *International Action to Avert the Impending Protein Crisis.* Economic Social Council.

Uphoff, Norman. 1981. "Political Considerations in Human Development." In *Imple-*

menting Programs of Human Development, edited by Peter T. Knight. Staff Working Paper No. 403. Washington: World Bank.

Uribe, Consuelo. 1986. "Limitations and Constraints of Colombia's Food and Nutrition Plan (PAN)." *Food Policy* 11(1):47–70.

Uribe Mosquera, Tomás. 1980. "Food Coupons in Colombia: Origins, Current Situation, Replicability and Prospects." Submitted to the Health and Nutrition Division. Washington, D.C.: World Bank.

———. 1981. *Formal Programmes and Implicit Policy in Food and Nutrition within the Andean Common Market.* Bogotá, Colombia: PAHO/JUNAC/CHU.

———. 1983. "Appendix on Colombian Food Coupons." In *Report of the World Food Programme/Government of the Netherlands Seminar on Food Aid.* The Hague.

Urrutia, Miguel, and Berry, Albert. 1975. "The Income Distribution in Colombia." Editorial *La Carreta.* Medellin, Colombia.

———. 1978. *Sierra Leone, National Nutrition Survey, Summary Report and Recommendations.* Washington, D.C.: USAID, Office of Nutrition.

———. 1982. *Sri Lanka: The Impact of P.L. 480 Title I Food Assistance.* Impact Evaluation Report 39. Washington, D.C.: USAID.

Urrutia, Miguel, and de Sandoval, Clara E. 1974. "Fiscal Policy and Income Distribution in Colombia." *Revista del Banco de la Republica* (July).

U.S. Agency for International Development, Office of Nutrition. 1973. *Planning National Nutrition Programs: A Suggested Approach.* Vols. 1–2. Washington, D.C.: USAID.

———. 1982. *Sri Lanka: The Impact of P.L. 480 Title I Food Assistance.* Impact Evaluation Report No. 39. Washington, D.C.: USAID.

U.S. Congress. House. Democratic Study Group. 1976. "Special Report on Food Stamps." Washington, D.C. Mimeo.

U.S. Congress. House. Committee on Agriculture. 1985. *A Review of the Thrifty Food Plan and Its Use in the Food Stamp Program.* 99th Cong., 1st sess.

U.S. Department of Agriculture. Economic Research Service. 1962. *Effect of the Pilot Food Stamp Program on Retail Food Store Sales.* Marketing and Economic Development, Ag. Econ. Report No. 8.

U.S. Department of Agriculture. Economic Research Service and Agricultural Research Service. 1962. *Food Consumption and Dietary Levels under the Pilot Food Stamp Program.* Ag. Econ. Report No. 9.

U.S. Department of Health and Human Services. 1979. *Summary, Yemen Arab Republic National Nutrition Survey.* Center for Disease Control. Atlanta, Ga.: U.S. DHHS.

U.S. Food Research Action Center (FRAC). 1981. *Food and Nutrition Issues in the Food Stamp Program.* Washington, D.C.: FRAC.

Valdes, Alberto, ed. 1981. *Food Security for Developing Countries.* Boulder, Colo.: Westview Press.

Vicziany, M. 1982–83. "Coercion in a Soft State: The Family Planning Program of India." *Pacific Affairs* 55:373–402; 557–92.

Viteri, F. 1971. "Considerations on the Effect of Nutrition on the Body Composition and Physical Working Capacity of Young Guatemalan Adults." In *Amino Acid Fortification of Protein Foods,* edited by N. S. Scrimshaw and A. M. Altschul. Cambridge, Mass.: MIT Press.

————. 1974. "Definition of the Nutrition Problem in the Labor Force." In *Nutrition and Agricultural Development,* edited by N. S. Scrimshaw and M. Behar. New York: Plenum Press.

————. 1982. "Nutrition and Work Performance." In *Nutrition Policy Implementation: Issues and Experience,* edited by N. S. Scrimshaw and M. B. Wallerstein. New York: Plenum Press.

Viteri, F. E., and Torun, B. 1974. "Anemia and Physical Work Capacity." *Yearbook of Physical Anthropology* 3:609–26.

Wallerstein, Mitchel. 1980. *Food for War: Food for Peace.* Cambridge: MIT Press.

————. 1982. "Dynamics of Food Policy Formulation in the U.S.A." *Food Policy* 7(3):229–39.

Warwick, D. 1979. *Integrating Planning and Implementation: A Transactional Approach.* Cambridge: Harvard Institute for International Development.

————. 1982. *Bitter Pills: Population Policies and Their Implementation in Eight Developing Countries.* Cambridge: Cambridge University Press.

Waterbury, John. 1978. *Egyptian Agriculture Adrift.* American Universities Field Staff Report 47. Hanover, N.H.: The Wheelock House.

————. 1983. *The Egypt of Nasser and Sadat: The Political Economy of Two Regimes.* Princeton: Princeton University Press.

Waterston, A. 1965. *Development Planning: Lessons of Experience.* Baltimore: Johns Hopkins University Press.

Weber, Max. 1947. *The Theory of Social and Economic Organization.* Glencoe, Ill.: The Free Press.

————. 1978. *Economy and Society.* Edited by G. Roth and C. Wittich. Berkeley: University of California Press.

Weicher, J. 1984. "The Safety Net after Three Years." In *Maintaining the Safety Net,* edited by J. Weicher, 4–6. Washington, D.C.: American Enterprise Institute.

Weingrod, A. 1967. "Patron, Patronage, and Political Parties." *Comparative Studies in Society and History* 10:376–400.

Weisbrod, B., and Helminiak, T. 1977. "Parasitic Diseases and Agricultural Labor Productivity." *Economic Development and Cultural Change* 25:505–22.

Wildavsky, A. 1979. "Implementation in Context." In *Implementation,* edited by J. L. Pressman and A. Wildavsky, 163–76. Berkeley: University of California Press.

Wilford, W. T. 1975. "Comment." *Economic Development and Cultural Change* 23:337–40.

Windham, C.; Wyse, B.; Hansen, G.; and Hurst, R. 1983. "Nutrient Density of Diets in the USDA Nationwide Food Consumption Survey, 1977–1978: 1. Impact of Socioeconomic Status on Dietary Density." *Journal of the American Dietetic Association* 82(1):28–34.

Winikoff, Beverly, ed. 1978. *Nutrition and National Policy.* Cambridge, Mass.: MIT Press.

Wisner, B. 1980–81. "Nutritional Consequences of the Articulation of Capitalist and Non-Capitalist Modes of Production in Eastern Kenya." *Rural Africana* 8–9:99–132.

Wolf, E. R. 1966. "Kinship, Friendship, and Patron-Client Relations in Complex Societies." In *The Social Anthropology of Complex Societies,* edited by M. Banton. London: Tavistock Publications.

Wolfe, B., and Behrman, J. 1982. "Determinants of Child Mortality, Health and Nutrition in a Developing Country." *Journal of Development Economics* 11:163–94.

———. 1987. "Women's Schooling and Children's Health: Are the Effects Robust and with Adult Sibling Control for the Women's Childhood Background." *Journal of Health Economics* 6:239–54.

Wolgemuth, J. C.; Latham, M. C.; Hall, A.; Cheser, A.; and Crompton, D. W. T. 1982. "Worker Productivity and Nutritional Status of Kenyan Road construction Laborers." *American Journal of Clinical Nutrition* 36:68–78.

World Bank. 1976. *Egyptian Agriculture Development: Problems, Constraints and Alternatives*. Report No. 931b-EGT. Washington, D.C.: World Bank.

———. 1978. *Arab Republic of Egypt: Economic Management in a Period of Transition. Vol. 1: The Main Report*. Report 1815-EGT. Washington, D.C.: World Bank.

———. 1982. *World Development Report, 1982*. New York: Oxford University Press.

———. 1984. *World Development Report, 1984*. New York: Oxford University Press.

———. 1985. *Ensuring Food Security in the Developing World*. Washington, D.C.: World Bank.

Wotecki, C. E., and Cordaro, J. B. 1979. "Nutrition Research Policy: U.S. Progress in the Past Decade." *Food Policy* 4(4):285–94.

Wunderle, R. E. 1971. "Evaluation of the Pilot Food Certificate Program." Ph.D. diss., Cornell University.

Yambi, O.; Jonsson, U.; and Ljungqvist, B. 1990. "The Role of Government in Promoting Community Based Nutrition Programs: Experience from Tanzania and Lessons for Africa." Pew/Cornell Lecture Series on Food and Nutrition Policy. Ithaca, N.Y.: Cornell Food and Nutrition Policy Program.

Contributors

Richard H. Adams, Jr., a political economist, is a research fellow in the Special Development Studies Division at the International Food Policy Research Institute. He has done extensive research on international migration and remittances, and the ways in which governments use local agricultural institutions to reduce rural poverty.

Margaret S. Andrews is an analyst at the Office of Analysis and Evaluation, Food and Nutrition Service, U.S. Department of Agriculture. She was formerly an assistant professor in the Department of Agricultural Economics at Rutgers University. Her research has dealt with issues related to U.S. food and agricultural policies, suburbanization, and agricultural development.

Katherine L. Clancy is a professor in the Department of Nutrition and Food Management at Syracuse University. She was formerly a resident fellow at the National Center for Food and Agricultural Policy at Resources for the Future in Washington, D.C. Her research has been mainly in the areas of domestic food policy, sustainable agriculture, food safety, and state and local food systems.

Alain de Janvry is a professor in the Department of Agricultural and Resource Economics at the University of California at Berkeley. He has served as chairman of the Giannini Foundation and as a project specialist for the Ford Foundation in Argentina. He has been a visiting professor at Catholic University of Chile, Santiago, and at the Indian Agricultural Research Institute, New Delhi.

Neville Edirisinghe has been a research fellow at the International Food Policy Research Institute and a consultant at the World Bank, the Food and Agriculture Organization of the United Nations, the International Monetary Fund, and the U.S. Agency for International Development. He formerly served as general manager of the Paddy Marketing Board of Sri Lanka. He has done research on the nutritional and economic effects of food-subsidy programs, intrafamilial food distributing behavior, and comparative advantage in crop production.

265

John Osgood Field is a professor in the School of Nutrition at Tufts University. He was previously a member of the International Nutrition Planning Program at the Massachusetts Institute of Technology and before that was a research associate at MIT. His main areas of research have been in nutrition planning, policy and program implementation, and famine and famine management.

Raymond F. Hopkins is chair of the Political Science Department and director of the Public Policy Program at Swarthmore College, Pennsylvania. His research and teaching include the political economy of food and nutrition policies.

Urban Jonsson is senior advisor in nutrition, UNICEF/New York. He spent many years in Tanzania, first as chief of the Nutrition Planning Department, Tanzania Food and Nutrition Centre, and then as UNICEF country representative. He has concentrated his work on improved conceptualization of the problem of nutrition in society.

Michael C. Latham is a professor and director of the Program in International Nutrition at Cornell University. A medical doctor with training in tropical medicine and public health, he was based for several years in Tanzania, where he was director of the Nutrition Unit of the Ministry of Health. His research deals mainly with nutritional problems in the Third World.

Michel Petit is director of the Agriculture and Rural Development Department at the World Bank in Washington, D.C. He formerly held the chair of economics at the Ecole Nationale Supérieure des Sciences Agronomiques Appliquées in Dijon, France.

Per Pinstrup-Andersen is director general of the International Food Policy Research Institute. His past positions include professor of food economics at Cornell University, director of the Cornell Food and Nutrition Policy Program, associate professor at the Danish Agricultural University, and economist at the International Center for Tropical Agriculture in Colombia. He has extensive experience in food and nutrition policy and, in addition to research and teaching, has served as a consultant to many government and international agencies.

David E. Sahn is an associate professor at Cornell University and director of the Cornell Food and Nutrition Policy Program. He was previously a research fellow at the International Food Policy Research Institute and has served as a consultant to numerous international organizations, including the World Bank, Food and Agricultural Organization of the United Nations, World Health Organization, World Food Council, and United Nations University. His research on the effects of agricultural and macroeconomic policies on incomes, consumption, and nutrition has focused on poverty-alleviation issues and distributional concerns.

John Strauss is a professor of economics at Michigan State University. He was formerly a senior economist in the Human Capital Department of the Rand

Corporation. Earlier he was an associate professor in the Department of Economics and an associate of the Economic Growth Center at Yale University. His primary area of research has been in the economics of household behavior in developing countries, particularly in relation to child nutrition and health issues.

Shankar Subramanian is an associate professor at the Indira Gandhi Institute of Development Research, Bombay, and is presently a visiting scholar in the Department of Agricultural and Resource Economics, University of California at Berkeley. His main areas of research have been in computable general equilibrium modeling and applied econometrics.

Tomás Uribe Mosquera is Colombia's minister-counsellor for trade and economics to the European Communities. He formerly held a similar position in his country's diplomatic mission to the United States. Earlier he was an associated investigator with FEDESAROLLO, Colombia's leading economic policy research institution, a Takemi Fellow in International Health at the Harvard School of Public Health, and the first director general of Colombia's National Food and Nutrition Plan. His main areas of research have been in the economics of household behavior, especially from the standpoint of food security and dietary consumption "rationality."

Peter Utting is a research fellow at the United Nations Research Institute for Social Development in Geneva. He is currently engaged in research on the social dimensions of environmental degradation and conservation schemes in developing countries. Throughout the 1980s, he was based in Nicaragua where he specialized in research on food-policy issues.

Index